THE
HERMETIC TREE
OF LIFE

"Mistele has distilled thousands of years of wisdom into an accessible and practical guide for anyone who wants to ensure that humanity thrives and succeeds. He elucidates the many nuances within classic metaphysical domains while teaching us how to fully autonomize as a species and become conscious architects of our future."

ELYRRIA SWANN,
AUTHOR OF *HOW TO BECOME A MERMAID*

"William Mistele is one of the few Goldilocks magicians practicing—not too hot and not too cold. This 'just rightness,' how easy it is to overshoot or undershoot the supernatural world, is often overlooked: it doesn't matter whether you miss by a little or a lot. Mistele shows what it takes to not miss, to find the numinous in the maze of the obvious."

RICHARD GROSSINGER,
AUTHOR OF *BOTTOMING OUT THE UNIVERSE*
AND *DREAMTIMES AND THOUGHTFORMS*

THE HERMETIC TREE OF LIFE

Elemental Magic and Spiritual Initiation

A Sacred Planet Book

William R. Mistele

Destiny Books
Rochester, Vermont

Destiny Books
One Park Street
Rochester, Vermont 05767
www.DestinyBooks.com

Destiny Books is a division of Inner Traditions International

Sacred Planet Books are curated by Richard Grossinger, Inner Traditions editorial board member and cofounder and former publisher of North Atlantic Books. The Sacred Planet collection, published under the umbrella of the Inner Traditions family of imprints, includes works on the themes of consciousness, cosmology, alternative medicine, dreams, climate, permaculture, alchemy, shamanic studies, oracles, astrology, crystals, hyperobjects, locutions, and subtle bodies.

Cataloging-in-Publication Data for this title is available from the Library of Congress

ISBN 978-1-64411-744-6 (print)
ISBN 978-1-64411-745-3 (ebook)

Printed and bound in the United States by Lake Book Manufacturing, LLC

10   9   8   7   6   5   4   3   2   1

Text design and layout by Virginia Scott Bowman
This book was typeset in Garamond Premier Pro with Tacitus Pro used as the display typeface

To send correspondence to the author of this book, mail a first-class letter to the author c/o Inner Traditions • Bear & Company, One Park Street, Rochester, VT 05767, and we will forward the communication.

CONTENTS

INTRODUCTION

The Hermetic Tree of Life: Elemental Magic and Spiritual Initiation is based on the Kabbalistic Tree of Life. I began reading books on this topic in the early 1970s, beginning with Dion Fortune's *Mystical Qabalah,* William Grey's *The Ladder of Lights,* and Gareth Knight's two-volume *Practical Guide to Qabalistic Symbolism.* There are currently a great number of books that pursue the meaning of this magical diagram.

The Tree of Life theme has many advantages. It brings into one place psychology, astrology, planes of consciousness, spiritual quests, and all manner of initiations. As a road map to the spiritual world, each individual can use it to gather together the variety of his spiritual experiences.

As a spiritual anthropologist, I have studied and meditated with about sixty masters and gurus. I notice that a master from the oldest Taoist lineage in China has quite different goals and methods than a master from the oldest Buddhist tradition in Tibet. A Hopi Indian shaman works with the spiritual and physical universe in a different way than the Wiccan, Druid, Muslim, or Christian.

Put simply, the various traditions on Earth do not share each other's dreams. What is sacred in one tradition is given no attention in another. They seem oblivious to the astral plane with its global dreamtime that supports every soul, regardless of the individual's path and the religion or wisdom he practices.

My purpose is straightforward. In spite of all the advantages that technology offers the human race, the survival of our species remains at risk. To use properly the immense powers that we hold in our hands, we need an equal level of wisdom to guide and inspire us.

And so my task is to study all the various traditions to which I have access. I have sought to distill and extract from them the universal aspects of their training systems. The goal is to bring this wisdom together in one user-friendly book that is neutral in regard to beliefs, doctrines, and religion.

I offer directions so that you may experience the wisdom of many traditions for yourself. Then you can decide what is useful and what you wish to discard. The focus is on your needs and not on the preservation of a tradition or lineage.

The chapters of this book follow the ten *sephiroth* of the Kabbalah. A *sephirah* (or *sephiroth* in plural) is a metaphysical domain. The sephiroth are extremely useful because of their wide-ranging and universal approach to life experience. And for each sephirah I present various themes.

The *Basic Quality* indicates the obvious and tangible aspects of the sephirah.

The *Virtues/ Vices/ Negative* section lists vices that waste your energy and undermine positive motivation, virtues that strengthen your energy and support positive motivation and negatives that seek to destroy.

The *Challenge* section is something to accomplish.

The *Magical Practice* is a method.

The *Common Virtue* focuses on a psychological skill unique to that sephirah.

The *Magical Virtue* section describes a power of transformation belonging to the sephirah.

The *Divine Virtue* section is what you might experience once you know the sephirah inside and out.

The *Dream* section is an animated visualization or symbolic picture through which we can use our imagination to bring the sephirah to life.

The *Initiation* section is about embodying the sephirah in yourself.

And finally, the *Mystery* section involves conflicts within the archetypes of the collective unconscious. For example, there are conflicts between the four elements in nature, within the astral plane, in the quest for truth, in the attainment of oneness in personal relationships, and in the relation between the personality and the higher self. The Mystery section also involves perennial questions: Why are we here? What is human nature? What can we become? What is missing from life? It is the mystery that surrounds us and is a part of us.

Each of the ten domains in this book has its own unique emphasis as well as its own purposes, gifts, and obstacles. And each is inexhaustible—we can explore any one of them for an entire lifetime.

Caught up in physical world, having to deal with the necessities of survival? This is Malkuth/the Earth. It is all about mastering and overcoming our limitations. And equally it offers us a way to be grounded so that we transcend the limitations of life.

Need some sort of relief, perhaps a dream that brings renewal and new hope? That is Yesod/the Moon. It is the foundation. It is the pleasure, sensations, and feelings found in sex, intimacy, family life, and the appearance of new light on Earth.

Need to solve a personal or a global problem? Hod/Mercury assures us that every problem has a solution and every conflict a resolution. In the end, nothing will remain hidden.

What about love, attraction, art, empathy, and personal integration? That is Netzach/Venus. Here we can observe how attraction and love have magical effects.

What is life all about? Why is there suffering and how do we find the inspiration that transforms us? This is Tiferet/the Sun. Find this inspiration within you and victory is close at hand.

Do you like to put aside each day a designated time to train your body, soul, mind, or spirit? That is Gevurah/Mars. But do not stop once you can best your competition. Gevurah reveals how to unite with the creative powers unfolding the universe. Now you are ready to pursue missions that transform the world.

Interested in wealth in all forms and in all planes of existence? That is Chesed/Jupiter. Why not start out from the beginning envisioning yourself having every need met so that you are in a position to give to others what enriches their lives?

And Binah/Saturn says, "Experience everything you can. Satisfy your every desire. But also discover your deepest lessons in life. Then take the time and make the effort to learn them. Life is whatever you want it to be. Just remember this command—attain freedom."

And then, too, there is Chokmah/Uranus. Now we deal directly with Divine Providence to transform society and to create a new world. You see reformers all the time wheeling and dealing with Uranus. They like to ask themselves, "How much can I change the world?" Reformers often fail because they fail to take human nature into account.

And finally, Kether/Neptune. Its basic quality? It grants completion, closure, satisfaction, and fulfillment. Anything you need, just ask. Well, that is, ask in the right way at the right time with the right motivation—such requests can never be refused.

◆

For me, the prime directive governing all souls who incarnate on Earth is *Become your own creation*. This book is my attempt to assist others in the pursuit of this declaration of spiritual freedom.

ON FRANZ BARDON

Franz Bardon was a master in the Western system of Hermetics. He died in 1958 in Czechoslovakia. Bardon emphasizes in his first book, *Initiation into Hermetics,* a careful, systematic, and step-by-step guide to training. The idea is to develop the student's body, soul, and mind so they are in complete harmony.

One of the unique features of his system is his focus on the four elements of Earth, Air, Fire, and Water as energies and vibrations to master in ourselves. The Earth element leads to being practical, productive, and effective in the physical world. You are down-to-earth. The Water element develops sensitivity, empathy, love, healing, and nurturing qualities. The Air element develops artistic sensitivity, detachment, openness of mind, playfulness, cheerfulness, and an appreciation of freedom. The Fire element develops resolution, willpower, determination, and commitment to accomplishing your goals in specific time frames. Through the exercises with the elements, the student takes what is weak in his soul and makes it stronger. He takes what is negative or passive and makes it positive and active.

At the end of *Initiation into Hermetics,* after a massive amount of training in the basics, Bardon guides the student to enter the realms of the four elemental beings on the astral plane. There the student makes direct contact with mermaids, sylphs, gnomes, and salamanders. Insisting on direct, firsthand, and personal experience, the student is to learn all he can from these beings. In effect, you are making these magical realms a second home.

Franz Bardon's second book, *The Practice of Magical Evocation,* continues where *Initiation into Hermetics* left off. In this book, Bardon gives clear descriptions of the heads of the four elemental kingdoms. After that, Bardon introduces 360 higher spirits that dwell on the Akashic plane of the Earth. These spirits too are described one after the other.

Going beyond the aura of the planet Earth, Bardon describes spirits that surround the Moon, Mercury, the Sun, and Jupiter. Bardon only gives the names of the Mars spirits since they are dangerous and, given that they specialize in power, they can be used for negative purposes.

Of course, it is wise to succeed in the basic training before working with these higher spirits. All the same, some students are sufficiently psychic that they can immediately sense, talk to, and interact with these spirits. Bardon's whole spiritual system was so new to me at the beginning that I spent three years studying in detail the auras of a large number of these spirits of the planetary spheres.

For me, some of these spirits have turned into lifelong consultants on various projects I pursue. Some have very practical suggestions since they specialize in different areas of human endeavor. Some are very useful in business. Some will produce—almost immediately—very dramatic experiences with love. Some specialize in assisting writers, poets, musicians, and other artists. Some deal with geopolitical issues. Some will assist the magician in acquiring psychic perception, magical equilibrium, magical protection, or the wisdom to make the best choices in life.

In some cases, contacting a spirit is like going and sitting in a class in quantum mechanics at MIT. If you have already worked through the requisites for the class, you can understand immediately what is being taught. If you do not have the math or background, the classwork is unintelligible.

And then contacting other spirits is more like walking in on "Hell Week," the Navy SEALs' most brutal training. The activities are so intense that you could injure yourself or worse in just three minutes. But Bardon's course of training is not hand-holding, and it is not designed to make you comfortable and secure. It is designed for those who wish to assist the human race in its extremely challenging path of working with nature and understanding itself. The student of Hermetics will seek to offer assistance to others in whatever way he can.

In Franz Bardon's third book, *The Key to the True Kabbalah*, Bardon describes twenty-seven cosmic letters. These letters are energy fields created through concentrating at the same time on a color, a musical note, and a physical sensation. The cosmic letters embody the creative forces unfolding the universe. They are physical-spiritual quantum fields that underlie matter, energy, space, time, history, life, soul, mind, and spirit. An example is the letter *U*, which has a shiny black color and represents consciousness operating outside of or prior to the manifestations of space and time. The letter *U* refers to the fifth element that originates, supervises, and dissolves the other four elements of Earth, Air, Fire, and Water.

In my working with Buddhist masters from many traditions, I noticed the similarity of the cosmic letter *U* and the empty mind and studies of the void that Buddhists pursue. As I mentioned previously, all things arise from the nothingness of the cosmic letter *U*. It sustains, refines, and restores all things, and dissolves them again when their purposes are complete so that there can be new beginnings. It contains all things within itself, is one with all things, oversees their transformations, and yet in itself it is absolutely nothing.

As with the letter *U*, practicing the cosmic language takes you beyond a religious context and enables you to approach states of consciousness in a professional manner. For example, you can consciously create magical and spiritual states of awareness at will. And you can immediately observe practical applications of those states of awareness in everyday life.

With letter *M*, we learn to create an icy cold, blue-green energy. Concentrating on it creates an energy field similar to the vibration of the mermaid realm on the astral plane as well as the vibration or magnetic field that underlies all water on Earth.

The letter *A* embodies the enlightened state of mind I described under the mystery of Hod. Since these letters operate on four planes—the physical world, the astral and mental planes, as well as Akasha*—they have a great variety of applications.

Although scientific questions may arise concerning the notion of

---

*For more on Akasha, please see the box on page 10.

an "ether," Akasha as used in this book is primarily a physical sensation. You can approximate this sensation by imagining that your body is emitting a dark violet light that penetrates through space and time. And then imagine that you are this vast space. The idea is that with sufficient training, anything anywhere in time or space that you concentrate on can be perceived as being immediately in front of you.

The Akashic body does not need thoughts to think, emotions to feel, or concrete sensations to perceive. It acts through intuition. In its awareness, it can penetrate through space and time.

As intuition, it can simultaneously be completely detached from, completely one with, and aware of all relationships of whatever it is focusing on. Spirit, or Akasha, incorporates into itself all experiences on the physical, astral, and mental planes without being subject to the limitations governing their perceptions and activities.

Spiritual or divine ideals are often associated with the Akashic plane or Akashic body. In terms of the Water element, we might encounter universal experiences or ideals, such as cosmic or all-embracing love. On this level, we learn to feel one with all beings and also to develop an inner peace in which we feel one with the universe.

Put simply, Akasha oversees the introduction, development, and fulfillment of the deeper purposes of life.

◆

I once sat and meditated with the Dalai Lama's weather controller. Letter *A* enables you to learn to place your mind directly into storms and winds and exert an influence over them. That may seem like the stuff of fantasy, but I know at least four people who can cause rain to start or stop within minutes.

Applied to the astral plane, the letter *A* also heightens your artistic sensitivity. We can observe in the element of Air how the vibration of one tuning fork causes another tuning fork to vibrate with the same tone. The letter *A* in the astral body is similar. You observe a social activity or pursue a certain subject matter and the heightened sensitivity of the letter *A* enables your brain waves to reflect what you are observing. The letter *A* is also a mental form of empathy that awakens deep feelings while simultaneously remaining detached.

The point of the cosmic language is to assume the role of a creator. Through a highly trained concentration, you create energy fields that heighten perception, feeling, intuition, understanding, and volition. In other words, you can choose to work with spirits who are masters in themselves. Or, with the cosmic language, you can run your own spiritual workshop in which you assemble and forge the mental and spiritual tools you need to accomplish your purposes.

Akasha

Akasha refers to the fifth element in nature alongside Earth, Air, Fire, and Water. It also refers to a plane or level of consciousness. In both examples, it is formless and timeless; it is a state of awareness penetrating through space and time without restriction.

Akasha is like a quantum field extending throughout the universe. It is a state of awareness *without form or image*. You enter Akasha in a state of trance. You focus on penetrating through space and time and there is nothing else in your awareness. Humans have the four elements along with Akasha in their spiritual makeup. The presence of Akasha does not make a person better or superior. But it does enable a higher learning curve and the ability to make new things happen that are not a part of the unfolding of history or hidden in the complexities of nature.

RULE 10

MALKUTH/EARTH

Kingdom, Physical World

Basic Quality	Focus on physical reality
Virtues, Vices, Negative	Solid/Rigid/Oppression
Challenge	Pursue something of value that you are passionate about
Magical Practice	Observe your routines
Common Virtue	Well-being
Magical Virtue	A quiet ecstasy
Divine Virtue	Silence
Dream	Mastery and love
Initiation	Bringing nature into one's role in society
Mystery	The five elements in the personality, society, and the biosphere

In Kabbalah, the sephirah of Malkuth relates to the physical world. Here, you can encounter every kind of vibration from the densest physical to the highest light. The physical world has great variety. You can ride on a bus and have a drug dealer sit on one side of you and a saint on the other side.

In life, there is horror and great suffering as well as wonder and immense love. Formulate a plan. Experience all you can. Then share with others the wealth and knowledge you have acquired.

BASIC QUALITY
Focus on Physical Reality

The basic quality of Malkuth is focusing 100 percent of your attention on the physical world that we share in common with other people.

There are many things that can interfere with our ability to see clearly and understand the world. Among these are strong emotions, fixed beliefs, and attachment to ideologies, philosophies, or metaphysical systems. Or simply a failure to appreciate the opportunities and lessons that the physical world offers.

VIRTUES, VICES, NEGATIVE

Virtues: Solid, stable, down-to-earth, reliable, adaptable, conscientious, hardworking, enduring, persevering, self-assured, and self-determining.

Vices: Rigid, inflexible, nonresponsive, insecure, anxious, eccentric, aberrant, stuck, greedy, self-centered, grim, menacing, feeling abandoned and without a home.

Negative: Oppression, exhaustion, failure, defeat, exile, slavery, bondage, jail, captivity.

CHALLENGE

The challenge of Malkuth is to find something worth doing that is right for you and totally captivating.

"Worth doing" means it uplifts others' lives and produces something of value to society. "Right for you" means that by doing it your life is enhanced, your values furthered, and it is satisfying just to be involved with it. "Totally captivating" means that the pleasure and satisfaction in your feelings, will, and intellect are strengthened, deepened, and working harmoniously together.

The challenge is also to do whatever it takes to make a home for yourself in this world.

Warren Buffett accumulates billions of dollars by buying high value companies and then, with great insight, he picks managers to run those companies who are honest, sincere, and love to work as Buffett himself loves to work. Buffet's attitude, like a gnome (an Earth elemental), is to "find something you love and then work at it with all of your heart."

To do this, you will need to make peace with reality. If you have bills to pay, you will need a job. And yet, as Warren Buffett points out in the next section, never stop searching for work that you love. The assumption is that if you are doing what you love, you will succeed (success includes happiness, health, and well-being) far easier than you would by working at anything else.

Find something worth doing that gets you out of bed in the morning and gives you a sense of belonging because you are a productive member of society. And yet there is another task. Do things that give you a sense of peace and well-being such that you feel you are a part of the greater universe.

With the onset of puberty, your hormonal system goes into high gear. It throws everything it has at you to get you to put aside your inner child who is in need of protection and supervision. It attempts to force you to become an adult who determines his own course of action and finds his place in the world.

We are social creatures often requiring constant feedback and interaction with others to feel healthy and whole. Operate without contact with others and your overall energy level is greatly reduced.

Experience everything you can. Satisfy your every desire. Realize your potential. Make use of your talents. You have received the gift of life. Give back. Leave the world a better place than the one you entered.

MAGICAL PRACTICE
Observe Your Routines

Review your daily life. Ask yourself, "Is there something else I can substitute for some of my routines that might produce better results? How does my daily life support my long-range goals and express my deepest values?"

Some individuals may be able to visualize what they did during the day in a way similar to watching an instant replay on a TV. Others may want to keep a journal. Find what works for you so you are fully aware of your routines and how they affect you. Over time, enlarge the time frame of your review. Consider where you have been, how you got to where you are now, and where you hope to be.

Get in the habit of sitting each day and just thinking.
WARREN BUFFETT

COMMON VIRTUE
Well-Being

"Well-being" is the feeling that enables us to fully appreciate the physical world. With it, the world is far more alive, full of hope and love. We see more of what is going on around us and are open to new experiences. Without the feeling of well-being, the world is cold, menacing, and hostile. And this can lead us to narrowing our focus, since our primary concern becomes survival.

For individuals with well-being, an individual's identity is not defined by the goals he pursues or what he accomplishes. There is, instead, a feeling of being directly connected to nature that exists as an inexhaustible source of peace and renewal. Life is seen as being sheltering and fulfilling. This appreciation occurs on a level far deeper than the conscious mind, for it has nothing to do with beliefs, doctrines, theories, ideas, or positive thinking.

There is continuity. If I lose something important to me at one point in my life, it can be found again later during another stage. For these individuals, even relationships do not really end. What is begun in one relationship can be carried on and fulfilled in another relationship. One such person said, "I feel like I am in a river, flowing, and accepted. I don't have to do anything. I can just be. Things just happen."

✸ Exercise: The Feeling of Well-Being
Recall times in which you were completely happy and satisfied, held and loved by another. Or you may have experiences, even moments, from childhood in which you felt completely safe and accepted by another person.

Review three of your best moments, when you felt at peace being here in this world. Now hold these experiences before your mind. Let the feelings in each flow into and through the others. This is what people with high well-being have inside of themselves all of the time. Joy and wonder, acceptance, and peace are constantly before their eyes.

Well-being creates a different perception. Independent of physical circumstances, you feel that being here on Earth is being home.

MAGICAL VIRTUE
A Quiet Ecstasy

In fairy tales, the elemental beings who associate with the Earth element are called gnomes. Of all beings, they feel most at home in the physical world.

I said to one girl, "You have the vibration of a gnome."

She asked, "How so?"

I replied, "There is this feeling in your aura of being in a cave beneath the ground that is perfectly silent and still. And yet there is also a sense that you are a part of everything physical, as if matter itself is alive and imbued with spirit waiting to be awakened."

She said to me, "Yes. That is the way I feel all of the time."

✦ Meditation on the Feet ✦

Your physical body is what enables you to be here in this world. Without it, you are on the astral plane among the departed or somewhere else. To be fully alive and active, make a point of keeping your body healthy. Exercise regularly. Eat with care. Monitor your stress levels.

There is a connection between the Earth element, which is analogous to the sephirah of Malkuth, and the lower area of the body—from the feet, lower and upper legs, up to and including the buttocks, genitals, and pelvic bone.

For some people, focusing on the feet as a meditation can get rid of some kinds of headaches—for example, from eye strain. And it also balances the typical focus of our awareness in our upper body and head. Over time it makes us more down-to-earth and grounded.

If it is comfortable for you, sit in a chair with your feet flat on the ground. Then focus your full attention on your feet. Become aware of everything you can about them without being distracted.

Sense the bottom of the feet as they touch the floor. Notice the toes, heel, and all sides of the feet. Visualize or imagine the bones, tendons, and muscles. Sense the skin moisture, sensitivity to hot and cold, and tactile sensations such as texture and pressure. The skin surface will likely be warmer than the surrounding air.

Also imagine or sense the blood flow through the feet and/or the pulse of the heartbeat. When you breathe deeply in, see if you can sense any tingling sensations or presence of increased vitality in your feet as you do so.

I often begin by focusing on a tiny dot of white light in the center of the upper part of each big toe. Then after a few breaths, I focus on the entire big toes. And then I focus on both feet at once.

You might be able to sense the effects of the parasympathetic nervous system. As you relax, the blood vessels near the surface of the skin dilate, increasing the blood flow and producing warm sensations. Since blood is around 83 percent water, you may be able to sense or at least imagine the sensation of water flowing through the feet. We will focus more on the element of Water in the next chapter.

Also, there is the experience of "zoning." Zoning is when you are immersed in a stream of sensations and feelings without any thoughts occurring. In this awareness of the sensations and feelings within the feet, you may experience dopamine and endorphins released into the blood stream. When this occurs, you may produce yogic experiences of bliss and shamanistic experiences of ecstasy.

Try this. Immerse yourself in a pure, sensory awareness of your feet. You can also move up from the feet through the ankles and lower and upper legs to the pelvic bone, including your buttocks and genitals.

At a certain point, you may feel the awareness of your lower body expanding into and including other aspects of nature—an awareness of rocks, mountains, and forests. Again, over a period of time—weeks, months, or years—the energy system of your body begins to shift. You may welcome the increased balance produced by being more connected to the Earth element in yourself.

The Earth element has a power that Warren Buffett points out regarding the mind: "The thing to do is to keep your mind when the world around you is losing theirs."

I sometimes meditate with individuals who have unusual auras. A few women I know are like the incarnation of gnomes. They have a woman's body but a gnome's soul.

When I have them meditate with me on their feet, I notice that they have a very powerful connection to the Earth element. I have not encountered any human masters who have an awareness of the density of their bodies to this extent. I have to concentrate on my feet being made out of solid steel to even approximate their awareness.

If you have a strong connection to the Earth, then 90 percent of the things that are upsetting in life vanish. It is a good idea to give your emotions your full attention to see what they are saying to you. But it helps to have a sense that keeps you focused on what is important under all circumstances of life. This is part of the purpose of the feet and lower body meditation.

DIVINE VIRTUE
Silence

*In silence the universe reveals itself as moving unobstructed
toward its goals.*

I like to tell the story of the time I attended my first Vipassana session. It was on Oahu. I went into a house as others were coming in. There was no talking. Everyone was silent as we sat down on cushions arranged in a circle. We sat for about an hour. It was just quiet sitting. At the end, everyone got up and left, again, without any words spoken.

I thought to myself, "This is perfect. This is the kind of group I have always been looking for." The next week went pretty much the same. Except at the end, one of the two "instructors" talked for about twenty-five minutes on the nature of Buddhist meditation.

I was shocked and appalled. How can someone take a divine virtue such as silence and twist it into a religious practice that requires conformity of belief and action in order to gain group affiliation? But I am not complaining. I never went back.

Silence is an unknown terrain and an invisible mountain range. No army can climb it. No commander or general can penetrate it and no reconnaissance plane can fly over it. You can neither lay siege to it nor assault it.

It is a country whose borders are guarded by nightmares, terror, and whirlwinds of despair. But those who cross over and explore these unknown lands find wealth beyond compare.

Silence is where dreams originate, visions are born, and passions enter to be transformed.

In war, silence is the element of surprise. It is the unthinkable. It does what the opponent cannot imagine. Whatever the odds, there is always a moment when success becomes inevitable. Silence sees what is invisible to everyone else's eyes.

Silence is beyond light and darkness, form and emptiness. Though silence never tampers with the ordinary and familiar, its response is always new.

Silence is the ability to take the most difficult of fates and karmas and turn them into something wonderful, because you see the beauty within them. Law and limitation bind things, giving them weight, shape, and place. But silence grants freedom because it knows how to wait. In the greatest darkness and the loneliest prison, silence finds gates leading to liberation. In silence, sorrow falls asleep in the arms of peace.

Silence is the inner strength individuals need to fashion the missing links between beginnings and endings, between dreams and their manifestations. This is because amid the routines and activities of life, silence maintains an open space inside them. In this space the highest ideal can be present without being contaminated, compromised, or put off to the side. Silence strengthens inner visions so there is never any doubt or uncertainty about their reality.

To summarize, in silence we shut down the world so it becomes still like a moment frozen in time. Though remaining completely detached, we look around in wonder. Here is the mysterious and at times crazy ongoing experiment of life—a mixture that we blend together of human and divine; ever so fragile, life is always willing to be shaped and transformed through our inner visions and the work of our hands.

※ **Biographical Note** ※

I am the son of five generations of men who had great faith in God. They practiced the most powerful work ethic on Earth—the Protestant Ethic—which is successful because it declares that your personal faith connects you directly to God, who will bless you in whatever path of life you take.

On the other hand, their weakness was that they were total extroverts. They lacked self-reflection other than their commitment to maintain the morality of their religious community. In a way, this extroversion and their orthodox faith worked well for them. It empowered them to focus 100 percent of their attention on the external world.

Being an extreme introvert, I inherited five hundred years of the intuitive insights given to them but which they ignored. Everything they might have learned through reflection and contemplation was deposited into a bank account with my name on it.

I know someone who was struck by lightning and survived. The lightning came right through the living room window and hit her. But it was okay. It cleared out her sinuses.

I was struck not by lightning but by silence. Unlike the girl struck by lightning, the silence was a shock to my nervous system. And this was because the religion I inherited had no guidelines, no manuals, and no information on how to view the world through spiritual perception.

Growing up, my Protestant teachers and university professors were incapable of comprehending a state of awareness in which the mind is fully alert but does not use thoughts. And to stand back and focus on not just your own behavior but on human history as if you are looking at it from outside—this level of detachment and intense scrutiny is necessary if the human race is to survive and to thrive.

DREAM

When you're associating with the people that you love,
doing what you love, it doesn't get any better than that.

WARREN BUFFETT

Imagine a room with different windows. As you gaze through each window, you are looking into a dream. One window is the world as we know it. Another window expresses our worries, anxieties, and fears. And a third window shows the world in which everything has gone right. Life is bright and fulfilling.

Each sephirah has a window that shows the best experiences in life. Regardless of our actual situation and circumstances in life, we can still dream life as it is meant to be.

For Malkuth, the kingdom, this dream can be where we have mastered our work and profession. You feel at peace, at home in this world, secure, and surrounded by those you love.

In the tarot, there are cards that illustrate this, such as the ten of pentacles and the ten of cups. The ten of pentacles is a master sitting at a gate. And the ten of cups is a family beneath a rainbow who are filled with love and joy.

But this window is not just a way of looking at the world. We can imagine we are there in the picture by lucid dreaming while we are fully awake. Put yourself into that state of well-being and peace. Make this picture a part of yourself.

INITIATION

In initiation, something happens to us. We change. Some aspect of ourselves is transformed. Consciousness shifts and we see the world in a new way. The result is that the various forces within us—desires, dreams, motivations, and inspirations—are amplified, deepened, and redirected.

In the context of this book, initiation draws together the various aspects of the sephirah and integrates them within us. In the first five sephiroth, we are also uniting with nature in terms of making an inner connection to the four elements—Earth, Water, Fire, and Air. In doing so, something of the wonder and beauty in each element is transferred into us in a way that enriches our daily lives.

The initiation in Malkuth is not a rite of passage. There is no graduation ceremony from high school or college, no certificates, no medals or ribbons, no secret handshakes, no anointing, and no patches to wear. There is no one welcoming us into an ethnic or religious group. In the initiation of Malkuth, we are on our own.

Imagine going out into nature. Perhaps you are in a forest grove in a valley surrounded by mountains. Perhaps you are sitting on top of a mountain surrounded by a vast view of a mountain range and ocean beyond. Perhaps you are in a location like Sedona or the Grand Canyon in Arizona, Joshua Tree National Forest or Yosemite in California, or Monument Valley in Utah.

You sense the silence and enduring presence in the features of the landscape. You relax. You feel at peace. And something of that rock-solid landscape and geological time becomes a part of yourself.

There is no need for others to validate or recognize your experience. This is an inner connection to nature. But it is not enough to be immersed in the timeless peace of nature when you are in such a setting.

The goal is to bring back this silent, timeless quality of nature so it exerts its presence in your daily life. Your role in society is then strengthened by feeling solid, down-to-earth, and timeless in being. The result is that you possess a perseverance, patience, and incredible self-reliance that is far in excess of others who have no such inner connection to nature.

It is, of course, possible to go live out in nature for a week, months, or longer. But in another sense, we can exercise our imagination a few minutes each day as we evoke a feeling of being out in the wilderness.

Certainly, there are simple things many people are already doing that connect them to nature. Having a pet is one thing. Dogs, for example, have been with us for twenty thousand to forty thousand years. They were our friends far back into the Paleolithic era. Human-animal contact reminds of a time when we were immersed in nature.

Having a garden is another thing. Agriculture began at least twelve thousand years ago. There are simple activities that briefly suspend the rush of daily life and reconnect us to nature.

MYSTERY
....
The Five Elements in the Personality,
Society, and the Biosphere

> *Water purifies and flows. Fire makes things happen. Air clarifies and balances. Earth ensures that our results are stable and enduring.*

We live on an amazing planet. It is in the Goldilocks zone in relation to the sun, meaning it is not too hot and not too cold. This enables liquid water to exist on the Earth's surface. The iron in the moving magma in the Earth's outer core generates the magnetosphere that protects life from solar radiation.

The active core also accounts for the movement of the tectonic plates that produce a vast range of ecosystems with their variety of life-forms. And, after billions of years of development, our atmosphere has become rich enough in oxygen to enable animals to exist on land.

Human nature is analogous to the main characteristics of our planet. The sky, embodying the Air element with its clarity, harmonizing influence, and freedom of movement, is like the mind and intellect. We have the ability to solve problems, resolve conflict, and to be curious—always probing and discovering new things.

The enduring presence of the physical materials of our world is present in human beings as the capacity to work, to innovate, and to shape nature. The Fire element, especially seen in our technologies and industries, grants us mastery over the world and the power to take charge and command.

And the Water element, with its receptivity and nurturing capacities, is similar to the receptivity and animating quality of feeling that enables us to bring things to life and to feel fully alive. And with feeling we have empathy—the ability not only to sense but also to feel that we share in the life of those around us.

But our planet comes with a high level of difficulty. Go back seventy thousand years and a volcano named Toba erupted on Sumatra in Indonesia sending twenty-eight thousand times more ash into the air than Mount St. Helens. Such eruptions produce miniature ice ages.

Genetic research concludes that at that time *Homo sapiens* may have shrunk to as little as one thousand adults, perhaps even to forty breeding pairs. We are very lucky to be here. In the geologic record, there is a list of intelligent beings like *Homo erectus* and Neanderthals who were less lucky than us and are now extinct.

The Fire element in volcanoes can produce climactic changes that threaten our survival. Similarly, the other elements have their dangerous aspects as well. Oceans produce rogue waves, storm surges, and tsunamis. The weather can cause famines, droughts, hurricanes, and tornadoes. And other forms of life can attack us with poison and violence as well as through plagues, illness, and diseases.

And so, in a similar way, since we embody aspects of the four elements, our minds can be at odds with our feelings. In a rush to survive and to dominate, we often abuse and kill those with less power. In our race to discover new technologies, we fail to put in place safeguards to prevent their misuse, or we give these technologies to the worst people on Earth who immediately turn them to malicious ends.

Though water covers 71 percent of the surface of the Earth, we barely have any sympathy for those of a different nation, race, religion, or culture. Though water accounts for around 80 percent of the volume of the blood, freely offering its nurturing, healing, purifying, and renewing presence, human beings have almost no capacity to feel what other people feel.

Back in the Paleolithic age when we were hunter-gatherers, we needed to stay focused on the well-being of those in our own tribe. Now, with a global community, one national leader or corporate CEO is in a position to threaten or damage the well-being of the entire planet.

Generals and politicians command the expansive and dynamic aspects of Fire. Scientists, artists, and musicians enjoy the clarity and dramatic presentation of the Air element. Societies and economies diligently preserve in producing wealth and material goods.

But our philosophers, psychologists, sociologists, anthropologists, and ministers and priests have not yet brought the Water element into their consciousness. The consequence is that human beings take risks that threaten their own survival in order to feel more alive.

When our capacity to feel is so weak we are in a very dangerous situation. And thus, we have this mystery—even the greatest of world teachers can talk about and illustrate love and compassion, but so far they have not figured out how to teach these things.

Throughout this book, we shall return again and again to the psychological and spiritual aspects of the four elements. They are the key to discovering that nature is at the core of our being. And they are part of the answer to the questions "What is missing from life, and what are we capable of becoming?"

RULE 9

YESOD/THE MOON

Foundation, Soul, Astral Plane

—When will I be happy?
—When you discover you are the source of your own happiness.

MERMAID QUEEN ISAPHIL

Basic Quality	Entering dream states at will
Virtues, Vices, Negative	Strength/Idleness/Narcissism
Challenge	Discover what makes you happy, fully alive, and at peace
Magical Practice	The five senses
Common Virtue	Self-acceptance as a gate to the inner self
Magical Virtue	The element of Water
Divine Virtue	Creating peace, happiness, contentment; comprehending opposites
Dream	Physical bliss
Initiation	Self-renewal
Mystery	The astral plane, spiritual anthropology, global dreamtime

In Yesod, we focus on our soul, our astral body, and the astral plane. We also explore sensuality, contentment, bliss, and what it is to be fully alive.

In Malkuth, we have a history of our experiences in the outer world. In Yesod, we have the flow of our inner life. In Malkuth, we formulate plans of action as we pursue our goals. To succeed, we will need to be practical, down-to-earth, and hardworking.

In Yesod, there will be times when we can accomplish far more in life by creating and living a dream. This dream can be so real that others become inspired by it and desire to make it their own.

There is a sequence. First become active, responsible, and successful in our physical world activities. Pass through various social stages, mature, and move toward our goals. And then, under the influence of Yesod, we add imagination. Here a dream, when strong enough, shapes reality.

BASIC QUALITY
Entering Dream States at Will

In Malkuth, we focus our five senses 100 percent on the physical world. Here in Yesod, we learn to create and enter dreams at will. Conscious dreaming goes in two directions. You can use the dream to step back and disengage from the stress of daily life. Or, having experienced feeling fully alive within the dream, you can then use the dream as a guide for what you wish to manifest in your life and share with others.

Since a dream is your creation, you can experience such things as relaxation, release, bliss, and renewal. You can also explore feelings that may be less familiar, such as love, ecstasy, peace, serenity, happiness, wonder, harmony, and illumination. With some skill and effort, you can experience the future as you desire it to be.

In music, movies, computer games, and novels, we step outside of daily life and experience vicarious pleasure in the scenes and actions of real or imaginary characters and events. To condense entertainment down into its essence, imagine sitting in a dark room in which there is a faint violet mist or soft light surrounding you. The magical quality of this mist is that any images appearing within it take on a vibrant feeling of being alive. As in a lucid dream, even a far-fetched fantasy becomes as persuasive as reality.

The astral plane is full of emotionally charged images that contain a full array of inspirations that enable an individual to wake up and fully engage with life. We have many people inside of us—there are kings and queens, presidents and generals, A-list actors as well as the lost and the impoverished homeless. In Yesod, the outer world and the inner world of our soul work together to fulfill our purposes.

VIRTUES, VICES, NEGATIVE

Virtues: Strength, independence, depth of feeling, knowledge of the inner self, innocence, happiness, contentment, satisfaction, self-acceptance, serenity, wonder, awe, being centered, balance, feeling complete.

Vices: Idleness, complacency, conformity, frigidity, moodiness, irritability, depression, guilt, humiliation, shame, being jaded, promiscuity, addiction, compulsion, obsession, insatiable cravings, self-deception, denial, paranoia, co-dependency.

Negative: Narcissistic personality disorder, loss of self, no personal boundaries, mental illness, insanity, self-hatred, illusion, feeling worthless.

CHALLENGE

Discover what makes you happy, fully alive, and at peace with the universe.

As I meditate on Yesod, I feel that what is within me and what is around me are in harmony. Desires still exist, but there is no urgency or concern about being satisfied. I sense that the satisfaction of all desires happens spontaneously, without effort or worry.

Being friendly is perfectly natural and effortless. There is no loneliness or isolation. My body feels saturated with contentment and love. The mother-infant connection of pure affection and intimate, physical pleasure/gratification is also present. There is a sense of being gentle and innocent. This energy vibration is so natural that there is not a trace of selfishness or ego present.

When you look around at your own activities and at other people, you perceive immediately what you want to do and where and to what extent you wish to be involved. You will know when you are focusing correctly on this vibration. You feel saturated with love, affection, tenderness, and kindness. You feel peaceful and content. You appreciate the world around you and nothing is pulling you off-balance or making demands. You are centered in yourself.

> *There is an absolute contentment*
> *In which the inner self*
> *Is at peace with the universe.*

We are responsible for our feelings. As Shakespeare pointed out, we may not be able to control external situations and circumstances, but we can still choose how we respond to events in our lives.

Feelings such as jealousy, anger, envy, and so forth carry a certain power. It is not these emotions but how we respond to them that counts. The challenge in Yesod is to produce in yourself calm serenity and inner peace that continuously renew and transform you from within.

MAGICAL PRACTICE
The Five Senses

Sight

I used to not think in pictures and, for some reason, I had a hard time recognizing faces. To compensate, I tried attending life-drawing classes for a year.

One art teacher said to the class, "Imagine as you move your pencil on the paper that you are actually touching the model's skin." He was trying to add touch to sight to better engage the brain.

After that, I took photography lessons for a year. With a good computer program, you can easily spend an hour editing one photo. There is cropping, resizing, and rotation. There is contrast, exposure, highlights, backlight, and shadows. There is brightness, tint, warmth, hue, tone, saturation, black and white, and color variations.

By editing a picture, your ability to visualize gradually develops. You can make the same photographic adjustments with your mind on something you are looking at. Ordinary sights become artistic compositions. You may look at something and think, "Wow. What a great shot that would make!"

The Hermetic magician Franz Bardon requires his students to do substantial work concentrating on each of the five senses. For Bardon, sight depends on light—which is created by Fire. Fire is powerful, expansive, explosive, and dynamic. It can refine and transform.

Visualizing a task to accomplish or a problem to solve is like being able to say, "I see things as they are now, but I can also see them in a different way. I can visualize step-by-step how to get from where I am now to where I want to be."

✳ Visualization Exercise

Visualize people you have known. If you cannot hold a visual image in your mind, then hold a picture in front of you and glance at it whenever you need to refresh your memory. This practice produces clarity and dispels confusion. You can process your feelings endlessly, but "to see" by visualizing clearly whatever you call before your mind is both reassuring and illuminating.

Visualize a picture in your mind that takes you into another world where you experience peace and bliss.

Sound

If you are a bird watcher, you have the songs of different birds in your memory. If you are vocalist, you may have perfect pitch. A pianist may be able to play entire arrangements from memory. Beethoven could conduct Symphony no. 9 when he was deaf.

A linguist or an actor may be able to mimic accurately nearly any accent he hears. Then again, Hopi Indians claim that they have a glottal stop among the consonants of their language that no linguist has yet been able to hear.

We are surrounded by the sounds of nature, those in our environment and those we hear in music, song, stage performance, and movies.

Different individuals, according to their background and training, will hear the sounds of the world in different ways.

✳ Sound Exercise

To heighten sensory perception, it helps to be able to recall accurately a sound, song, and spoken language. Take any sound from your environment and practice imagining you can hear it again at will. There is the song of the bird, the cat meowing, the dog barking, the wind chimes or the wind howling, falling rain, thunder, a wave breaking, and so on.

Take a song you know and imagine hearing it sung by a different voice or played by different instruments. Take one of your favorite songs and listen to it in your mind. As you listen, focus on the feelings the song creates for you. In addition, try to sustain the feeling without the song that called it forth.

Touch

To sight, the eye. To hearing, the ear. To smell, the nose. To taste, the tongue. But to touch? The hands?

The entire surface of the body is skin, all the nerves internal in the body registering pleasure, pain, pressure, temperature, electrical and magnetic energy, and more. The aura itself responds to contact and vibration.

To develop awareness of tactile impressions, Franz Bardon mentions such things as focusing on sensations of hunger, thirst, tiredness, and so forth.

And yet, in exploring body sensations, we are opening the door to our entire nervous system. Addictions, obsessions, and fascinations all involve strong body sensations rooted in neurology, biochemistry, and biography. Yet many of these sensations are subject to conscious control.

The more acquainted you are with your body—breathing, tension and stress, your ability to relax, the stomach and digestion, your heartbeat, your internal organs, and the whole spectrum of body sensations from prenatal to adult—the more you understand yourself and the more creative you can be in interacting with others.

✴ *Exercise: Zoning*

I previously mentioned "zoning" under the foot meditation in Malkuth. As you focus on physical sensations, the sensations themselves change. The body and consciousness transform each other.

If you focus on your feet or any body part, the sensations may become all that is in your awareness

Descriptions of Zoning

1. Effortless.
2. You are fully alert.
3. It requires no thoughts, no ego, no validation, and so there is no fear or sense of insecurity.
4. It is ongoing.
5. It is filled with bliss.
6. It is ecstatic in that it immerses you in an experience that is outside of your normal, conscious, social identity.
7. In being ecstatic, it also unites you with the natural world.
8. It is relaxing and releases tension.
9. And the zoning I am describing is not fantasy. It takes place within the physical world.
10. Everything happening is within the now.

Zoning is a part of a more formal process called focusing. In focusing you can ask about what you are sensing, "What is this like?" or "What does this remind me of?"

For example, when focusing on my feet, a vast variety of images or other sensations appear. My spontaneous response to the above questions might be, "The sensations in my feet have the solidity of a redwood tree five hundred years old," or "It reminds me of when I touched one of the stones in a stone circle on Mull Island off Scotland."

To better understand zoning, you might try briefly assembling a series of your own experiences relating to bliss, ecstasy, feeling at peace, happy, and so on. Some of these will be tranquilizing and others energizing and some both at once. In some you can notice the effects of adrenaline, dopamine, estrogen, testosterone, or a wave of pleasure in all its many aspects flowing through you.

Smell

A few memories: The first time I caught the scent of the smoke of burning cedar—that for me is pleasure and satisfaction. We each have our favorite smells, like freshly ground coffee.

To catch the scent in the air of moisture and cooler air indicating an approaching wind shift and a distant thunderstorm you do not yet see—that is bliss for me.

To feel that the air that I inhale is part of the sky and that its winds flow through my chest.

The scent of plumeria in the air when I get off the plane after returning to Honolulu.

I recall the first time I caught the scent of the sea. It grabbed hold of me, offering a kingdom of wonder and enchantment.

To wake and to literally smell the hair of a woman filling the room, the woman who was lying next to me in my dream, a woman I have not yet met:

> *In the end no matter where we go*
> *How much we seek to be free*
> *There remains this final mystery*
> *Like the fragrance*
> *Of a woman that fills the air—*
> *Love is everywhere*

Smell, like taste, serves to ground us. Taste and smell relate to the denser aspects of matter and physical being.

Animals have a highly developed olfactory sense. For example, the perception of scent in bloodhounds is many times more sensitive than that in human beings. They can follow trails that are several days old.

Bears, such as the silvertip grizzly found in parts of North America, have a sense of smell seven times stronger than bloodhounds. Bears can detect the scent of food from up to eighteen miles away.

Each sense brings with it its own delight, joy, and feeling of being alive. Explore your perception of smell as well as the other senses. Together, the five senses reveal the mysteries of the natural world.

Taste

Taste has five aspects—salty, bitter, sweet, sour, plus umami. Umami is often tasted for example when you eat pizza. Different cultures add their own specific kinds of taste to this list.

Like the sense of smell, taste strengthens the stability of your consciousness. Sight, sound, and touch can be used to take you away into imaginary worlds, but focusing on the taste of what you are eating brings you back immediately to your body.

There are cultural, psychological, and physiological aspects to taste and our choice of diet. We often associate feelings of well-being and festivity, family life, and love with certain diets and menus. Switching to a different diet, an individual may get the same or better nutrition but lose something in the process.

As you practice taste, try to notice your own cultural and psychological preferences. Notice also the vibration of the food and energy that your sense of taste perceives.

Some women say, "I experience bliss just by eating."

The difference between my approach and Franz Bardon's is that Bardon wants you to be able to concentrate on the sense of taste for five minutes and then later for ten minutes without a single thought appearing in your mind.

What you totally miss when you practice in this way is wonder, awe, and mystery. The five senses are gates leading to infinity. Through them we are able to discover all that can be known about the universe on all planes of existence.

There are entire astral kingdoms within each sense and each sensory perception or sensation. If I focus just on the taste of grapefruit juice in my mouth, it is very easy for me to become the grapefruit tree, its roots, its awareness of seasons, its blossoming and ripening of fruit, and its transmission of seeds. I am within the tree's awareness of time, its relation to the sun, to air, to the elements, and to the Earth.

When I taste grapefruit juice, I am not only aware of nature. I become a part of nature. Taste and smell join you to this world and to the celebration of being alive. I call that feeling of union that the heart celebrates *joy*.

Every now and then take a moment and recall what you have eaten in the last twenty-four hours. Note how hungry you were, the various tastes of the food, and the degree of satisfaction you felt afterward.

COMMON VIRTUE
Self-Acceptance as a Gate to the Inner Self

> *Blessed are those who pass through their inner darkness*
> *without fear or shame, for they shall attain freedom.*

We have hidden desires. We embody contradictions and live with unresolved conflicts. It is our ongoing effort to maintain balance while unmet needs from the past and new desires and longings are welling up within us.

Sigmund Freud indicated that even a rational and responsible individual can be overwhelmed by the id that contains blind and insatiable instinctual, infantile, and primitive desires. These cravings can be so powerful that they can take possession of the individual and leave a trail of destruction if, even briefly, they gain control over our lives.

By contrast, for Carl Jung, the unconscious is like the Library of Alexandria that contains the collective experience of the human race. These collective experiences are embodied within archetypes that inform and guide us through life.

And yet the archetypes themselves are in conflict with each other. Love and a respect for universal life compete with power and the need to survive. Tradition and the wisdom forged from experience are in conflict with new and unexpected opportunities that sudden appear before us.

And then there is the more accessible subconscious—the part of our personalities that contains memories, desires, and purposes that are near to consciousness. Some point out that the subconscious has its own language and mode of communication. For example, it does not respond to thoughts or reason. Rather, it notices the degree of confidence, self-assurance, and command with which you think and speak.

The subconscious deals with the now. It is not sufficient to plan a future in which you are a better person. The subconscious wants to see a picture of the final result you are after as if that result is real and fully present right in this moment.

The subconscious says to the conscious mind, "You are all the time speculating about possible outcomes without making a serious commitment. Show me right now the final result of what you are after, and how certain you are of obtaining it, and I will tell you whether I can supply you with the energy and emotion you need to get there. If you are going to mix in doubt, worry, or uncertainty, then I have much better things to do with myself. Come back when your plans are the substance of reality rather than the stuff of dreams."

As I study the vibration of self-acceptance in myself, traumatic events that happened in the past seem inevitable. It is as if the stress and tension I went through arose from having to learn through trial and error how my inner self and the external world actually work.

In accepting myself, I feel free of an internal judgmental voice. I accept the diversity of myself, of all of my different selves. As Ursula Le Guin says, "We all have many people inside of us," and Shakespeare, "One man in his time plays many parts." Each part of ourselves has its own needs, dreams, and desires to satisfy.

In the process of knowing ourselves, we may discover aspects of ourselves that operate in opposition to our conscious purposes. For example, we may encounter projection, denial, codependency, blaming, hypocrisy, narcissism, regression, self-deception, inflation of ego, guilt, shame, self-doubt, and lack of confidence. Coming to terms with these things is part of our journey.

✶ Exercise: Speaking with Your Subconscious

A simple way to study your conscious/subconscious interaction is to talk to yourself before you go to sleep at night. You can use words but you are more likely to get better results if you use feelings and images. For example, make a picture and add the feeling of how you wish to sleep during the night. And then add how you want to feel when you wake up in the morning.

You can, for example, tell yourself you are going to experience a deep peace as you sleep and that you will wake up happy and ready to get up and go. Briefly, make a picture and feel what this would be like. Thank your subconscious in the morning when you succeed.

It may take time to learn to work in this way. But there is no one sitting next to your bed at night saying you can't do this. It is your subconscious. There are obviously a lot of things that can interfere with this process. But ultimately sleeping and dreaming are you spending quality time with yourself.

The Shadow

Jungian psychology gives us the symbol of the shadow. The shadow by definition is the part of ourselves that we consider inferior and humiliating. If we focus on it, we may be aware of it, but it seems foreign or in opposition to who we are.

When it asserts its presence, we may feel awkward, embarrassed, ashamed, or even afraid that it is there. Its presence is hard to accept. For Carl Jung, the shadow is a dark, primitive, and instinctual part of our personality. It is ever with us as part of our motivation, emotions, and drives, and yet it eludes our understanding.

The shadow has no conscience and no awareness of our overall objectives. All the same, the shadow contains things of value that are hidden from consciousness. If this content is denied, the individual may lose a degree of vitality, spontaneity, charisma, and creativity.

One way you can observe your own shadow is by noticing when you dislike or hate other people. This can involve projection. The very thing in them that you find obnoxious or evil is a reflection of what is in yourself. It may be that what you dislike is that the other person is giving vent to something active in you that you have repressed or deny.

The shadow is a paradox. If you give in to the shadow and surrender to its demands, you act in gross and unwholesome ways. If you deny or repress it, again, you may lose your creativity and momentum, for it has the power to undermine your motivation.

The shadow reminds us that we are not yet fully alive. When we define ourselves in a specific way, we automatically leave out much of what is active within us. This can be instinctual cravings, desires, needs, ways of acting and being that we not only dislike and disown but that we have in some way managed to convince ourselves do not exist within us.

The shadow requires of us, then, that we invent new ways of living. And this requirement that we acknowledge and redirect these shadowy, instinctual desires continues through our entire life; the shadow points out to us in what ways we find ourselves restrained and inhibited by our conventional lifestyles and normal ways of thinking.

It may require a lifelong search and massive effort to reconcile who we are in our social identity with what is inside of us. Like so many things in life, the shadow demands that we give it our full attention, if only because it has important things to say. And it requires we remain ever vigilant so that it does not end up laying traps that defeat us.

We are on a spiral circling back on itself as each loop moves onto a higher level. We repeat what we did before but each time with greater success and creativity. And yet there comes a time when we see that we are the entire spiral—the darkest beginnings and the highest perfection are joined together within us. The higher self understands that it could never have ascended without undergoing the entire journey.

There is a point where we can look back and see that every desire will be satisfied, every need met, every dream manifest, every ideal made real, every vision fulfilled, and every quest attained. Self-acceptance on this level means that we have made the universe our friend.

Hormones Related to Happiness

In addition to the psychological aspects of self-acceptance, happiness depends in part on hormones that are tied to our behaviors. Here are four hormones related to happiness—dopamine, serotonin, oxytocin, and endorphin.

Dopamine

Dopamine released into the bloodstream produces good feelings as you make progress toward a goal. You feel excitement and energy as you are about to get something you want. There is a feeling of strength, as in "We are almost there. Let's finish this."

The steps can be small or large and the goal can be near or far. It is the sense of movement that produces the reward. Put the garbage by the door so it is ready to take out. Do some background research on what you are about to buy. Check something off on a to-do list. In each case, you are closing in on accomplishing something.

You can observe this in yourself. There is a feeling of satisfaction in moving toward a goal. Consider setting up your daily schedule to cash in on this hormone's contribution to your energy level.

Serotonin

This is a favorite of Tony Robbins, a famous life coach. Serotonin is stimulated by confidence. Remind yourself of your successes and things are you are doing right. Keep the best image of yourself in front of your mind.

Serotonin fights off anxiety and depression, so it is valuable addition to your neurochemical cabinet of natural medicines. Make a habit of challenging yourself to excel even in very minor ways, like adding a new exercise to your daily workout. Read something informative every day. Keep on top of the things you need to get done.

Serotonin in your bloodstream carries with it a feeling of being confident without the need to be pushy or dominant. When you trust and feel in control of yourself everything is so much easier to do.

Oxytocin

Oxytocin is strong when you have a feeling of connection to other people. It supports emotional bonding. Expressions of affection like hugs, kissing, and sexual intimacy release it into the bloodstream. Pet your dog or cat for five minutes and you heighten its effect.

Stay in touch with your friends. Compliment others when appropriate, and show gratitude. Be altruistic. Help others in need. In talking to others, disclose personal details about yourself that enrich the conversation.

Oxytocin heightens awareness of social cues that are present in group activities. There is a greater support for actions that preserve group survival. Oxytocin reduces fear and anxiety and heightens trust of others and a feeling of security. It can also act as an antidepressant, and with injuries it reduces inflammation and accelerates healing.

Oxytocin is strongly related to empathy. In an evolutionary context, the male gender is less affected by oxytocin since they are more likely involved in hunting and warfare activities that require less empathy in order to succeed.

Endorphins

Endorphins are released into the bloodstream to reduce pain and stress, to increase pleasure, and boost mood with the result of enhancing well-being. They enable us to keep functioning in spite of injury and pain.

They are responsible for euphoric states found in the runner's high, vigorous exercise, in sex, in listening to music, in dance, and in eating spicy foods or dark chocolate. Laughter, yoga, skilled meditation, and simply enjoying a favorite movie can also produce it.

Acceptance of ourselves is the first step of an inward journey. Know yourself and take care of yourself. The journey has no end.

MAGICAL VIRTUE
The Element of Water

Of the many states of consciousness described in this book, the vibration of Water is the least known and understood. One Taoist master said to me, "It is impossible to teach Westerners how to meditate on the Water element." He taught the other elements but not Water.

Of the fifty or so masters I have taken seminars from, none of them had the vibration of Water in their auras. There is no lineage, no tradition, and no temples of the Water element or of mermaids and mermen. Jesus said of his disciples, "Out of their bellies shall flow streams of living water." But this prophecy has not been fulfilled even after two thousand years.

Though there are token uses of water in religious rituals, there are no serious prayers, sacraments, or liturgical practices that evoke the healing and purifying virtues of Water. If you watch an outdoor baptism, it is like the baptized individual is trying to get out of the water as fast as humanly possible. Water is an unknown domain within the landscape of the soul.

On the other hand, as difficult as working with Water may be, Water offers fabulous benefits for those who unite their consciousness with it. Those with the vibration of Water never lose their innocence. This means that traumatic past experiences do not limit their ability to give all of themselves in the present moment.

Water is self-purifying. Its vibration dissolves fear, sorrow, unhappiness, sadness, anxiety, and depression. Water annihilates loneliness.

Water offers renewal. It fulfills your dreams. It makes things whole and complete. Christopher Columbus put it this way: "And the sea shall grant each man new hope, as sleep brings dreams of home."

You will notice, for example, after you succeed in Water meditations, that people otherwise indifferent to you now enjoy being around you. They do not understand why, but your energy makes them feel more alive, more whole, and new.

✦ Water Meditation ✦

As we did with the magical virtue in the previous sephirah of Malkuth, we can begin meditating on the feet. Recall that blood is around 80 percent water. Using our imagination, we can put off to the side the other components in blood and concentrate on the Water content.

Focus on the feet and imagine just Water instead of blood is flowing through them. Some people will be able to feel this sensation directly, but it is sufficient to imagine the sensation. There are both physical sensations and feeling aspects to this awareness. Flowing Water has these properties. It is cool, yielding, receptive, purifying, endlessly adaptable, receiving energy into itself, storing it, and then releasing. Become fully aware of these aspects of Water so that they are the only thing in your awareness.

Along with the physical sensations of flowing Water, there are the feelings that accompany or are behind and underneath them. Water is soothing, nurturing, renewing, healing, serene, calming, refreshing, bringing to life and making fully alive, and vivacious.

Selfishness, jealousy, and resentment are foreign to its nature. Though protective, sheltering, and nurturing, it does not allot any time to the need to feel important, validating one's identity, or being posses-sive. Put simply, Water is innocent and endlessly giving. But be careful thinking it easy to exploit and to direct. There are also no ends to its depths, and it embraces all that exists.

This meditation can be done every day. You can begin focusing on the sensations of Water flowing through the feet. You can then extend this flowing sensation up to the lower legs and gradually through the rest of your body. Or you can begin with the feet and then imagine Water flowing through the entire body.

The feelings associated with flowing Water may appear spontane-ously. Or you can focus on each feeling by itself, such as the calming sensation or a spontaneous feeling of happiness.

Later on, you may feel it is effortless to sense a connection between the flowing Water in your body and images of Water in nature such as a mountain waterfall, a stream, a river, lakes, an ocean bay, and the sea. Alternately, you can use your imagination to drop the temperature of Water so it moves from feeling cool to very cold. Colder Water height-ens receptivity and healing capacity due to being able to absorb more heat quicker. And, again, as the meditation succeeds, you may notice you can begin to relieve simple things like headaches and tension in yourself as well as in other people.

For more on the Water element, see my books *Undines: Lessons from the Realm of the Water Spirits* and *The Four Elements*.

DIVINE VIRTUE
Creating Peace, Happiness, Contentment; Comprehending Opposites

The divine virtue in Yesod is the ability to create specific feelings at will. We can do this by imaginatively reentering situations where these feelings were strong. When I say "reenter," I mean treat a memory like an actor about to walk on stage to play a part in a well-rehearsed play. You review a situation in your mind. And then you enter it and live through it as if experiencing it for the first time.

Actors possess skills. They put everything else off to the side so there is no distraction. They respond to cues and actions as they are happening so they are in the present moment. And they create a backstory that explains why they think and feel as they do, so as to better internalize their role.

But you have an advantage over actors. You have had the actual experience. Your memory can be revived so that it takes on the quality of a lucid dream. Everything appears real regardless of how unlikely it is.

Consider situations that were cold, hostile, or unfriendly. Go back and relive a few of those memories.

Next consider the opposite—situations where people were warm and friendly. If you succeed in this simple exercise, you are in effect creating within yourself whatever feelings you wish. Demonstrate to yourself that imagination can command both the positive and the negative.

Continue to the next step. Hold both positive and negative feelings before your gaze at the same time. Imagine, for example, you are in a theater and the stage is divided in two at the center with a curtain. On one side is the memory you have lived through of a positive experience, and on the other side is a memory of a negative experience. Imagine you are able to visit each side of the curtain as you wish.

Consider the paired opposites:

Sadness	Happiness
Disapproval	Approval
Hate	Love
Loneliness	Intimacy

Pick one or two pairs from the above list or choose your own pairs of opposites. Then recall a memory of one feeling and then its opposite. Again, as in the example of the divided stage, hold both positive and negative feelings before your gaze at the same time.

One aspect of the negative is that it needlessly wastes energy, time, and opportunities. It holds back and controls rather than freeing and liberating. Some individuals may discover they cannot imagine the positive version of a negative feeling. Their attachment to the past is too strong and the experience is still overwhelming. And this is important to grasp, because there are traumas, fears, terrors, and horrific experiences that are handed down from one generation to another.

Sometimes an entire family, a culture, a religion, or a nation is traumatized by a set of events from which it has the greatest difficulty recovering. Until it does so, the future is shaped by what the past contains rather than by what can be imagined, envisioned, or dreamed.

Sometimes more experience is required before an individual can distinguish between positive and negative. Through new experiences over the years, an individual may look back and be astonished that what he once accepted as normal he now considers to have been completely negative. In other words, there is a learning curve in which we replace the negative with the positive, the unhealthy with the healthy, and the weak with the strong.

In the above cases, the individual is not just attempting to become more mature and emotionally healthy. To move forward, he is working through the collective karma (sorrow, fear, failure, hopelessness) of a larger group to which he belongs.

Sometimes the conflicts of the individual are a reflection of conflicts within the collective archetypes of the human race. In such cases, we have a kind of hero's journey described by Joseph Campbell in which the individual engages in a journey that leads deep inside of oneself. On this journey, the individual will discover new allies and skills and also encounter major obstacles and unknown dangers. If he succeeds in his journey, he is able to return to the familiar world of society with new knowledge or a gift that enriches the world.

Negative and positive experiences both have learning curves. You begin where you are now. And then you imagine what you wish to be. Reality—the changes you can produce in yourself—will be your best test for determining your progress.

The end result of imagining both the positive and the negative is that an individual ends up feeling clear inside. There is an appreciation that there are things that needed to be learned and experiences that had to be lived through before self-understanding arises. One further result is a feeling of gratitude that life grants us the opportunity to take who we are and become transformed.

Recapturing Projection

We see ourselves reflected in other people.

There is healthy give-and-take in relationships. Each person has something to give to the other. Part of the attraction may be that the other person reflects back to us something hidden in ourselves. The other has a calmness, confidence, beauty, playfulness, vivaciousness, or a feeling of being alive that we do not have.

If the relationship ends or does not progress, we may feel we have lost something. We may feel less alive or less valuable. But whatever it is that the other person has we can recapture to some extent. In which case, the other person served to introduce us to something wonderful that we are now meant to make a part of ourselves.

For example, there is a girl in Siberia who for me has the soul of a sylph, an Air spirit. She is very spontaneous, loves play, and has a marvelous sense of independence and an outrageous feeling of joy. She is not frivolous, because in fact she has a strong work ethic. She holds down three jobs. Rather, in her soul she feels free. And she can give herself totally to the experience of a moment without worrying about what others might think. She has the ecstasy of the Air element.

If I try to reproduce her energy in myself, it is the feeling of being high up in a blue sky. I feel totally weightless, floating, and free of any restricting influence. And though I sense my body, I also feel more relaxed than I have ever felt before in my life.

If there is turmoil or trauma or intense things going on in my life, it would be exactly like being up there in the open, clear, blue sky and watching on the horizon a thunderstorm's lightning pounding the Earth with its shock waves. It would seem beautiful and full of wonder in its own way. But that thunderstorm, or difficult experience, does not weigh on me or restrict me.

What I just did is take a woman and translate my attraction to her into an awareness of being a part of nature. To some extent, a man may look at the woman as being more of nature, a natural feeling he wants in himself.

For most women it is usually the opposite. She looks at the man as being a part of society—productive, making his own decisions with confidence and a strong sense of self. Of course, with the actual girl we can do very creative and fun things together. But I do not feel undue loss if she is not available. This is because I can sense how she is within and part of me.

That is an example of taking a hard look at what another person means or feels like to you and reproducing that individual's energy in yourself. In psychology, this is called "recapturing projection," though psychologists may not turn to nature to find those energies.

I also study the Water element and incarnated mermaids. When I was younger, I always felt that society was hiding the nature of the feminine spirit from me. It was not until I was twenty-nine years old that I met a woman whose aura reflected the element of Water in nature. It would be another thirty years before I would meet a second incarnated mermaid. And during those thirty years I did not even know how to describe this aspect of femininity that is missing from society.

And so the question, How do you do what such women do? They are totally in the moment, totally receptive, completely giving of themselves. There is no ego weighing them down, no guilt, no loss of innocence, and no insecurity that might awaken jealousy or bitterness.

Their energy is literally that of a stream, a mountain pool, an ocean bay, or the entire ocean itself. I was once meditating with a mermaid queen and she said to me, "Shut up and give me ten minutes in which you just immerse your consciousness without any thoughts in the experience of being inside of an iceberg."

Because I was using a high level of concentration, this was not difficult to do. She was pointing out a basic rule of magic. Experience things for yourself firsthand. Then you can understand it.

What was I projecting on mermaid women? For me, literally, their brain waves are the vibration of Water. They are as I describe—flowing, releasing, soothing, calming, purifying, healing, nurturing, giving, without any ego being present.

To become flowing like Water in your feelings without your thoughts arising or evaluating the process is nearly impossible for a human male to accomplish. He would have to forget about the girl and go spend a great deal of time studying and imagining he was Water in nature in one or more aspects. And this is not something men do. It is not something gurus, masters, or teachers in any tradition on Earth do either.

You want to recapture projection in regard to a mermaid in human form? Then forget about the women. Find nature at the core of your being.

But to be fair to the process, I actually do not want to become a merman equivalent of an incarnated mermaid. I want the watery sense of flowing, being in the moment, and giving, but I still want to maintain all my other abilities and purposes. Recapturing projection, then, is not just reproducing in yourself what you are attracted to in the other person. It is also integrating it into yourself in a harmonious way.

To summarize, recapturing projection is taking a hard look at another person who we feel attracted to. The other may do for us what no one else can. All the same, we can also imagine how we would be different if that other person was a part of us. Instead of being dependent on another or feeling loss if the other does not respond, we become a stronger and more independent person.

Perhaps the other person's role in your life is not to make things easy for you. Instead, she has introduced you to a journey of self-discovery. Her gift to you is to assist you in finding something in yourself you did not know was there.

In my novel *The Admiral's Mermaid,* the admiral asks the young girl, "Who are you?" She replies, "I am the part of you that you will never find on your own."

DREAM

The dream of Yesod is being in a physical state of bliss. For example, it is easy enough to notice bliss in advanced practitioners of yoga. Through stretching and breathing, they produce in themselves a mind that is calm, emotions that are serene, and a nervous system that is saturated with a refined pleasure.

We can carefully brew a cup of coffee that has a crisp taste on the tip of the tongue. It has body and a soothing, strengthening stimulation. We can make a wine that is balanced, has intricate flavors, and a distinct and pleasing aroma. We can also produce refined pleasure and ecstatic sensuality in our bodies.

Under the section on Magical Practice, I mentioned that each of the five senses has its own experience of bliss. So does the entire body. Breathe in. Relax. There is food and liquid in the digestive track, air in the lungs, muscles that are toned, and a harmonious metabolism. Enter a dream in which you can say to yourself, "Every desire is satisfied beyond what I could have wished for or imagined."

In a state of bliss, endorphins and dopamine run thick in the bloodstream. Many people produce this vibration through external means such as surfing, skydiving, mountain climbing, or winning in some sport. They enter a zone in a rush of adrenaline.

We can experience bliss through activities in the outer world and then internalize the experience. We make them part of ourselves. There are not just the golden days of our youth when we challenged ourselves by pressing ourselves to the limit. There is the wonder of being alive that is always with us. Look within. Use the magic of your imagination. Find a source of bliss in yourself that continuously overflows.

INITIATION

The initiation of Malkuth was to be out in nature on your own without need of social validation or support and to internalize that sense of well-being, of being solid and grounded, as well as an inner silence. And then to bring that feeling back with us so it energizes our work in society.

In a similar way, the initiation of Yesod is to draw together the powers of the inner self—a sense of happiness, of contentment, self-acceptance; the purity, healing, and innocence of the Water element; the ability to create feelings at will; and the bliss of the dream.

Work with your shadow, the untutored and primitive part of yourself. Give your emotions your full attention. Unite with the Water element. Put aside your ego. Enter a purely receptive state of mind and focus your awareness so that only flowing Water exists in your consciousness.

Recall and focus on the very best feelings you have had in life.

Hold them before your consciousness. Relive them. Make them part of yourself.

The sephirah of Yesod is all about the inner world of the psyche that sustains us from within. Turn your inner life into a dream that nurtures you and grants you strength and renewal. Fulfill the divine imperative to participate in the unfolding of the world—become your own creation.

MYSTERY
The Astral Plane, Spiritual Anthropology,
Global Dreamtime

The mystery of Yesod is that, while supporting our individual ability to feel, the astral plane contains a vast range of emotional life that is as yet unknown to the human race.

Astral body: The astral body pertains to the realm of the soul, to feelings and emotions. The astral body is in the shape of the physical body but is made of a subtler substance. It is receptive and responsive in the present moment to who you are with and the situation you are in. The depth and variety of feelings expressed through the astral body are what enables us to feel fully alive.

Astral plane: The astral plane surrounds and penetrates the physical world. Sometimes referred to as the "other side," the "world beyond," or "the next world," the astral plane contains many realms and kingdoms.

According to firsthand accounts, the astral plane can be visited through astral projection, psychic perception, meditation, lucid dreaming, near death and out of body experiences, and other means.

The astral plane offers elemental energies that nurture our souls the way food, water, and sunlight provide energy that keeps our bodies alive in the physical world. Without the benevolent support of the astral plane, when people die there would be nothing left of us, since there would be nothing to sustain the soul when it is not attached to a physical body.

The astral plane operates by different laws than the physical world. Matter in our world has shape, weight, chemistry, and density. A rock can exist for billions of years in the same form, as do some meteorites you can find lying around on the ground. And this dense matter of the physical world stores immense amounts of energy. Ten pounds of uranium can destroy a city. No one goes around destroying cities on the astral plane.

Our physical world is governed by linear time producing history where one event follows another. Work hard. Produce material and cultural wealth and what you accomplish enriches the world. At the same time, the physical world is characterized by limitations that we strive to overcome in order to survive and to succeed in our endeavors.

By contrast, the astral plane has no planting and no harvesting, no sex and no reproduction. The soul is sustained by an energy field that encompasses the planet. If you imagine something, unlike in our world, there is no delay between what you imagine and what manifests.

Time and space as well are different. If you wish to be somewhere then you are there. No need for horse, boat, bus, or plane. In the physical world you will meet people with whom you have nothing in common. This does not happen on the astral plane. People associate with others who are of a similar vibration.

If you love and are free of fear, then those individuals who are similar to you will be easy to meet. If you are competitive and defensive, then similar souls will be near you. Your aura and vibration determine the settings and beings you encounter on the Other Side.

All the same, the astral body attaches itself to what it is familiar with. The past shapes what we feel and think. Traditions unite groups of people, defining goals and offering strategies.

When someone dies, they do not say, "Oh. I am no longer bound by a physical body. I can now assume any form I wish. I shall be as brilliant as Einstein, as artistic as Beethoven, as perceptive as Shakespeare, and as dynamic and determined as George Washington and Lincoln." But they do not say this. They feel closely tied to the body they once lived in and the social matrix in which they existed.

It seems the astral plane produces experiences that seem real the way dreams at night seem real to us while we are dreaming. But dreams at night are like a carnival house of mirrors. They reflect our daily lives. They remind us of the past, confronting us with repressed fears and desires. They warn us of possible futures. They are stimulating, reviving, and a kind of pressure valve, a place to release tension and stress.

The astral plane, by contrast, is like a sea of energy that we are all immersed within. It supports every feeling, every personality, every culture, every religion, and every path of life. And it stores a nearly incomprehensible spectrum of sensations, feelings, and ecstasies, many of which are outside of the human imagination.

You can be an adept at lucid dreaming where you wake up in your dreams each night. And in your lucid dreaming you can also shift from personal dreaming to moving among the kingdoms of the astral plane. And yet all the explorers of human history have only made brief excursions into these mysterious astral realms.

✴ Dream Exercise

A simple exercise for working with the astral plane is to explore your dreams. Take one or two of your best dreams and then enter them again while you are awake. Play with the imagery. Make changes and edits. Fashion them in whatever way you want.

For example, imagine you have a close friend who is highly skilled at listening. This individual does what no one else can—he gives you 100 percent of his attention. He hears everything you have to say, grasps every feeling, and is always there for you. You feel perfectly safe, always accepted, and always understood. This experience is an astral creation available to everyone.

Using your imagination in this way, you gain the ability to follow your feelings through various imaginary landscapes of history, mythology, religion, and the domains of astral beings as well. This is called a pathworking—you take an image, an idea, a person, or a spirit, and then imagine in a dream state of mind what it would be like to interact in some way with it.

Warnings

It would not be fair to discuss the astral plane without warning about the dangers of premature contact. There is a reason why most people find it difficult to interact consciously with the astral plane. To keep themselves alive, they need to stay focused on the physical world.

On the other hand, some individuals suffer from an overexposure to the astral plane. Imagine trying to do all the things you do each day while in any moment you may "see," "hear," or "feel" things that are not part of our physical reality.

It is one thing to see fairies and the spirits of dead people. These perceptions are part of legends, oral traditions, and mythologies. They may be part of your ethnic or family tradition. But what if an individual also sees dragons, werewolves, hobgoblins, wood elves, jinn, leprechauns, various UFO entities, gargoyles, banshees, and/or monstrous beings of every imaginable kind?

What if a leprechaun returns to you each year offering a pot of gold in exchange for a few favors that greatly reduce your ability to feel? Or perhaps your life is in a rut? Are you down and out? Why not imagine you are a great prophet who is here to warn the world of impending dangers? We certainly have enough dangers that need warning about. Or perhaps you are being cursed by some astral being who has nothing better to do than spend all of his time and energy trying to make you fail in life?

Or are you like Narcissus? You catch a glimpse of yourself and fall in love with what you see? Everything else in the world is now dim by comparison. The astral plane vastly amplifies ordinary emotions, turning them into ladders leading up into the light or down into darkness.

It is one thing for a highly trained individual to use a magical ritual to interact with spirits. He operates following traditional rules, one of which is maintaining secrecy. It is totally different if an individual wants to share with others his experiences with a glittering array of beings that inhabit the astral plane. It can be very exhausting to listen to someone ramble on about such experiences, unless of course you write fairy tales and love firsthand accounts.

There are also experiences on the astral plane that are so enticing they make life in our world appear to be shallow and meaningless. Some people even commit suicide because they have had a taste of the peace and bliss of the astral plane.

As enticing and inviting as it may be to turn to the astral plane for relief, it is like trading gold for straw. You can learn more in one life-time on Earth than you can learn in many lives lived out on the astral plane. And yet the astral plane remains close by. There are people and spirits that will mentor and assist you, and there are people and spirits that will try to exploit and destroy you. As with all things, check out the product or what is being offered before you buy.

The Beautiful Park
An Interview with Ronda Starkey

Ronda is an amazing psychic and healer. When she lucid dreams each night, she makes contact with a great number of people and spirits on the astral plane. Among other things, Ronda acts as a greeter for the newly departed. This material is from an interview with her.

Some people experience being in a beautiful park on the astral plane after they die. It is a place to help people transition from the life they have left behind so they can move on. But you do not have to die to experience it. You can imagine it and enter it now through meditation.

Relax. Now imagine you are in a beautiful park. For example, the park could be a composite of the best of the sixty-two national parks in the United States, except here the colors are far more vivid than anything we experience in our world. The blue of the sky has twenty or more shades of color. The clouds are so soft and real it is like you can reach out and touch them or climb up on one, lie down on it, and float along in the sky.

The songs of birds are enchanting. They sing to you that whatever you may have ever lost is now returning to you and found again.

The flowers are exquisite in form and beauty. The scent of a flower is like sipping a wine that is full of mirth, joy, and play.

And if you touch a tree, placing your hand on its bark, it feels as if you are touching the body of a woman. And like a woman you love, the tree invites you to become one, to share the innermost feelings and dreams within your soul.

There are no heavy feelings here. Your body feels nearly weightless. And, if you thought about it, you would notice there are no fears or threats here and no need to struggle to survive. You feel absolutely safe, secure, and filled with a wonderful sense of well-being.

When you breathe, you do not breathe in air but rather you feel light flowing through your body. And the sunlight touching your skin is a healing caress, rejuvenating and granting you the vigor and exhilaration of youth.

It is as if the divine world has created this park as a way to feel what is so rarely felt while being alive—that nature is within you. And with this perception you also feel welling up from inside an inner peace with the universe.

Here a great harmony embraces all things. Discord and conflict have been transformed into beauty and wonder. There is a faint sound in the distance of a magnificent symphony. And if you listen carefully, you might hear a voice gently saying, "What you experience here is an act of creation. All that you feel and sense is within your power to create at any time and in whatever world you exist."

If I focus on this beautiful park, there is a prelude. I am drinking a bottle of rare wine with friends who have already died. The taste heightens the imagination, opens perception to other realities, and takes you just outside of space and time.

And then I am here, in the beautiful park. There is a still lake, gorgeous trees of all colors, and an exquisitely designed gazebo. A violinist is walking around the lake playing joyous melodies. There is a hot-air balloon floating in the sky with passengers sipping champagne.

And over in the distance, Alexander the Great is riding an elephant. Sitting next to him is King Porus of Punjab, India. But instead of recalling their war with each other, they are traveling in an alternate reality in which their wise men have established peace throughout the world.

In such a world, knowledge is such that the innermost thoughts and feelings of any man are fully revealed. This is the beautiful park for me, not just soothing to the senses and serene. It is a place of magic and the fulfillment of dreams. And, as you can see, it is not so far away. In fact, the entire spiritual universe, with a little imagination, is available to experience firsthand.

Realms, Kingdoms, and Domains
within the Astral Plane

Perhaps the most familiar realm of the astral plane is the place where the dead and those not yet born reside. It is where people "enter the light" when they die and, as we have seen, here is a beautiful park for new arrivals. And there is a life review in which you relive every moment of your life.

From individual accounts of those who on a daily basis visit and have assigned duties on the astral plane, each individual's experience of the afterlife is different. In general, however, newly departed often carry with them from their previous lives their unsatisfied desires and unfulfilled dreams. Since the astral plane is so responsive to imagination, these souls spend some time experiencing all that they wished they might have experienced while still alive.

If you wanted to but did not win an Oscar while alive, then you can walk the red carpet as many times as you want on the astral plane. You are in effect the protagonist living out the movie script you have written. Others form communities where they associate with people of the same mental and soul vibrations.

At some point, however, whether in a happy spiritual realm or in a self-created realm of fantasy, an individual will tire of the routine and begin to long for new, more challenging experiences that offer a higher learning curve. There is no place like the physical world in which to be confronted by challenges and to learn new things.

We can also speak of a "lower" level of the astral plane. Here are found lost souls, some of whom have died traumatically. They cling to the life they left behind even though the physical world has changed and no one there remembers their name. And here are larvae and phantoms—creatures created subconsciously through emotional or sexual excitement and obsessive compulsions.

Beyond the realm of the newly departed, the astral plane has a vast array of realms and kingdoms. There is an entire bestiary—there are unicorns and dragons, giants and medusas, gorgons and harpies, banshees and werewolves, and more. Anything you can imagine is present somewhere in some form because these astral beings are not constrained by physical reality.

Some of these races are present in folktales and legends. The Sidhe, for example, which are associated with Irish and Scottish mythology, are similar to fairies and elves. They are sometimes viewed as living in an invisible world that coexists with our own.

There are stories of jinn, such as the Fire spirit that is the genie in the story *Aladdin*. Mermaids appear in a great many legends. Homer mentions the sirens, and the Greeks had water nymphs and a number of other nature spirits. There are flower fairies, wood elves, trolls, and hobgoblins to name a few. All of these beings are part of the reports of those who are sufficiently clairvoyant to see and interact with them.

Some individuals in our world reach out and speak with fairy queens and even marry them. Others visit these realms at night when they dream. And this is not so strange. Some who are adept at lucid dreaming can easily meet and interact with other people who are asleep and dreaming. When they awake in the morning, they remember experiencing the same things together. In these lucid dreams, they are on the astral plane, and so many of these astral beings are free to appear to them.

Again, because the astral plane is so responsive to imagination, visualization, feeling, and suggestion, it is quite possible to create an individual or shared dream. Most notable are the gurus, saints, and masters of various lineages. Part of many ritual practices involves making contact with deceased lineage masters who offer advice and assistance to the living.

Religions have their own versions of heaven. Each has its own specific range of vibrations derived from its ideals and what it values as sacred, holy, life-giving, and enduring. With sufficient will and skill, you can create your own magical realm. Invite others to share it with you or else populate it with a vast number of creatures your imagination calls into being.

The astral plane is not so hard to experience vicariously. You can do this by playing a computer game that has characters leveling up, a story line, artistic scenes, captivating music, and mythology. You are in effect entering an imaginary dream developed by many writers, artists, and programmers with voices supplied by actors accompanied by an array of dramatic music.

The video game industry has begun making more money than movies and North American sports combined. In its first year, *Conan Exiles* sold over a million copies. You can even play it online with others joining with you or with your clan. If you play *Conan Exiles, Skyrim, Enderal,* or other games for a month, pause and review your experiences. Recall what you felt at the beginning, as you discovered new things, during conflict, and as you approached the endgame.

Think about it. The game imagery generates feelings of wonder, surprise, and delight as well as frustration, confusion, and a respect for what you did not know you were up against. You may have started over a number of times and you may have determined to solve whatever problems confronted you.

When you play a game online, there may be ten thousand other people active in the same imaginary landscape along with you. The astral plane is slightly different, however. The dreamlike images you encounter are often archetypes. Here is the entire human race with all the dreams, motivations, inspirations, drives, desires, and ideals that have determined the course of their lives.

The Four Elemental Realms

On the astral plane are the realms of the four elemental beings. The souls of these life-forms embody the vibration of one element from nature—Earth, Air, Fire, or Water. In other words, they are nature itself in an intelligent form.

✳ Biographical Note ✳

In one of my roles, I am a "mermaid greeter." I offer assistance to mermaid spirits who have incarnated in human bodies at birth and have grown up usually thinking that they are human. Having studied mermaids in their own realm on the astral plane, I have been able to say to them when they are here living among us, "If you have any questions about being here that you want answered or if there is any way I can assist you, let me know."

Some of these women do an internet search for "mermaid" and "woman," and then they find my essay "Traits of Mermaid Women."

They then write me and say, "You are the first person who understands who I am," or, "It is like you are inside of my head."

My exploration of the four elemental realms on the astral plane and with those who incarnate from those realms began forty-five years ago. Just out of college, I met a freshman who was the daughter of Presbyterian minister. Unknown to her parents, she was also the granddaughter of a hereditary Scottish witch. In that esoteric, oral tradition, the grandmother passed down the Wiccan craft to the granddaughter without the mother knowing anything about it.

She told me how a Wiccan coven in Canada wanted her as its priestess, in part because she was a natural-born psychic and had the Wiccan tradition in her blood. This group was doing everything in its power to compel her to join them. Wiccans I have spoken with deny that this could happen. But human beings are human beings. When people associate together in a group, they can become greedy, selfish, abusive, and malicious.

So there I was. I just finished a major in philosophy at a decent college. I studied with a well-known philosopher at the University of Chicago. And then I run into a girl who is multidimensional in consciousness; she is able to directly perceive the astral plane.

She could see spirits moving through a room. She could perceive the state of the souls of the dead as she walked through a graveyard. She was clairvoyant, telepathic, and clairsentient.

I encountered something my entire Western tradition—from Socrates to Martin Heidegger and Paul Ricoeur—knows nothing about. For goodness' sake. The Brothers Grimm, with all the fairy tales they collected in Germany, never ran into this. Dante, having written about hell, purgatory, and heaven, knew nothing about this. Dante populated the astral plane of his Divine Comedy with figments of his own imagination, following the vices and virtues laid out by bishops who forbade their practitioners to study the spiritual world.

I went around and consulted with any religious authorities I could find. They basically said, "We have no knowledge of the astral plane or of the actual practices of other religions. Try prayer. That is all we have to offer."

Consider our technology. It is okay to rewrite DNA, to send the

Voyager outside the solar system, to invent AIs, to create temperatures in laboratories hotter than the sun, to design bombs that can destroy cities with nuclear fission or fusion, to have machines roaming the sands on other planets, to give weather reports on exoplanets in other star systems, to create direct neurological links between computers and the brain, and on and on.

But religious authorities do not wish to upgrade their perception so as to perceive through firsthand experience the nature of the spiritual realms that surround us in every moment of time? I am not so coy, complacent, or void of curiosity.

However, it took me another twenty years before I was in a position to accurately read her aura. The girl was not a human being or an incarnated mermaid. She was a spirit of the Air element, a sylph, incarnated in human form. Sylphs have the ability to perfectly attune to you "as if you are inside my head reading my mind."

Incarnated sylphs, like the sylphs in the sky, cherish freedom above all things. They like to appear and then disappear, going their own way as does the wind. It was not the girl I was attracted to. My attraction was to the entire astral plane that she introduced me to. And so over the decades I have entered all four elemental realms on the astral plane, gotten to know some of their kings and queens, and set down my experiences in two books published by North Atlantic Books.

The young natural-born psychic, heir to a Wiccan lineage and an incarnated sylph, left my life behind as if we had never met. But first she took me a few miles from my college and introduced me to what was perhaps at the time the largest occult library in the world, which was at a local Theosophical Society. I spent so much time there reading books that were not in the libraries of Harvard, Stanford, or Oxford that the librarians used to have me watch over things when they left for afternoon tea.

✦

The Four Elemental Realms

Salamanders are Fire in action
Lava flowing, volcanoes exploding,
Tectonic plates unfolding

When a thunderstorm's lightning
Shatters and shakes
Darkness quakes
A salamander emits willpower
The way Fire emits light.
Grasp their power
To fight for what is true and right.
For the Fire element:
There is an electrifying
Enthusiasm and conviction
Such that when others see you
They see an ideal now real
Sylphs are light and clear as air
Free of bondage and fear
In the atmosphere they are everywhere
They balance these opposites—
Hot and cold,
Low and high,
Wet and dry,
Calm and turbulent,
Electric and magnetic—
Bringing harmony to the sky
Kiss a sylph on her lips
And you may taste enlightenment
In the Air element:
There is outrageous good cheer
Free of all fear—
Walk through life with freedom
Delight and rapture illuminating
Every sensory perception.
A mermaid's love like water flows
Beyond what the human mind can know—
Innocent, embracing, forever giving.
Who can become
A waterfall, a stream, a lake, or a sea
When they dream?

Her love is the part of nature
Human beings have not yet seen
And yet it is this planet's deepest dream—
To fill the Earth with love
As water covers the seas.
In the Water element:
There is a love that with complete ease
With another becomes one
You will know when you have it—
There is no end to your giving.
Gnomes are as pure and solid
As precious stones
Silence is their home
Their work is transforming the Earth
If you follow them where they roam
If you make their reason and logic
Your own
Then you may hold the philosopher's stone
Its gift of immortality is well known.
In the Earth element:
There is an inner silence so complete
So filled with peace
The unknown universe uses your voice
When it wishes to speak
Or you find things to work at
That you love with all your heart and soul.

Dreamtime

*There are many mansions within the soul that no one has
ever entered, though the doors are unlocked and the gates
thrown open.*

Our personal dreams move within familiar landscapes. Even when we
wake from nightmares or an impossible, blissful fantasy, our dreams are
our own. They do not stray from the feelings that come to us during
the day or that follow us down through the years.

Dreams have purposes. Our desires may be frustrated. A dream can compensate. It can remind us of what might have been, or of being loved, or of a love that once was.

Dreams may speak with the voice of our instincts. Hungry, prowling desires lurk in the darkness of our unconscious waiting for an opportunity to break free and stand in front of us. The dream, speaking with the voice of our subconscious, says, "Here. It is your turn to deal with this."

Dreams can speak with the voice of our conscience. Things we may consciously deny the dream declares we still feel inside—guilt, remorse, sorrow, and loss. Occasionally, the dream speaks plainly—happiness is right here in front of you if only you would let your conscience guide you.

Sometimes when I dream, I am aware that I am not just within a lucid dream that I have imagined. The amount of energy present and the richness of context indicate there is more. The dream is a message from the future.

Sometimes I feel all my dead ancestors drop in from the astral plane. They stand behind me looking over my shoulder. They whisper in my ear from the Other Side, "Satisfy the desires we could not satisfy; experience what we could not. Though we are dead, through you we live again. Set us free!"

And sometimes when I dream, I enter the dream that is the astral plane; it weaves together all that humans and other beings are capable of experiencing. Here are global archetypes and other dimensions of awareness.

Spiritual Anthropology

Dreamtime is a word used by the Aborigines of Australia whose history reaches back fifty thousand years. In dreamtime, the events of the physical world somehow blend and unite with mythical time, the source of sacred beginnings.

A fundamental aspect of dreamtime is its vast landscape. This landscape does not have coordinates such as past, present, and future. Rather, this landscape is a world to be explored. In it there is no end to what can be discovered, felt, and experienced.

Each tradition formulates its own ideals, goals, theologies, origin myths, quests, rituals, ceremonies, and methods of transforming both the individual and the community. They assist as best they know how to live a responsible life and also experience wonder, awe, beauty, and mystery.

What is observable is that gurus and students in a spiritual lineage share the same realm of the soul with its illumination and inspiration. The images that embody these vibrations are transformers of motivation; they step up and down the forces that drive us forward in our lives.

Yet religious communities often take hundreds if not thousands of years to agree on what is sacred. Charismatic individuals and prophets play an important part. They take what is "seen through a glass darkly" (the archetypal images radiant with astral light) and hammer out doctrines and creeds for the faithful to believe.

Then, through rituals and ceremonies, dreamtime is made available to us, offering us its energies of renewal and inspiration. When effective, we are saturated with deep feelings that briefly enable us to experience the timeless and transcendent world that surrounds us.

But by necessity, there are boundaries that guard our souls. Authority figures, custodians who oversee our traditions, mark and guard these boundaries. They insist that we not experience certain feelings, placing them off limit, or they declare certain attitudes to be hostile and unwelcome. Some feelings are alien to our personalities and the opposite of what we are—a threat and danger to the stability of personal identity and society.

And so groups build psychological and spiritual barriers to keep others' dreams from contaminating the astral light they hold dear. Consequently, the dreamtime of one group, religion, or culture almost never overlaps the dreamtime of another.

When they dream at night, Catholics do not change like a shaman from human form into a wolf or a deer. They do not run in a lucid dream through the woods at night in state of exaltation free of fear. A god of the sea such as Neptune or those of sunrise or the night sky will never appear.

The Wiccans and Druids do not dream at night of a formless god. They do not wrestle with him for a blessing that shapes the destiny of many nations. It just never happens.

The Hopi Indians do not share their dreamtime or their ceremonial secrets with Navaho Indians or even with plains Indians who have the same clan totems like sun or eagle. Hawaiians do not share their spirit guides and inner plane teachers with Australian Aboriginal clans or vice versa.

Christians do not share the same dreamtime with Jews. A rabbi who used to write for the *Jerusalem Post* insisted that Christians have a completely different God than the Jews. The Jewish God expected Jews to participate in the work of salvation, whereas for Protestants salvation is accomplished by God without human support.

Muhammad had the archangel Gabriel dictate the Koran. Gabriel has a totally different outlook than the prophets of the Old Testament, and Gabriel's vibration rarely appears within Christianity and almost never within Judaism. Here we have three closely related religions which, nonetheless, have totally different dreamtimes.

Buddha formulated a different dreamtime than that of Hinduism. Without benefit of spirit guides, guru, or lineage, Buddha attained enlightenment on his own. There is nothing like this pure, mental clarity that unites with the void within Hinduism. Even Shiva, the transcendent one, took consorts and lovers.

And where in all of the Western world is there a trace of the depth of understanding of the physical body that the yogis of India have mastered? There would be no existentialism if Sartre and Camus had attained bliss just by sitting, breathing, stretching, and meditating.

And the yogi or Buddhist master does not dream of a postindustrial society in the information age in which the individual is responsible for monitoring and eliminating corruption in government. And the modern artist, with his hypersensitivity, does not dream at night of being called to fulfill a vision. Often drugs sustain his drive and charismatic performance. Our artists and rock stars have no divine commission.

The general does not dream of loving a woman with all of his heart. And the scientist on his quest to know all that can be known about the universe does not dream of what is so real to some—being able to feel what anyone else on the Earth feels.

And so the problem—*if we cannot easily share other individuals' dreams and if groups (religions, cultures, nations) cannot experience what is sacred for others, then no wonder people do not get along or understand each other.*

There Is A Reason For This

I have never heard of a master in one tradition actually referring a student to a totally different tradition. Human spiritual traditions do not dream other groups' dreams.

There is a reason for this. In the Hermit tarot card, the man seeking wisdom holds a lamp illuminating a few feet before his path. On this planet there is no one switch you can flip that lights up the world so that all darkness is banished.

All around us is mystery. And to peer into this mystery? The joy is so great, the universe is on the verge of exploding in trying to contain it, and beauty is so filled with wonder it is absolutely terrifying. It is good to have a home port and a place to call your own where love is assured. In other words, how lucky you are if your beliefs are certain and offer you reassurance.

Early in my life, when I was just out of college, I was exposed to a massive amount of writing on Western and Eastern esoteric traditions. And yet, even then, I sensed there was a global dreamtime, an awareness underlying all traditions of the human race.

And so I used to sit on the ground outdoors at night and meditate. As I meditated, I listened to the silence of the planet Earth. Here there is no tradition, no lineages, and no social engineering involving endless attempts to promote newly invented ideologies in order to better allocate scarce resources.

I was in geological time. Here there is no Darwin's survival of the fittest. Instead, there is the beginning of life, its journey through time, and all the many ways in which it can be fulfilled, attain freedom, and ascend into higher dimensions of being.

The planet Earth has her own dreams. She dreams of uniting with the sun and of feeling one with the universe. And she waits for an intelligent species to arise that will share her dreams, to feel what she feels in her heart. This is the dreamtime I was searching for—it includes all the dreams of the human race and yet it is infinitely more.

Another way of approaching or encountering global dreamtime is to ask, "What feeling or love, what kind of receptivity, underlies and supports the dreams of all individuals, groups, societies, religions, and lineages, including the vast array of beings that exist on the astral plane?"

Global dreamtime, the astral plane, offers support, nurturing, shelter-ing, and protecting without judgment or criticism. Being all-embracing and one with all things, it just gives.

Take a moment. Imagine that your love is at the core of every being offering support and promising the fulfillment of every dream. But where can you go to celebrate such love without having to commit your-self to rituals or beliefs, doctrines, or eschatological schemes?

There is a spirit in the system of Franz Bardon that specializes in the mysteries of silence. When I contact him, I feel I have entered a temple where people come to meditate. Enter this place and you find all the great masters of the Earth sitting and meditating together.

Their silent meditation is like a prayer for the human race and the planet Earth. These masters are seeking to offer through conscious endeavor and meditation what the astral plane itself offers to departed souls—the inspiration and emotional support that enables each person and group to be fulfilled in every possible way, without preaching or telling others what to do; for what individuals are to accomplish is to make the world new through the visions in their hearts.

There is a vast array of spirits that are part of the Akashic plane of the planet Earth. One set of spirits oversee human evolution. Cigila, for example, specializes in offering divine missions to those who are trained as magicians. But he requires that you first work through your personal issues—that you pass through your "inner darkness," confronting the parts of yourself you do not as yet know—before you are given the keys that transform the world.

The common denominator in his assignments? The goal is to reduce suffering on Earth. There is a stillness about Cigila. And in this still-ness that embraces all paths of life, he holds the world within his heart.

People can learn things sooner or later, through great suffering or by utilizing understanding and wisdom from the beginning. Cigila is the kind of spirit who prefers people learn things sooner and without unnecessary suffering.

We all dream at night. The dreams of other people and the dreams of the planet Earth are sitting by our side waiting for us to awaken.

RULE 8

HOD/MERCURY

Glory, Splendor, Quest for Truth

Basic Quality	Clear and concise speech
Virtues, Vices, Negative	Alert/Dull/Criminal
Challenge	Develop clarity of mind
Magical Practice	Observing without thinking; understanding all sides, contemplation
Common Virtue	Vivaciousness
Magical Virtue	The element of Air
Divine Virtue	Faith and conviction
Dream	Making others more alive and words that transform the world
Initiation	A clear mind amid confusion
Mystery	The enlightened mind

Hod/Mercury is your high school teacher and college professor trying their hardest to get you to think clearly. Isolate the parts and variables. Study and define. Compare and contrast. Cross check, test, and verify. Be systematic and thorough. Arrive at a perspective that integrates everything into one whole.

If you train in a college curriculum like business or science, you develop a mind that is sharp, investigative, and analytic. If you work more with the humanities studying drama, literature, poetry, music, dance, or painting, you develop an artistic sensitivity that heightens your perception and awareness of the nuances of each moment. If you study law, economics, and somehow combine those with deep contemplation on the lessons of history, you develop a sense of justice and an understanding of the forces that control the fate of nations.

By contrast, sitting in a Zen monastery, you acquire calmness and clarity of mind. Sitting in a Tibetan Buddhist monastery, you might develop depth of mind. Working with a shaman who is deeply aligned with nature, your mind might become grounded and solid with an enhanced awareness of how to heal and restore harmony. Studying with great martial art masters, your mind becomes centered in your body and also electrifying, explosive, powerful, completely focused on your immediate physical situation.

Going further, if you have the chance to study with incarnated mermaids, you might develop brain waves that are flowing like water and empathy that is all-embracing like the sea. If you study with an incarnated sylph, you may learn to be playful, cheerful, and outrageously relaxed and joyous. If you study with a gnome, an incarnated Earth spirit, you feel grounded as if your inner self is as solid as a granite mountain. Incarnated salamanders, Fire spirits, are slightly trickier. Their entire being is focused on power.

In Hod, we meet the mind in all aspects. The goal is to be fully aware, alert, attentive, and intuitive in order to make the best choices and expedite the solution of problems.

BASIC QUALITY
Clear and Concise Speech

The basic quality of Hod is speech that is clear, concise, and that expresses exactly what you mean. Dale Carnegie has books and even online classes on this topic. He has helped many people with their communication skills; for example, in one course description you learn to "communicate logically, clearly, and concisely."

VIRTUES, VICES, NEGATIVE

Virtues: Alert, assertive, truthful, clear, brilliant, objective, concise, to the point, a judicial temperament, tolerance for ambiguity, persuasive, engaging, sincere, consistent, curious, and communicative.

Vices: Dull, dishonest, insipid, shallow, superficial, narrow-minded, intolerant, argumentative, opinionated, moralistic, attached to ideologies, pessimistic, overly mental, off in the clouds, rude, secretive, facetious, social phobias.

Negative: Criminal, liar, thief, hacker, con man.

CHALLENGE

The mind is as open and vast as the sky, as detached and clear as a mirror, as deep and as receptive as the sea, as creative and still as the empty space that shelters the stars and galaxies. Find this mind within yourself and live your life free of confusion and doubt.

MAGICAL PRACTICE
Observing without Thinking;
Understanding All Sides, Contemplation

Learn to perceive without thoughts intervening. This is the foundation of all magical traditions. This requires that you learn to stop your thoughts and, fully alert, sit in silence as you observe.

✳ Exercises: Open Mind

✳ Part I: Observing Your Mind
Once every so often, take some time and observe your mind. This action is not predefined. You are not a judge or a referee, not a life coach or a cheerleader, not an arbitrator or a therapist.

Rather, you get to decide for yourself the best way to observe your own mind. You can be playful, funny, humorous; artistic, a story teller, or passionate; silent, still, or sacred as the atmosphere of a temple or shine; detached, inquisitive, investigative—it is up to you to discover your "inner observer" who will reveal how your mind works.

As with the physical world and with the realms of the soul, there is no end to the exploration of the mind. It might help to remember that, like life itself, your mind is free to reveal itself in endless new ways. Notice when it reveals new sides of itself.

In the books written by Carlos Castaneda, the Yaqui sorcerer Don Juan has a practice he calls "stopping the world." It is perceiving without thoughts arising. When you stop your mind from thinking and look around, you are in a different world.

✳ Part II: Tolerating Ambiguity

Learn to argue both sides of any position with equal clarity and enthusiasm. Make this a lifelong ambition. That is, before you take a position, make sure you understand the strengths and weaknesses of opposing points of view and what all parties are feeling.

You can also observe the mental processes in other people. For example, watch a news report on TV. Then ask yourself, "Is the anchor reporting facts as best he can or does he distort the facts in order to express a political agenda?" For some people, once an idea, ideology, or perspective enters their minds it becomes too painful for them to see things in a different light.

In arguments and discussions by news anchors and politicians, we often see them using red herrings or the straw dog argument. Knowingly or not, they present a biased version of another's positions. They then dismiss the opposing points of view by simplifying or misrepresenting them.

A more skilled politician will discuss accurately a position that opposes his own and the reasons why people hold that position. He is then far more persuasive because now he is speaking in a fair manner to those on both sides of an argument. This leads to the compliment that even his enemies respect him because he speaks the truth.

Someone with a judicial temperament is able to tolerate ambiguity. He weighs evidence and considers case studies without the need to form an opinion in advance. To do this, you practice thinking other's thoughts without bias or prejudice. Police negotiators, screenplay writers, mediators, and skilled scientists are trained to do this.

Then again, some people will never acquire such skills in this lifetime. "Being objective" is beyond them because, out of insecurity and lack of basic training, they need to feel from the outset that they are right and that others are wrong.

✳ Part III: Contemplation

> *The mind is capricious, feverish, unstable, restless, turbulent. It is*
> *harder to subdue than taming the wind.*
>
> ARJUNA, FROM THE MAHABHARATA

> *Blessed are those who minds are as open and clear as the sky, for*
> *their peace shall be as a sea that has no shores and as a stream*
> *that flows from the dawn of time to the end of eternity.*

When confronted with a new problem or difficulty, a master will very carefully examine it in all aspects until he formulates the right question that brings him close to the answer he seeks.

This is similar to contemplation. You take any concept, doctrine, theory, image, ideal, or spiritual principle and you consider it from all sides and aspects. You recall your experiences and bring together any observations that bear on your topic.

And then you place your mind in a receptive state and see what impressions, intuitions, and feelings arise.

Contemplation is holding before your gaze all aspects of a situation without having to use thoughts to analyze or evaluate. It is the "perceiving without thoughts intervening." It is perception free of prejudice, of an urgent need to form conclusions, and without utilizing previous systems of interpretation.

✳ Method

Visualize someone who is interesting to you. Recall when you first met and what occurred, what you thought and felt at that time. Review the course of your getting to know or work with this person. What things surprised you or were new for you? What was the best and the worst of the relationship?

Gather together all your experiences with the other and hold them before your mind at the same time. You are also imagining the other's inner life as compared to that individual's outer life.

Use your empathy. Put yourself in this person's position and see the world through his or her eyes.

Having done this preliminary work, now just remain gazing at what you have seen so far. You are focused, and yet your mind is empty and in a receptive state. Notice the insights, intuitions, impressions, and feelings that arise as you do this.

I review my experiences with a person I recently met from the beginning to the present. I note the various feelings I have had. I notice the other's way of relating to me. I take in the highlights, the insights, the dramatic moments, the revelations, the unexpected, the new things I learned, and the deeper feelings that underlie our connection to each other.

This is similar to an individual who sits in the audience and watches a play on a stage. He continues to sit in the empty theater when everyone has left. And there the whole play again unfolds before his eyes, each moment frozen in time and available to be recalled and relived. Like recalling a play, you also become aware of the underlying themes, the conflicts, the resolutions, and the epiphanies that occurred.

There is a question behind my contemplation, like the playwright himself might ask, "Have I told the story well? Do I feel what the other feels? Is there any sense that there is something vital and important I have left out or that is missing? What have I learned? What gifts did we give each other? How close or distant is the other person now and in what way?"

You can also contemplate problems you have and brainstorm solutions. You can imagine the future when a problem is resolved and try to reverse engineer how that solution was obtained. You can contemplate a goal, a plan, or enter a dream you have for the future.

✳ Symbols

Symbols are suitable for contemplation. An individual can also be a symbol as can an institution, a ritual, a ceremony, a mandala, or an image. A good symbol captures your attention and is endlessly fascinating. It is graphic and sufficiently physical and familiar that we can relate to it. At the same time, it is slightly outside of everyday consciousness so that it provides insight and challenges to us to let go and see the world through new eyes.

For a symbol to be effective, it cannot be reduced to a specific intellectual explanation. You cannot use words to define exactly what it is. If you take it literally, it loses its power of transformation. If you overspiritualize it or treat it as an abstraction, it no longer speaks to you individually. A symbol resists analysis, which has this benefit: it enables a response from that part of ourselves that is more profound and inclusive than the intellect.

A Tibetan lama I once studied with was annoyed with one of his students who talked too much. So he told him casually, "Go into the temple and meditate on the Tibetan letter of *AH* for six hours." The lama wanted the student to refine and upgrade his quality of speech.

Tibetan symbols, yidams, and tantras do not appeal to me. But I loved the idea. You take something that captures your attention and has unknown depths to explore and spend some serious time meditating on it. I used to go sit for six hours at a time in the Senoran desert outside of Tucson, Arizona. There I would contemplate one of the ten sephiroth of the Kabbalistic Tree of Life.

This worked for me. I was in a state of contemplation where my body, soul, mind, and spirit all worked together in harmony to reveal truth and insight. This book is one result of that practice. A sephirah combines very practical and down-to-earth considerations even as it reveals the profoundest mysteries of life.

COMMON VIRTUE
Vivaciousness

The essence of my being is a love that gives all of itself in every moment and never loses its innocence.

Part I: To Flow Like Water

What feeling best brings to life our interactions with others? Being vivacious. Synonyms for *vivacious* are scintillating, sparkling, animated, effervescent, cheerful, bubbly, upbeat, high-spirited, full of life, and lively, to name a few.

Being vivacious is observable in the choice of words an individual uses, vocal pitch, intonation, the moment to moment give-and-take on a verbal and nonverbal level, and so on.

Some individuals may have ten observable nonverbal responses in any thirty seconds during a conversation: the fullness of the lips, the tension in the facial muscles, the eye movements, expressions of the chin, and turning of the head.

Actors in Hollywood often have ten or twelve facial gestures they repeatedly use for dramatic purposes—a shoulder shrug, a characteristic smile, a glance, eye contact—a way of responding that they repeat in movie after movie. It does not seem to matter what movie these actors are in. They walk into the studio, get in front of the camera, and then speak a few lines. It is often their stage presence and charisma that captures the audience's attention, not their acting skills.

And then you have genuinely vivacious individuals who are fully alive in each moment. They respond to you, not with ten or twelve, but thirty to a hundred different nonverbal gestures. Some responses they seem to reserve just for you.

This enhanced attention and customized receptivity make you feel fully alive in the present moment. They are responding to your responses, which awakens and stimulates your nervous system and emotions.

In each moment, like flowing water, a vivacious person adapts and changes, altering to respond to the situation without regard to what may have gone before or what is to come next. This purifies and refreshes. The effervescence gets inside of you and make you feel new.

✳ Exercise: Feeling Vivacious Energy

An actor can focus on being vivacious by responding to the subtle cues and observable body language in a situation as well as to the subtext (the unseen dynamics of the situation). But vivaciousness also has an energy, a state of mind, and a receptivity of soul.

Visualize a man or woman of the opposite gender in front of you. Now imagine that the two of you are standing in a bubbly and pure mountain pool with water splashing down from a falls. There is the cool air, spray and white foam, the waves and ripples, the currents, and the water flowing over the rocks. Perhaps a thin spray rises in the air lit with rainbow colors as it is caught in the sunlight.

Instead of identifying with your social identity, you are identifying with the energy of nature and sharing this with the other person. There is now a current of watery, renewing, life-giving energy circulating between the two of you.

This meditation is not a concept. It is not even a set of images. It is an actual watery energy you can feel flowing in and through each other.

How to Tell When You Are with a Mermaid Woman

Slightly outside of human experience are mermaids. Unlike human women who embody all five elements, incarnated mermaids embody the one element of Water in their auras. How do you distinguish a mermaid woman from a human woman?

Once you know what to look for it is impossible to miss. She is like the snow at the North Pole—it can sit there for ten thousand or ten million years and still remember the tropical forest that went before—she is Water: that nubile fertility of pure receptivity never disappears.

It is in the way she receives your energy. There is no riptide pulling you to where you do not want to go; there is no undertow pulling you down so you have to struggle to keep your footing on solid ground; there is no tsunami, emotions dredged up by the superego, pushing you back with that muddy, choppy tumbling of emotional jealousy or angry demanding. She has no ego, no fear; the desire to take from you never appears. It is impossible for her to feel neglected—she has no human needs; she already feels complete.

When with her you feel like you are the sun and she is ice. She willingly melts in the presence of your energy because that is the nature of her beauty. She gives freely without attachment to form or identity.

You feel like you are the sun and she is the sea—without difficulty, she absorbs your heat (your desires, everything you can imagine or dream). The warmth she radiates at night, her very being testifies to your presence in her life.

There is more.

When you are with her, you feel like she is a stream and that you are gravity—every single movement she makes is shaped by your presence.

Do not take my word on this. Observe a stream. Memorize its sound, touch, scent, taste, and the way it feels as it flows around your body. And then look at her face as you speak: there is not a trace of distraction. Gentleness, tenderness, affection—there is a feeling of letting go into the flow—that the two of you have become one soul.

She may look, talk, and act human, but I will tell you this: once you discover that this way of being exists, when you experience it again it is impossible to miss.

In summary, her face has that grace, a gift to us like the North Atlantic Current. There is the silent peace of the ocean trench; the warm sensuality of a wave breaking on a tropical beach; and the pristine purity of an iceberg breaking free from a glacial plain at the edge of the Arctic Sea. You may not be able to see or feel these things, but when you leave her presence, you may sense for the first time that when you were with her you felt fully alive.

We all have mermaids and mermen inside of ourselves. The whole point of the ten rules and the ten sephiroth of the Tree of Life is that the greater universe is reflected inside of us. Work with some of the Water meditations in this book. Celebrate the beauty of the universe!

Part II: Active Listening

People are often unaware of their own emotions as they talk. They may not realize they are angry, sad, enthusiastic, or worried. In active listening, we paraphrase the content—the ideas—of what a person has said. Separately we describe the feelings the person has toward his topic.

Active listening is a form of feedback. You do not have to be accurate, only close. When people look in the mirror, they may be surprised with how good they look or how bad. But until they look, they do not have that information. Active listening gives another the opportunity to look inward and become more conscious of what they are feeling.

Part of active listening involves noticing incongruities—the difference between what a person is saying and the feelings expressed though body language—facial expression, gestures, intonation, or even word choice.

An individual says "It did not bother me," but his face darkens, his eyes turn hard, his voice changes pitch, his muscles tighten, and so on.

This is an incongruity between what is said and what appears in the body. In a case like this, you can simply point out the changes in body language.

Another example: "As you talked about her, you started speaking slower and with a quieter voice than the way you were talking before. You seem to take more time to process your feelings."

Or: "You say you love him, but you also mentioned some terrible things he did to you. But I do not see you expressing any anger. Are those feelings there also?"

I briefly explained to a woman a scale of physical reactions and emotions relating to anger. I then asked, "On a scale of one to ten, how angry were you with him?" This is where a guy took her to the high school prom and then left her there, going off to do something else. It seemed that in her body language and word choices she was expressing anger at around a five when the events suggested it might have been much stronger. She said that on a scale of one to ten her anger was a twelve. Her response to my question gave us both a clearer picture.

Active listening is often useful during conversations with highly opinionated and narrow-minded people. This is especially true where the other individual is so insecure that he demands you agree with him.

With active listening, you can carry on a conversation without being drawn into the vortex of the other person's confusion or hostility. Simply give the other person your full, undivided attention. Again, listen and paraphrase back to the other the cognitive content of what is said and separately how they feel about what they are saying.

You are not agreeing with them. You are acting as a mirror that is neutral in reflecting the other's thoughts and feelings. The reason this often works is because you are giving the other person the kind of attention that perhaps no one else has ever given him before in his life. And you are not placing one idea in conflict with another idea. Rather, you are enabling this individual to speak from his own, firsthand experience.

Practicing active listening, you are perceiving without thoughts intervening. You are not thinking about anything at all. You are just 100 percent present, clear, and reflective—acting as a highly skilled and committed listener.

All the same, active listening does not work with someone who is committed to being negative. The negative person will not be satisfied until you are drowning in confusion or hatred the way he is.

There are a great many directions in which you can take active listening. After all, we are dealing with life, and life is nearly infinite in variety.

To summarize, the active listener reflects back to you like a mirror what you say, and separately the feelings you have when you talk about something. A very skilled active listener is so empathic that he or she is simultaneously completely detached from you while listening and also completely one with you the way a mirror perfectly reflects every photon of light that shines upon it without distorting or interpreting.

You will notice when you have a good listener. You feel the other person's voice at times is the voice arising from the core of your own being and the depths of your heart—the still, quiet voice of your own soul. Most people will go through life without ever having had another person really hear what they have to say.

Skills Relating to Active Listening

Tracking, summarizing: Tracking and summarizing are similar to empathy. In this case, you make multiple observations and then tie them into a question or general observation suggesting a possible pattern.

For example, "You began by mentioning that you did not really remember much from that year. And then you went into great detail about several life-defining events that occurred shortly afterward. It seems that now you are better able to cope with what you went through than you were then. Is that true?"

In this case, you are mentioning differences that have occurred at two different points in time and then asking why.

In another example, I pointed out to one person that as he told the story of his life, he looked most alive and enthusiastic. His face lit up when he talked about a drawing class, and the colors of the paints when he was age five. So I asked if he might consider doing more with painting or working with colors in some way now later in life. The comment gave him a chance to review his own feelings and experiences.

Self-disclosure: Self-disclosure (sharing your own experience) has the risk of shifting attention from the other person to yourself. The idea is to share and then immediately return the focus back to the other person.

Self-disclosure encourages the other person to reveal more about himself. You do this when your experience resonates with the person you are listening to. It is one of the few times that comparison is helpful because it enables the other to go deeper into the past by asking new questions about what was experienced.

For example, "What happened to me when I had a similar confrontation was that I never spoke with anyone again about that topic. What did you do in the situation you mention?"

MAGICAL VIRTUE
The Element of Air

The sky, the atmosphere filled with Air, is open, vast, clear, and, in a sense, free of gravity. We breathe in Air, which provides life force and vitality. Air vibrates in our feelings, encouraging humor, playfulness, cheerfulness, and a sense of freedom.

Air is in our minds, symbolizing mental clarity, detachment, and the investigative capacity that seeks knowledge and understanding. And it has a spiritual component offering, as with the stars in the night sky, a sense of stillness and cosmic harmony.

Here are two practices for exploring it.

✳ Exercises: Air

✳ Part I: Uniting Your Breath and the Wind
Think about your breath. As we inhale, we draw in comparatively dry, cool, low pressure, and oxygen-rich air. As we exhale, we release relatively moist, higher pressure, warm, and carbon dioxide–rich air. The expansion and contraction of chest and diaphragm moves the air in and out of our lungs.

Breathing is similar to the movement of winds in the sky. In the sky, however, it is the turning of the Earth, the temperature changes over land and water, the interactions of hot and cold, moist and dry air, and the changing of the seasons that move the winds.

Think of your body as a hologram that has open space inside. As you breathe in, imagine that Air fills this hologram. The Air moving in and out as we breathe is similar to the winds in motion over the entire surface of the Earth. The Air in our bodies is the same Air surrounding us as the atmosphere.

Be aware of both at once—the Air moving in and out as we breathe and the weather in the planet's atmosphere. Think of them as one expanse. Feel united from within to the sky.

✱ Part II: The Sensation of Weightlessness

The Air element can also be explored by concentrating on the sensation of weightlessness. Here are three ways to do this. Visualize yourself sitting on a chair on the other side of the room. Imagine your body is again a hologram. Think of the Air in that hologram as being weightless as if it is floating like a balloon.

Now imagine you become that hologram across the room. Go back and forth between focusing on yourself as you are and the holographic picture of yourself that is floating weightless. In this way, we remove density and gravity from the sensory perception of our bodies.

A second way of getting a sense of weightlessness is to focus on breathing. As you inhale and exhale, focus only on the sensation of Air entering and leaving your body. Again, the Air is weightless. We are putting off the side all other sensations of the body and just immersing ourselves in the motion of Air.

This is not the practice of pranayama, which is interested in the vitality in breathing. This is the Air element itself, part of the atmosphere. Again, think of your body as being empty inside like a hologram and the Air moves in and out of this open, empty space.

As we did in the first part of this exercise, sense the Air around yourself for miles in all directions. Imagine you are this sea of Air so that as Air you are moving in and out of the open space of your body. It is not you breathing. It is the atmosphere moving in and out of you.

A third way of gaining a sense of weightlessness is to imagine you are up in the sky, say around forty thousand feet. All around you is the open expanse of light blue sky. There is nothing here but Air. You are a part of the sky.

✳ Experiences Underlying the Weightless Sensation

The first thing I notice when I imagine myself being weightless is a feeling of freedom. There is no gravity holding me down. I am not bound or limited by anything. This is the opposite of being depressed; instead of being weighed down, there is a feeling of being buoyant, elevated, and lifted up.

The Air element also carries with it a sense of detachment. The sky contains weather conditions, but the blue sky itself remains vast, open, and clear. It is unaffected by thunderstorms, hurricanes, tornadoes, hail, and whiteout conditions.

And with the sense of weightlessness comes clarity. To see clearly you have to actually look without bias or preconceptions. With Air and sky, nothing pulls you in one direction or another; nothing pushes you to make a judgment or draw a conclusion.

And with the detachment, with the feeling of being free, and with the openness comes artistic appreciation. There is a hypersensitivity that is able to feel within and a part of other people and situations. And, at the same time, it is extremely curious and investigative.

This is the attitude of an artist. You can look at a situation of conflict and see a story unfolding: "Take in every detail. Feel every nuance of the suspense as each moment unfolds. Which way will the story turn? What does each person feel and why do they choose to do one thing and not the other?"

On a physical level, the weightless sensation within the body produces a powerful feeling of relaxation. In Franz Bardon's book *Initiation into Hermetics,* the author mentions that concentrating on weightlessness enables you to feel so light that you do not feel your body at all.

The weightless sensation, like the Air element itself, also carries a sense of harmony. Air in the atmosphere is constantly balancing opposites of hot and cold, wet and dry, high and low pressure, calm and turbulent, electric and magnetic, sunny and cloudy, and night and day, and so forth.

When you feel united to the Air element, and, in this case, to the entire atmosphere of the Earth, you feel an endless, boundless outpouring from within yourself of freedom, harmony, beauty, and wonder that we can call joy.

And finally, with the clarity, vastness, and harmony is a stillness. This stillness is a wisdom that understands how the world unfolds; to everything a time and a season.

Summary

In Malkuth, the magical virtue is a quiet ecstasy. This involves being aware of our body united to the densest aspects of physical world. There we pursued an exercise involving concentrating on our feet.

In Yesod, the magical virtue enables us to feel united to the Water in nature. The accompanying exercise involves imagining our blood as water as it flows through our bodies doing what water does—purifying, healing, renewing, and making fully alive.

Here in Hod, the magical virtue centers on the Air element. The exercise has two aspects. First, we sense the connection between breathing, in which inhalation and exhalation are similar to the winds and weather conditions in the atmosphere. We feel united to Air in nature.

The second part involves exploring the physical, psychological, mental, and spiritual experiences that the physical sensation of weightlessness imply. Through uniting with the Air element, we can learn to produce in ourselves—at will—relaxation, openness, sensitivity, mental clarity, and a sense of a great harmony.

The study of the elements of Earth, Water, and Air unite us to the dynamic powers unfolding the universe.

DIVINE VIRTUE
Faith and Conviction

We can talk about faith in terms of how refined and pure it is. And we can also discuss its strength—how much of it someone has. There is quality and quantity.

An individual with faith brings out the best in any situation he or she enters. In this sense, faith is a union of willpower, self-mastery, single-minded focus on your objectives, and a highly disciplined concentration.

And, if only to a small extent, an individual with faith has a connection to the divine world. This connection is not through the cognitive and rational aspect of the mind as in "I know (or I believe) something to be true," though a clear mind helps.

Faith is an application of a higher or a divine level of awareness that takes hold of real situations in our lives. Without a direct connection to the divine or something "transcendent," faith is limited in scope and power. We see crude forms of faith quite often where it is expressed as obsession, fanaticism, self-righteousness, arrogance, and attachment to rigid ideas, ideologies, dreams, and fantasies.

Rather than enabling transformation of oneself and the world, this low-grade form of faith seeks to control others. It can mimic truth and light, yet it remains twisted, impure, inferior, and impatient for results. Faith in its lower forms focuses on believing in man-made doctrines. It is obsessive in demanding conformity to group norms. And it demands submission through obedience to human authority figures and to stagnant and obsolete traditions.

And yet, whether the faith is positive or negative, an individual with faith has certainty. He can see clearly what it is he wants to have happen in the future. He is adaptable, resourceful, and has a plan B. He is able to reexamine goals and utilize new methods. He is able to seize on opportunities as they arise. Never underestimate the power of faith as it operates on the dark side.

The positive version of faith is both detached and empathic, neutral and yet passionate. The individual possesses an electrifying excitement and yet he is calm and at peace. He is hardworking and committed to achieving results over the long term that are of enduring value.

And he is in the moment, constantly evaluating where he is, the effort and energy he is expending, and the best route to his objectives. And yet, in addition to tracking movement toward his objectives, he is equally interested in how he lives each moment. The future is present because the future is already alive within him.

✳ Exercise: Faith and Living the Dream

A powerful method for changing oneself and the world boils down to a simple formula.

Concentrate on what is desired as if it is real right now in this moment. Visualize it. Feel it. Think it. Affirm it.

Imagine you are in the future where it has become reality. Walk around. Observe firsthand what this is like. Take in the sights, sounds, and feelings. Participate in conversations. Repeat this on a regular basis.

Finally, state your case as if you are presenting a petition to Divine Providence. Be brief and concise. Answer questions with complete certainty about your purpose and about the value of what you seek to manifest.

As when the Supreme Court reviews a case, questions are put to the attorneys who represent opposing positions. The answers do not require brilliance, logic, or persuasion. In our case, the purpose is to see to what extent you believe in what you are doing. In the courtroom of spirit, it is not possible to deceive oneself or others.

1 to 10

Faith is about you and how you live your life. It is also world historic— we can study it in terms of ourselves and people we know; and we can study it in terms of individuals whose faith has shaped history.

Consider examples of faith on a scale of 1 to 10. To make a New Year's resolution and not follow through with it is a 0. To say your goal in life is to know God, but your only efforts in that direction are to go to church and pray, that receives a score of 1.

To say, "My conscience is captive to the Word of God . . . Here I stand, I cannot do otherwise." That is a 5. This is Martin Luther, the founder of Protestant Christianity. Like many others, Luther put his life at risk to begin the Reformation. But Luther offered no system of self-transformation nor any serious reform of the Catholic Church from within other than to demand of the Church, "Stop being so greedy with other people's money and stop selling indulgences."

To say when you were young that you always knew you would one day be wealthy (Warren Buffett, who become one of the wealthiest men on Earth) is a 6.

To say you are going to help other people accomplish their goals in life and then you help literally millions of people to do so (Tony Robbins, a life coach) is a score of 7.

To say, "In three days I can take my third army and relieve the siege of Bastogne"—this was General Patton who engaged more enemy troops than any general in World War II. This is an 8.

Patton focused on quality—he ordered his chaplain to write a prayer for the weather to clear so Allied bombers could bomb the Germans. And he focused on quantity—he sent that prayer to everyone in his third army asking them to pray along with him. The weather cleared.

An 8 is also to say, "In this sign shall we conquer." Constantine ordering his legions to place the sign of the cross on their shields before a crucial battle. Constantine united the Roman Empire under a new religion called Christianity. And he relentlessly demanded that his Christian bishops create one creed to define his state religion.

A 9 is to say, "I am going to invent an alternating current engine." This is Tesla. He did this when his boss, Thomas Edison, said to him that an alternating current engine is impossible to make. Tesla changed the world.

To go on fighting courageously with a ragged, starved, poorly clothed army and defeat the most powerful army in the world is also a 9. This is George Washington, who pointed out that if the opposing generals felt a small amount of his despair, they would quit the battlefield.

In 452 CE, Pope Leo left Rome without an armed escort and went out and met with Atilla the Hun. Through charisma and persuasion, he convinced Atilla to turn his army around and not attack Rome. This is a 10.

To defeat the Irish king's army by evoking the archangel Michael so you win, and lose not one man in the battle, is also a 10. This is St. Columba in sixth-century Ireland.

As you can see from a few examples, faith manifests in different ways. In some cases, it requires persistence and rugged endurance or commitment to an ideal and self-sacrifice. Other cases require a heightened imagination and reverse engineering—you envision what you want to happen (the end product) and then, proceeding step-by-step, you figure out how to get there.

Other times it manifests as charisma—there is a powerful confidence, massive experience, a radiant inspiration, and the sheer force of personality that implants in other people one's own conviction. Sometimes faith proceeds from discipline, self-mastery, and the power of command that puts a plan into action.

And sometimes faith produces something miraculous. One's intentions are reinforced by the divine world, which has placed its power within you. But when touched by the divine, be careful with your assumptions. The divine can abandon you in an instant. And with even a small mistake, there may be disastrous consequences that persist for centuries.

Checklist for Faith

Visualize what you want as being real right now—be graphic and concrete.

Describe it; explain it; justify it; state what purpose it fulfills. Speak aloud in a way that carries weight and force.

Put the full force of your emotions into it, like an actor who has internalized a part. Go into the future and walk around. Talk to people. Study how the future came into being.

Notice the extent to which you radiate your dream such that others begin to feel that whatever is alive within you they want alive within themselves.

Put the electric/yang energy into it. On a scale of 1 to 10, ask yourself how strong is your faith, conviction, and will? Is your purpose joined to a divine purpose?

Put the magnetic/yin energy into it—love, peace, serenity, and happiness. On a scale of 1 to 10, ask yourself to what extent you are willing to nurture your project once you have brought it into being. And does what you wish for arise from the depths of your heart?

You can certainly recall and put yourself back into memories of when you acted with daring and conviction. Recreate those electrifying and dynamic feelings in yourself.

You can also meditate on individuals whom you admire who acted with a strong faith. Visualize them. Get a feeling for the spirit within them and then imagine that same feeling is now within you.

And finally recall the exercise in Yesod. As you go to bed at night, visualize and feel as real what you wish to be. Get your subconscious on board as you fall asleep.

Problems in the Study of Faith: The Subconscious

There are many reasons for not being able to imagine what we want. We may feel unworthy, conflicted, doubtful, guilty, not sure we really need something, or, if we get it, we may end up abusing it or harming others as a result. And these conflicting emotions may be far more than subjective. We may have seen over and over in our lives patterns of intention, action, and results that in fact produce feelings of guilt, self-doubt, and harm to others. We could even argue that to get what you want always places you in a position of greater power. And power is always easy to abuse.

From one point of view, the subconscious views the conscious mind as being stupid. People say what they want, are planning, or wishing for, but they do not really believe it. To not be completely certain about succeeding when you make a wish is to plan for failure. And what is far worse from the subconscious point of view is that the conscious mind fails all reasonable tests when it comes to imagining in a concrete and graphic way what it wishes to accomplish.

Since part of the job of the subconscious is to contain and store energy, it is a waste of its time and resources to cooperate. The conscious mind acts arbitrarily, unreasonably, impulsively, and without any regard for the real issues of life. It is as if the conscious self intentionally refuses to speak the language of the subconscious or show any respect when it makes its requests.

The remedy for this situation is to demonstrate real conviction, feeling, and imagination when seeking to bring about a change in yourself. And again, the conviction is in part demonstrated by imagining that what you want is real right now in this moment.

And then there are your feelings. Consider enthusiasm. You search your memory and put yourself back into past situations through which you can evoke the feeling of enthusiasm. At this point, your subconscious will be able to say, "Ah, now you are speaking my language. Now I know what you mean when you say, 'I am full of enthusiasm.'"

And finally, you have to explore with your imagination what it means for your wish to be completely real right now, as something already accomplished. This is where daydreaming or imaginative explorations take on the power of magic. Ask yourself, "What would it be like if what I wish for has already become real?" Your subconscious would like to know the answer to that question. This is because the subconscious has to take all the energy it has allotted to one set of behaviors, beliefs, and emotions and channel that energy into a new set of behaviors, beliefs, and emotions.

If you just sit there saying what you want to be and feeling it as real, you are still making a half-hearted effort from the subconscious point of view. You have not really done your homework. Your subconscious wants you to enter that dream of the future as if you are living it right now.

After all, the subconscious produces dreams every night that seem completely real to the dreaming mind. If you want to succeed with the subconscious, you have to use its own tools and language. You have to convince your subconscious that the two of you are working together and listening to each other to accomplish your project.

If the dream of what you wish to be is 100 percent real to you, then you already radiate the energy of what it is like to be what you want. Your actions and thoughts then change in order to fall into alignment with this new self-image, energy, feeling, and thought.

Summary

Imagine the trouble individuals might get into if they fall in love with a fantasy or try to live a dream without bringing to it a massive amount of experience. Magic, or faith, accepts the world as it is and yet dares to make it into what it is meant to be. Getting results requires a highly trained imagination that can shape reality.

I have had people write me and say they have begun a course in training their body, soul, mind, and spirit. They want to know how long it will take for them to change their fate or else produce miraculous events.

I tell them, "Magic is not a shortcut. It is a study of how to make the best choices in life. The best magic is to love something with all of your heart. Then time does not matter, and work is a pleasure."

Or if you want the official, no-nonsense statement of Franz Bardon: The study of magic requires superhuman patience.

DREAM

The dream in Hod has two parts. The first part is to imagine yourself as being so receptive, vivacious, and giving that others feel more alive in your presence.

Sometimes after I meditate on Water, I notice that even individuals who are completely indifferent to me will sit nearby without any reason for being there. It is like they want to absorb my energy. They do not know how to talk about this. But their bodies feel invigorated, enlivened, and at peace.

This is part of the dream. You have a benevolent and spontaneous effect on others. Your presence is stimulating, energizing, and satisfying.

The second part of the dream of Hod has to do with your relation to truth. It is not about the content, the cognitive or propositional aspect of your ideas. Rather, it is how you present your ideas. There is an openness, radiant clarity, and immense flexibility. You are not attached to ideas. Instead, you facilitate solutions.

Sometimes this is just a matter of being a good listener. Other people want to be heard, to express themselves or to work through their feelings without you trying to solve their problems. Other times, they want someone to point out the obvious—the bottom line or the hard, cold truth—so they can move on with their lives.

And then there are times when someone needs to speak out and declare, "Here is what must be done." Things like "We have an O-ring problem and there is a strong chance the space shuttle will explode on takeoff. Here is the design flaw that will cause that to happen." Or "Bernie Madoff is running a Ponzi scheme. His investment firm must be shut down immediately before he harms thousands of people." Or "No, Mr. President. As much as you want these negotiations to succeed, you are committing an act of treason to proceed in this way."

Often to make changes in institutions, corporations, or political agendas, you have to put your career in jeopardy. It is easier to take bribes, promotions, or accept sealed settlements rather than stand up and expose corruption. Are you a team player, realistic enough to move forward without damaging longstanding values, or are you a rabble-rouser or disgruntled employee who wants to get even with a little fame thrown in?

Others will want control of your mind and thoughts because that is what they need to succeed with their plans. To speak the truth will at times require overturning long established traditions. In the United States, it often takes between six and forty years to change corrupt social or corporate institutions.

In a crisis, anger will not work. Rage is impotence. Rebellion or its complement—whining, complaining, and blaming—is self-defeating. Something else is required.

The dream in Hod is being able to speak the truth in a way that transforms other people and the world. William Blake puts it this way: "O for a voice like thunder, and a tongue to drown the throat of war!"

I spoke one time before the Hawaii State Board of Education. I had some great ideas, but there was no chance the board would take any interest in them. So I rehearsed. I imagined I was an Israeli commander reviewing our battle plans one last time before boarding a plane and landing in enemy territory. In such circumstances, you have to be absolutely confident, certain of your mission, your training, and the commitment of the men you are working with. And it helps to speak as if you are returning from the future, having already seen that your mission will succeed.

The person sitting next to me said afterward, "This is a 'you' I have never seen before." My recommendations were accepted.

INITIATION

The initiation of Hod is to be clear, decisive, and balanced when circumstances are confusing, uncertain, and problematic.

Question: How do you proceed in the face of the unknown? You start off in a place of ignorance, confusion, and conflict, unable to express yourself. And you end up where you completely understand all aspects of your problem and its solutions.

To do this, you remain calm amid a crisis. You investigate and question amid prejudice, presumption, and a rush to judgment. You are analytical amid superstition, flexible amid rigidity, openminded amid narrowmindedness, and unselfish amid corruption.

In glancing into the unknown, there can be moments of pure chaos where there is no definition, no pattern, no theory, and no paradigm to explain what is being observed. The unknown can be very frightening if your mind craves quick explanations.

Opposed to feeling existential insecurity in confronting the unknown is passionate curiosity. The thrill of discovering something new is one of the greatest pleasures of being alive. Look at scientists! Some spend a lifetime experimenting without knowing if their work will change the world for better or for worse.

Confronting chaos? In the sphere of Hod, insecurity, chaos, and the unknown are more than matched by an insatiable curiosity and a dauntless commitment to discovering the truth.

Regardless of the confusion in external circumstances or the conflicts in internal emotions, the mind retains an unshakeable clarity. Never let it go.

MYSTERY
The Enlightened Mind

We think. We solve problems. We formulate plans of action. We investigate, experiment, hypothesize, observe, and theorize. We test, research, and we draw conclusions. We use our minds to do many things. But what is the mind itself? What consciousness is behind all mental activity? And what is the enlightened mind?

In feudal societies, social mobility and personal volition were minimized. If you are a king or feudal lord, you do not like to be criticized or have your actions carefully examined. Why not have monasteries where the best and the brightest sit doing nothing? For the sake of social stability—to reduce political unrest—that would be perfect.

By contrast, in the modern world, society and government depend on the active participation of the people. As an ideal, government is of the people, by the people, and for the people. It is individual initiative that keeps government and society fair, free of corruption, and user-friendly. In terms of the sephirah of Hod, we want an enlightenment that liberates individuals and empowers them to play a dynamic role in their world.

I do not think of enlightenment as something embodied in a saint, guru, master, avatar, or world teacher. Rather, an individual is free to develop enlightened states of awareness that he can draw upon as he needs. Here is one form of enlightenment, though there are as many kinds of enlightenment as there are stars in the sky.

But first, a little humor. From *Stories of Magic and Enchantment*:

And seven mighty angels, lords of creation, stood before the throne of the Creator. And they petitioned him, asking for advice on how to deal with the human race. Sitting upon a throne that exists neither in space nor in time but rather is beyond, the Creator replies, "Did I not create the blue sky?"

And the first angel replies, "Yes, you did."

And the Creator asks, "Why did I do so? I could have left above the Earth darkness and clouds of dust and ash, or else impenetrable mists of dissolving acids."

And the angel replies, "You created the sky by day so that in one single glance men might see that regardless of the raging storms of life, regardless of being surrounded by death on all sides, and regardless of the horrors that pursue them from the moment they are born, the mind itself is open, pure, and clear."

"Is that it?" asks the Creator with a tone of voice implying the angel is missing the main point.

And angel, good at improvisation, replies, "And, in contemplating the sky that embodies freedom and the enlightened mind, there shall come a time when each man shall find the universe reflected inside of him."

Recall that a good symbol holds your attention and is captivating. It is sufficiently physical and familiar that we can relate to it. At the same time, it is slightly outside of everyday consciousness so that it provides insight and challenges to us to let go and see the world through new eyes.

The sky is useful as a symbol of the enlightened mind. The sky is open, vast, limitless, and luminous. You can gaze at the sky and then imagine your mind is the sky. Such a mind is detached, and in the same moment, it is astonishingly receptive and capable of understanding all aspects of any problem or situation. Such a mind is brilliant, crystal clear in thought, perception, and understanding.

Under magical virtue, I described experiences relating to the Air element that fills the sky: The first thing I notice when I imagine myself being weightless is a feeling of freedom. There is no gravity holding me down; instead, there is a feeling of being buoyant, elevated, and lifted up.

The Air element carries with it a sense of detachment; the sky contains weather conditions, but the blue sky itself remains vast, open, and clear despite them.

And with the sense of weightlessness comes the clarity you have when you look without bias or preconceptions; nothing pushes you to make a judgment or draw a conclusion.

The weightless sensation, like the Air element itself, also carries a sense of harmony; it is constantly balancing opposites.

When you feel united to the Air element, to the entire atmosphere of the Earth, then you feel boundless joy.

And finally, to reiterate, with the clarity, vastness, and harmony is a stillness. This stillness is a wisdom that understands how the world unfolds; to everything a time and a season.

To summarize, there is a state of mind that embodies clarity and freedom. Thoughts, feelings, sensations, perceptions, and experiences are things that appear within the sky. They may be wondrously beautiful, or horrible and terrifying. But the mind itself remains clear, luminous, open, vast, and free.

By focusing on the relation of breathing to the atmosphere, it is possible to develop a feeling of being connected to the sky. There is an ecstasy found in this connection that can be heightened to the extent one begins to realize that breathing is its own religion.

RULE 7

NETZACH/VENUS

Victory, Poise, Charm, Charisma, Personal Love

Basic Quality	Relating to others
Virtues, Vices, Negative	Unselfish/Lustful/Treachery
Challenge	Find someone or something you love completely
Magical Practice	Two examples of pursuing life goals
Common Virtue	Empathy
Magical Virtue	Magnetic love
Divine Virtue	Purity of motives
Dream	Oneness
Initiation	Personality integration
Mystery	Zen of love

To review: the Earth has the vibration of making something of value that endures. You enrich the world and life through your presence. When you do this well, the world is a better place for you having been here.

The sphere of the Moon is related to the astral body. Here, unlike the Earth, there is a sense of the unfolding of time—you perceive when and where dreams are fulfilled. And you attain an inner peace with the universe that is reflected in the calmness and serenity of your soul.

The sphere of Mercury intensifies the powers of mind. This sphere exists to solve problems and bring about the swift resolution of conflicts. Here is a concentration in which you consider and integrate all aspects of a problem. And equally there is a level of conviction that approaches near certainty. It is like the highest faith that exists, not faith as belief, but faith as making the best possible choices and manifesting the best outcomes in every situation you enter.

Venus draws together body, soul, and mind, which are embodied in the previous spheres of Earth, Moon, and Mercury. With Venus, love, happiness, and bliss unite in a state of ecstasy. Your inner self and your actions are in harmony. Here beauty reveals divinity. And in uniting with another, our awareness expands so that we are prepared for the next great step, which is to fuse all opposites within ourselves.

In doing so, the highest light of divinity is able to be reflected through us. This is no small task, and thus the ecstasy of Venus empowers us to move toward this goal—to find the motivation and inspiration we need to become fully aware of the beauty and wonder of the universe that surrounds us.

The sphere of Venus enhances knowing who we are and what we are best at doing. As a consequence, you learn to maximize your positive influence on others and the world to the greatest extent.

Venus enables you to get the most out of any situation. You are not stuck in your thoughts or caught in your emotions or slow in your responses due to your body's habitual reactions. You feel invigorated, alive, and ready to engage with what is occurring in the world around you.

There are also feelings of rapport, intimacy, and deep satisfaction that pervade this sphere. There is the sense of blending body, feelings, and thoughts so that the attaining of rapport between individuals becomes a high art. At the same time, this rapport is not a function of devotion, loyalty, or commitment to another. It is a way of seeing inside oneself and another person to create the highest level of connection.

Here it is the most natural of things to weave two individuals' separate identities into a oneness sustained by a sacred space of the heart. If there was a society that embodied this awareness, the individuals would have a vast variety of ways in which to share with each other all that they have ever experienced and all that they care about and love.

Venus provides an assurance that no need exists within oneself that cannot be expressed and satisfied.

But just because love is constantly being celebrated and cherished, it would not be wise to underestimate the power of this sphere. The spirits that dwell here know how to magnetize you so that you begin to see and feel as they do. Just as copper carries a current of electricity between two poles, rapport and intimacy serve to transmit the inner essence and spirit of one person to another.

And so naturally this sphere possesses profound knowledge of sexual magic, of personal beauty, attraction, charm, poise, and charisma. Here is the beauty of art, the mysteries of divine love, and the love bonding an individual to a deity or spiritual ideal. Here are found healers of body, soul, and spirit. And here is the inspiration and wisdom guiding those who search the depths of themselves or undertake spiritual quests.

It is possible to contemplate this sea of Venusian light from a state of mind that is calm, relaxed, and detached. Even so, the Venus oscillation contains a passion and a rapture that even the most intellectual and objective minds will find hard to resist.

BASIC QUALITY
Relating to Others

Relating to others in an attractive and engaging manner. Attraction creates the feeling of being one with another, a vision of one's path in life, and it binds us to our highest ideals.

VIRTUES, VICES, NEGATIVE

Virtues: Unselfish, empathic, poised, charming, charismatic, and personal magnetism. A beauty that draws together and harmonizes all aspects of oneself.

Vices: Lustful, selfish, deceptive, jealous, entangled, codependent, passive-aggressive, ruthless, envious.

Negative: Treachery, betrayal, abandonment, rejection, spite, divorce.

CHALLENGE

Find someone or something you love with all your heart, soul, mind, and strength.

✳ The Wrist Exercise

Certain exercises may have unforeseen side effects. This exercise suggests it is possible to immediately evoke a feeling of loving with all of one's heart. In practice, it is advisable to move slowly step-by-step in that direction. Love, like communication, is best expressed when it is sensitive to context and the particular individuals involved.

Focus on how your entire body feels. Notice your breathing, your digestion. Are you comfortable? Are you at ease, or is there tension in certain muscles?

Now hold one wrist with your other hand. Notice everything you can—the warmth, the pulse of blood, the shape of the wrist, muscle tension, the texture and moisture of skin, and the feeling of the wrist being held, the strength of the hand, and so on.

Without moving in any way, focus the feeling into the wrist of "I love you with all my heart, soul, mind, and strength."

You may notice additional sensations and feelings at this point—for example, an awareness penetrating into the wrist, a heartfelt feeling of embrace; or the warmth is altogether different, perhaps it is giving and healing, and there is a sense of uniting, merging, and becoming one.

Let's go further. Continue holding the wrist in the same way, but put your mind and consciousness into the wrist being held. "Become" the wrist, aware from inside (so to speak) of the muscles, the bones, its solidity, heat, and blood flow.

Whatever else you may notice, you might sense that there is no longer a merging, uniting, or a becoming one. You have become one with the wrist. The process of overcoming separation is complete, though the oneness can always become deeper.

Return now to focusing on your whole body. Notice if your body also feels different in any way. When I do this exercise, I can feel not just changes in my wrist but also in my entire body. The electricity and magnetism in my body seem to have increased.

In this exercise, at first the emphasis is on how deeply you can love another. But equally in loving another we transform ourselves. As one Venus spirit put it, "You will never meet your real self until you love another in this way."

MAGICAL PRACTICE
Two Examples of Pursuing Life Goals

When you make the right commitments that bring meaning to your life, everything else falls into place. Everything else is the way it is meant to be. The struggle is then not a struggle. It is part of a flame of joy. You sense how the spirit within you is shaping your life experience into a reflection of love.

TRAPI, SPIRIT OF CAPRICORN
IN THE EARTHZONE

Get your life together. Know where you have been, who you are now, and where you want to go.

In this section I offer two examples of how to pursue your life goals. The first comes from Tony Robbins, Life Coach: "Make a rigorous determination of where you are and what your goals are. Then make a 100 percent effort to reach your goals so they become real."

The second example is from Ira Progroff, who recommends using an Intensive Journal to review the major stages of your life: "Ask yourself, 'What were my inner feelings during those stages compared to the outer world events?' View yourself with both objectivity and with compassion. Then, with renewed trust in yourself, you can now move forward into the next stage of your life, which stands open before you."

✷ Exercise: Life Coach Tony Robbins: "Unleash the Giant Within"

(Based on Tony Robbins' Aura Readout)

Tony's Outer Presentation and Inner Motivation

Inner Source of Inspiration: "Let's work with large numbers of people and find ways to change them and the world."

Outer aura: The most remarkable feature of Tony Robbins' aura is how energized he is. He has a very self-contained and self-generating energy system. And while retaining his own energy, he manages to transmit some of his highly energized feelings to others.

Inner aura: Tony feels totally at home at a seminar surrounded by thousands of people. He says that every fourth day he is either leading a seminar or on his way to one. He has literally worked with millions of people.

Personality: Tony is very direct, engaging, and a great listener with a skilled mind. He has a large repertoire of tested methods for assisting others to solve problems.

Inner personality: In spite of his outer groomed and well-honed personality, Tony is a wild man, out of control and excessively demanding that others change their lives. As he says of himself, "I am obsessed with what makes the difference in the quality of people's lives."

Images come to mind like an elephant on a rampage or a bull charging a matador. But it is actually easy to understand if you translate his obsession into words. He says (my words), "I accept people exactly as they are, and then I find ways to change their lives for the better."

And this works for him because:

1. People do make changes for the better (that is what they pay him for).
2. In practicing his methods without fully understanding why they work, people fall under his "authority." That is, following his teaching is a little like riding a roller coaster—a lot of exciting things happen in a short period of time. At best, people attain their goals—

and at the worst they are stupefied but nonetheless in awe of his charismatic power.

Summary of Robbins' System

1. Put yourself in your best state of mind. Identify your beliefs, your deepest values, and the standards you want to live by.
2. Answer the questions, "Who am I, and who do I want to be?"
3. Define the goals that will give you meaning and make your life worth living, that inspire you and give you the drive to do the work you need to do to succeed. As Robbins says: "Whatever you hold in your mind on a consistent basis is exactly what you will achieve in life. If you talk about it, it's a dream. If you envision it, it's possible. If you schedule it, it's real."
4. Relax. Now imagine that you have achieved your goals, that in every way they are real to you right now. Relish how this makes you feel, and take note of the person you have now become.

According to Robbins: "Practice the future. Focus on where you want to go. Whatever you focus on, that is where you are going to go and that is what you are going to get more of.

"Remember: your brain can't tell the different between something you vividly imagine and something you actually experience."

As we move toward manifesting our goals, we are going to live our lives with joy and thankfulness. We are going to operate at a peak level of performance.

We are going to have loving and satisfying relationships. We are going to feel fully alive. And because from the core of our being we feel certain about attaining our goals, we shall make a total commitment and put forth a massive effort.

Robbins: "The state we are in in any moment powerfully impacts the meaning that we assign to something. So part of your life's work is managing your state. Spend most of your time in pleasure rather than pain and the people around you feel less pain and a ton of pleasure.

"You are in control of how you feel in any moment of time."

And at this point Tony turns into your football, basketball, or other coach who demands—with great conviction—that you do even more than what you at first imagined. And if you do not believe this is possible, his charismatic presence transmits to you that you indeed are capable of doing just that.

A Few of Tony's Strategic Interpretations

"It's never the environment; it's never the events of our lives, but the meaning we attach to the events—how we interpret them—that shapes who we are today and who we'll become tomorrow."

"Nothing in life means anything but the meaning you give it, so please give your past events an empowering meaning to build powerful and empowering beliefs. Out of our deepest pain will come our greatest gifts—but this can only happen when you take control of the meaning."

"Write down some events you think impacted you negatively, and instead of using it as an excuse to beat yourself up, look for a positive and empowering lesson: there are no tragedies if something good can eventually come of it. We are not our pasts unless we live there."

"Human beings have the awesome ability to take any experience of their lives and create a meaning that disempowers them or one that can literally save their lives."

"Successful people ask better questions and, as a result, they get better answers."

"Questions accomplish three specific things:

1. Questions immediately change what we're focusing on and therefore how we feel.

2. Questions change what we delete.

3. Questions change the resources available to us."

"The brain will search and scan all the options available based on the question we ask ourselves. If you ask ourselves 'How can I be so stupid?' as many of us do, guess what? You will find a ton of reasons . . . But if in time of difficulty you ask yourself 'How can I turn this around?' your brain will deliver ways to turn it around."

"A problem-solving question: What's great about this problem?"

"Emotional Mastery: the final goal of most things we do is to change how we feel. If you feel differently, you behave differently."

"How am I going to live today in order to create the tomorrow I am
    committed to?"

And now this is my question—What is missing from Robbins' system?
Though Tony talks about it, his training lacks transcendence—there is no
detached observer who is the playwright, director, and producer in the
audience watching the play of our life unfold. The emphasis is on getting
the script and scene right. The deeper meaning of life beyond the drama
of action, of attaining goals, does not appear in this theater.

If you want that, you will have to turn to a method such as Ira
Progoff's Life Journal.

And if you want to ask questions such as "What are the deepest
lessons in life for me to learn? How much time, effort, and what kind
of commitment will it take to learn them? And when I have attained all
my personal goals in life (if not before), what divine mission is available
for me to accomplish?" You will have to take a look at the next six
sephiroth.

(*Note:* See the twenty hours or so of free videos of Tony Robbins on
YouTube as well as various essays written by him on the internet, and
consider purchasing his organization's products.)

Ira Progoff's Intensive Journal

Tony Robbins emphasizes pursuing your goals. But his paradigm is
based on "What are your needs and problems right now? How can I
help you succeed and free up the tremendous amount of energy you
have within you?" His focus is on the world as we know it and your role
within society. Wherever you are, live each day with gratitude and have
those feelings right now that make you feel fully alive.

But Tony himself, in spite of all his philanthropic activities and
amazing work on finance, is not listening to the deeper issues of the
heart. If he were, he would be giving seminars on how to eliminate corruption in government. He would upgrade his magic of visualization to
eliminate wars. He would teach nations—rather than just individuals—
how to achieve their goals.

Tony's net worth is around 500 million dollars. It would be nice to think that those whose net worth is 500 million dollars or more would be able to shift gears and ask, "What work can I accomplish that is of such value that it will endure for all ages of the world and inspire anyone who is touched by it now or in the future?"

Tony's approach goes in the direction of becoming, on retirement, like Jay Leno—who had to build an airplane hangar to house his collection of 150 luxury cars and motorcycles. Robbins' methods do not go in the direction of producing a Ralph Nader or a Martin Luther King who challenge not themselves but society to live up to its ideals.

And so I present a second method for attaining goals that is more contemplative in nature and that involves listening to the process through which our lives unfold. This is Ira Progoff's Intensive Journal. Here is my simple paraphrasing and adaptation of one exercise at the beginning of his practices.

✷ Exercise: Ira Progoff Intensive Journal Steppingstones

The Steppingstones portion of the Intensive Journal enables us to see our lives as a whole from the vantage point of the present moment. All the diverse threads and themes of our life begin to weave together, offering us strength and integration. We gain a generalized sense of how our life has been unfolding and its outer and inner movements. This activity generates new energy that helps carry us forward into the next phase of our life.

There is, for example, a feedback stream that is achieved simply by writing down, in a detached manner, the inner and outer events of our life. As we reread these entries at different points in time, we develop a clarity and perspective on our lives amid the movement and change. A sense of personal integration generates greater creativity and spiritual growth.

1. Relax. Close your eyes if you like and be still. Allow your breath to slow and, without yet looking for details, sense the feeling of movement in your life. Get a sense of the continuity and flow of your life as it unfolds.
2. Observe whatever feelings, images, and phrases come to you. Notice the rhythms, tempos, and cycles of your life. Let them shape

and present themselves in whatever form or way they wish. Trust yourself to watch this process unfold without the need to edit, evaluate, or comment on it.

3. Now write down a list of eight to twelve "steppingstones." These are the events, images, sensations, thoughts, or milestones of your life that come to you as you review your life from the beginning to the present. To start the process you might simply write, "I was born," and continue from there. It is a spontaneous process. Let your intuition guide you as to which events are right. You do not need to be concerned if they are not in chronological order.

4. Write a short phrase or sentence for each of these steppingstones that allows you to quickly bring to your mind what you are referring to when you reread your list. For example, you can begin with "It was a time when . . . " and then describe what that milestone in your life was like. For example, "It was a time when I needed to be completely alone. So I decided to live for five months in a little cabin in the desert of Northern Arizona just off the South Rim of the Grand Canyon."

5. When you finish your list, read it over again. Read it from a neutral state of mind, again, just observing rather than commenting or evaluating.

6. Notice the patterns, themes, and the nature of these steppingstones of your life. What do you feel as you reread the list? What is the continuity or discontinuity? What does the list itself have to say to you?

7. Every few months, repeat the exercise. Notice the different things that come to mind at different points in time. Like hiking a trail through the mountains, the valley below appears in a different way according to the season and vantage point from which you gaze. The changes in your perspective may give you new insights.

Building on this, a second exercise is to select a period or stage of your life from your list. Then go deeper into it, exploring it in depth.

1. Ask yourself questions about the period, or start with general recollections. Feel free to use images, metaphors, short descriptive phrases, and sensory experiences.

2. Go into more detail—such as dreams you had, your hopes, ideals, goals, attitudes, relationships, frustrations, and feelings.

3. For example, you can focus on the inner flow of your life during this stage. What was going on inside of you amid the external events?

4. Find an image or accurate description of the inner flow of your life. Now compare the outer world events of this stage with your inner life. Notice when your inner and outer worlds were in sync and flowed together and when they had no connection or were in conflict. Note too in what moments, activities, or personal experiences did the inner and outer flow of your life best come together, and in what events or ways were they most separate?

5. Work up to the present with this process. This enables you to see your life and yourself with both detachment and with compassion. At this point, with trust in yourself and an inner sense of strength, you can now move forward into the next stage of your life, which stands open before you.

Ira Progoff offers quite a few additional exercises for fully entering into these different phases of life. For example, you may want to write dialogues between different aspects of your life during the time period, such as a dialogue with family, friends, and other important relationships; a dialogue with your health; your work; your religion/spirituality; an important event; or cultural or societal norms, attitudes, or values of that period.

As much as I enjoy the Dialogue method in Progoff, I modify it at times so it becomes active listening in which I am both the listener and the one speaking. Here is an example.

JENNIFER: Why don't you tell me about that phase of your life when you were living out in the desert south of the Grand Canyon?

JIM: What about it?

JENNIFER: You were all by yourself. Wasn't that kind of lonely?

JIM: I think I was too numb from my last year in college and I was still recovering from having been so involved with people day-to-day to feel lonely. No, I definitely was not lonely.

JENNIFER: So this was a chance for you to take a break, step back, and unwind in your own way and in your own time? And in a way you seem to feel very grateful for having that opportunity, is that right?

JIM: It was far more than a break and stepping back. I was in complete withdrawal from contact with human beings. And grateful? I just wanted to connect to something real. Nature, the planet Earth beneath my feet, the trees and rocks and animals—they were real. People seemed to me at that time to be obsessed with their social identities. I could sense the way individuals create illusions. Society was so conflicted in the late sixties and early seventies that it felt like a huge carnival with rides, amusements, haunted houses, all sorts of booths and games that test your strength, agility, cleverness, and will.

And I don't mind that. People are free to enjoy life and do with it as they please. Except that in the twentieth century they have discovered how to destroy all life on Earth. That is what I object to.

JENNIFER: So your "withdrawal" from human contact was perhaps more than just connecting to nature. As you talk, I can see your body language shifting as if you are back there living again in that wilderness. There is a steel-like quality about you now.

It is like you are not just into nature but into silence, an inner silence, a stillness like a mountain or a tree or a rock. Like you were after a way of sensing and a perceiving deeper than what is found in human interactions and conversations. And you weren't judgmental of human beings but desperately seeking more than the wisdom of human traditions and religions, is that right?

JIM: Inner silence? Yes, the Earth herself was my teacher. I wanted to see and to understand truth without having to rely on past traditions in which the so-called masters and priests, the gurus and wise men, are so incomprehensibly insecure they actually compare themselves to each other and rank themselves one as more important than other. And so they do not learn from the sky, the ground, the trees, the sea, and the rivers—which are the real teachers on this planet.

JENNIFER: You seem to have known what you were doing to be able to go off and live like that by yourself. Like you were activating some ancient knowledge you already possessed deep inside. All the same, maybe lonely is not the right word. Maybe in some way the extent of that withdrawal did affect you profoundly?

JIM: I admit. Looking at my own behavior during that stage of my life I desperately wanted to be a part of some community. But I had already had a wide range of experience with different social groups such that I could easily see the negative aspects of any group in which I tried to participate.

JENNIFER: So balancing your need to connect against your ingrained bullshit detector, you ended up invariably on your own, is that how things turned out over and over?

JIM: Exactly.

The above exchange enables Jim to "move" from one place of feeling and understanding in himself to another place. Seeing the past more clearly through the assistance of a good listener, he is able to better sense where he wants to go next with himself.

All the same, this is Jim's discovery process. It is his path. You cannot walk it for him. No matter how wise or experienced Jennifer may be, she will never be able to say to Jim, "Jim. Look. This is what you really want and this is how to get it."

It is very tempting for opinionated individuals, extroverts who are impatient for quick results, or for those trained in diagnosis to want to just tell someone what the events of their life mean. If you want that experience, you can join a traditional religion. They have creeds to believe that explain everything, or dynamic methods to unpack your emotions and attain your goals in the fastest way possible.

If, on the other hand, you want to view your life from a place of stillness where you can hear the still, quiet voice of conscience speaking to you, then a seminar like the Intensive Journal would be more appropriate.

Summary

I offer these two very different sets of practices so that you have a context for viewing the methods, groups, or institutions that appeal to you.

The goal is to acquire an integrated personality that brings together your body, soul, and mind so they are in harmony. Treat each part of yourself with respect. Unite them so you attain your greatest strength.

COMMON VIRTUE
Empathy

Empathy: To "read" what others are feeling and thinking; seeing through another's eyes, feeling what they are feeling. "Empathy is the capacity to understand or feel what another person is experiencing from within the other person's frame of reference, that is, the capacity to place oneself in another's position" (from Wikipedia, "Empathy"). There are many definitions for empathy. Types of empathy include cognitive empathy, emotional empathy, and somatic empathy.

These include caring for other people and having a desire to help them; experiencing emotions that match another person's emotions; and discerning what another person is thinking or feeling. Some believe that empathy involves the ability to match another's emotions, while others believe that empathy involves being tenderhearted toward another person.

People do seem to recognize the feelings underlying bodily movements and facial expressions in another by associating them with expressions in oneself. Humans seem to make an immediate connection between the tone of voice and other vocal expressions and inner feeling.

Empathy as a Statement of
Fact Followed by a Question

Larry King, a famous TV talk show host, often uses questions that establish empathy with the guests on his show. He will begin with a statement of fact and then follow with a question.

For example, Larry to guest: "You mentioned that this is a new job assignment for you in a field in which you have no previous experience. I am guessing that you have had moments of doubt about your abilities in the first few months?"

And then, even though the guest is on TV with millions of people watching, he will say something like "No one has ever asked me about this. Yes. It was a terrible struggle until the second year."

Although Larry had never met his guest before, Larry had just coaxed his guest to disclose something personal that he had never shared with anyone else. Even on a linguistic level, empathy is very powerful tool.

Try the above form of empathy. While listening to what someone says, state a fact that you and the other person regard as true about the other's experience with the topic. Then ask a question that links the statement of fact to something the other person has not yet disclosed.

Examples: "You have a job that requires secrecy. Does keeping secrets from your friends and family present difficulties for you?"

"You have been moving between different jobs, advancing as you go along. Is it hard to formulate specific career goals with so much change?"

"You know a great many people, yet you choose your friends very carefully. Is it hard at times to keep your personal life separate from your career?"

★ Exercise: Imagining Yourself as Another Person

A therapist I knew mentioned that when all else fails in a counseling situation he imagines he is the other person. Invariably, this gives him the insight he needs and also creates a rapport with the other person. When you imagine you are another person, people suddenly feel connected to you.

Try this. Imagine you are inside of another person's body sitting as that person sits. You imagine that you are speaking with the other's voice and using the other's body language.

Going further, you imagine thinking the other's thoughts, possessing the other's memories, seeing through the other's eyes, and feeling the other's feelings. You explore another's self-image until you notice a specific, concrete, and physical sensation in your body that arises in response to imagining you are the other person. When you get this sensation of being the other person, focus on it. Allow it to tell you something new about the person.

Then ask yourself, What is this sensation like? Is there an image or symbol that you could use to express it? What does it tell you about this person and the inner flow of the other's life? Do you sense how the individual feels right now, or do you sense something deeper like the force that shapes the person's life?

For example, if I imagine I am a young woman whom I consider to be amazingly complex, I get a sensation in my belly as if I have just eaten a piece of Godiva chocolate. It is sweet, warm, and satisfying. The sensation tells me that in spite of my ideas about her, she actually is what she appears to be—a sweet, young, and loving woman.

I imagine I am a stockbroker whom I just met. I get a sensation of being very relaxed, laid-back, and easygoing. This sensation is in complete contrast to his physical appearance, which is tense and in control. I ask him about this. He says he is looking forward to retiring and that I seem to know more about him than any of his friends.

Getting physical sensations in this manner gives a direct body-to-body and heart-to-heart connection to another person. For a brief period or longer, you are now connected to this person in a way that no one else in the world is. Consequently, you may notice an instant change in your body language and that of the other person.

Among other things, there is—as I mentioned—greater rapport. You and the other may feel more relaxed and comfortable so that words are no longer needed to confirm or validate the relationship. The level of connection is more fundamental than that produced by conversation or social interactions.

I taught a woman this form of empathy. Just after imagining that she was one with me, she paraphrased my conversation with her. As she did so, I felt that her words were like my own voice speaking to me from depths inside myself. I do not recall ever having had this experience before.

Almost everyone has had a life-long friend. In talking to such a person there is a feeling of trust, relaxation, an effortless ease, and satisfaction that accompanies the conversation. Yet no friend I have ever known speaks to me with a voice from the depths of my heart. This kind of empathy allows you freedom of movement so your consciousness can move back and forth between yourself and another. In so doing, you discover an energy and connection that joins both of you.

People often ask me, How do I make this relationship work? How can I overcome the barriers separating myself and this other person? How can I enhance the relationship so we feel really close to each other?

If you want help in a relationship, there are all sorts of things you can do. You can work with a counselor. You can create special experiences that the two of you share only with each other. You can help each other learn something or be there to help the other work through some sort of problem. You can really listen to the other person without trying to insert your own judgments.

But if you want the spice of divinity or the blessing of Divine Providence in your life, then think about making an effort that no one else you know is doing. As in the stories of the Buddha walking down the road, imagine you are the other person. Study the other as if you are reviewing your own life. Do it once a week. This is not the spontaneity of "falling in love." This is creating a sacred space through your art in which two separate people can meet and feel they are one.

I used to do divorce mediation. A divorcing couple is assigned a male and a female mediator who work together as a team. We would separate the man and woman who were getting divorced and listen carefully to each of their stories. The common denominator that was always there in each divorce was that the married couple lacked empathy for each other.

For example, the man thought his wife's role as far as taking care of the children and the house should have been easy for her to perform. She thought his role as a husband in making money should have been easy and certainly more enjoyable than what she was doing. They could not grasp the other's actual situation. They had ideas in their minds that prevented them from sensing what the other was feeling.

In mediation, we consider both points of view, what each feels, what each thinks, and the conflicts they have with each other. Then, combining empathy and clarity, we assist them to discover their common ground and how they can move from the present into a negotiated settlement that both parties can accept and live with.

✳ A Few Basics

Part I: Use your imagination in asking the questions, "What if I were this other person? What is this other person feeling? What does this individual think, and why do those thoughts arise in that person's mind?"

And also, "What is it like to be in that individual's body, to have grown up with that individual's biography, and to have faced the conflicts and sought the goals of this person's life? What was it like making those choices that defined this individual's life?"

Part II: Ask yourself, "What are others' innermost desires and needs?"

Make a picture and feel this picture as real of what this individual would be like when his needs are met, his desires satisfied, his conflicts resoled, and his dreams fulfilled.

MAGICAL VIRTUE
Magnetic Love

Magnetic love is holding another within your heart. It is caring for another as if the other person is part of yourself. It dreams the other's dreams as if those dreams are one's own.

In doing so, it creates a sacred space in which two become one. It is a sharing, but this sharing also includes everything the other person is and everything you are.

People falling in love often say, "I was in love with you from the first moment we met. I feel like I have always known you. Until we met, I did not know what was missing from my life; I was only half alive. Now I feel complete.

"You are a part of me. I can't imagine living my life without you."

✳ Exercise: Enchantment

Recall briefly times when you experienced some of these moments of enchantment—for example, feeling you were meant to be with someone or that you shared special moments together that you could never have experienced with anyone else.

Note the difference between happy, balanced, harmonious, and other satisfying expressions of love and those which are more needy, hungry, out of control, and painful.

Eros and Psyche

In this Greek myth, the goddess Aphrodite gives Psyche, a beautiful human princess, four tests that she must pass if she is to marry Eros, Aphrodite's son. In the fourth test, Psyche journeys into the underworld of Hades. There she has to fetch a vial of the Elixir of Eternal Beauty from Persephone, the consort to the god Hades.

It is no small feat for a mortal to negotiate with goddesses who are indifferent or opposed to her quest. And yet there is another, a fifth test, if we can put it that way. The king of the gods, Zeus, in disguise assumes mortal form and appears in front of Psyche. He asks her, "Tell me, young woman. What do you really want?"

Psyche replies, "To look at a man and feel that his innermost desires I understand. I wish to be one with him so that all separation is overcome. I want my words to be as real as the sun, the moon, the stars, the Earth, the mountains, and the seas when I say to my lover—'There is nothing in you that is not a part of me.'"

Zeus responds, "Until this moment love such as this did not exist. What being, mortal or divine, could ever have imagined or dreamed of a love so fine?"

Zeus raises Psyche up and makes her a goddess, placing her among the other gods and goddesses of Olympus. For though she was once a mortal, her love was immortal, timeless, and divine.

Psyche's choices reconstitute the archetypes in the collective unconscious, or put simply, she encourages the gods of Olympus to become more mature. Zeus discovers there is more to love than just lust, and so he overcomes his mad passion to seize mortal women to satisfy himself.

Eros has been operating like an impulsive child, out of control and without conscience. But it is not Eros that Psyche has to negotiate *with. It is Aphrodite, the mother of Eros. She acts from behind the scenes to exercise power over everyone, especially her own son.*

Eros has no chance of psychological development without Psyche originating a new form of love, turning even Zeus into her ally. In the end, Aphrodite affirms that Psyche has passed the fifth test: to reach the heights of heaven and to survive the dark depths of the Earth, love must mean more to you than your own self.

The Magnetic Fluid

From the Water element we described in Yesod, we can extract a more subtle vibration. We can call this the magnetic fluid. This magnetic force is analogous to magnetism in nature. It is cool and contracting. It is soothing, vivacious, and calming. It purifies and renews. It reveals what is missing from life and acts to make others feel fully alive.

In psychological terms, it is empathic, sensitive, and responsive. It draws together, bonds, joins, and unites. It accepts and affirms. Its shelters and protects. It heals and makes whole.

In spiritual terms, it presents us with feelings of wonder, ecstasy, and beauty. Like Psyche's quest, feminine magnetism reveals the deepest feelings and mysteries at the core of the self.

✶ Exercise: The Ocean of Love

In this exercise, we join physical sensations and feelings. Though you will not find a discussion of this in any texts of psychology, some people do this spontaneously. It is one of the powers of love.

Imagine that you are in the center of an ocean of water. This ocean extends in all directions around you. Imagine the water of this ocean as being cool, perhaps blue-green, pure, and flowing.

Now, add to these imagined sensations of a physical ocean the feeling of love. The water becomes a presence that is nurturing, healing, renewing, and fulfilling. It brings to life whatever it touches. We are now within and part of an ocean of love.

Some will be able to imagine the sensations of water surrounding them but have difficulty adding the feeling of love. Recall again that the sea brought life into being and that it sustains life. The magnetic field within the sea offers us dreams of the way our consciousness can be extended and refined. Once you sense the feeling that is inside Water, the sea becomes a powerful symbol. It embodies the sensations and feelings of all-embracing love.

Take a few moments to explore this imagery. Imagine that you are this sea of love. Identify with this vast field of energy, without referring to yourself as being in a specific location or even having a bodily form. You are love and this love is everywhere.

Now again visualize someone in front of you. Visualize the person's body as a hologram, as being empty inside. Next, imagine that as the sea you begin to flow through the top of this person's head, into his or her body, and out of the person's feet.

As you do so, sense everything within this person. Your cool, flowing Water heals, purifies, harmonizes, and nourishes. Pain and tension dissolve. Frustration and unhappiness disappear. The individual feels whole, complete, happy, and serene. In effect, you are uniting the individual with this sea of all-embracing love.

As you perform this exercise, retain the feeling that you are the entire ocean. Your energy and love are inexhaustible and everywhere. As the ocean, you are pure receptivity, and no obstacle limits your power to flow and to remain pure.

One woman to whom I taught this exercise was able to produce strong sensations of flowing Water combined with love in other people who were in no way psychic. It took two minutes to teach her the exercise. A minute later, with this simple meditation she was extending her aura through the body and mind of another person with effects that were unmistakable.

Another woman said to me after practicing the exercise, "I already do this every day with my boyfriend. I just never put it into words the way you do."

You can also use this meditation for healing. Hold another's hand or place your hands on a part of another person that is injured or needs healing. As you do so imagine this blue-green watery magnetic energy is flowing through the other person restoring him or her to health.

You can love and care for another person. But that is not the same as feeling there is a boundless source of love flowing from you through the other person. Because magnetic love is a force of nature, it is not prone to the insecurity, jealousy, and possessiveness of romantic love.

The ocean of love exercise teaches an individual to observe love as an actual flow of energy between one person and another. Because it arises from a boundless source, there is no ego present, no wounds from the past, and no insecurities relating to the future. One of the initiations or mysteries of Venus is to find such love in yourself.

DIVINE VIRTUE
Purity of Motives

To maximize your charisma and powers of attraction, others need to sense that you have pure motives. In this sephirah, we learn to be dynamic, in charge, assertive, direct, and persuasive. At the same time, to be fully effective, we learn also to be unselfish. People need to know that they can trust you, that if they work with you, they are not going to be disappointed or mistreated.

To be unselfish requires the three previous sephiroth: Malkuth's magical virtue of feeling solid inside, Yesod's ability to cultivate the best internal feelings, and Hod's ability to have a clear mind amid confusion. Then we are able to take responsibility for how we affect others.

To have pure motives you have to be able to recognize when you are being exploitative or abusive. And so we will also need self-refection. Someone may be predatory, exploitative, or coercive in regard to sex, but they may deny doing so not just to others, but also to themselves. Especially people with power often compartmentalize their emotions. They need to do so to maintain control over themselves and others.

But denial does not produce a trustworthy person. The narcissist is not trustworthy. They use other people as a way to meet their own needs. Being responsive or helpful to someone else is only a means to an end—getting what they want. And then some people believe their own lies. Survival for them requires continuously deceiving and playing others.

A religion can interfere with pure motives if it produces fanaticism, blindness, and insensitivity. Those committed to ideologies define themselves as being right and everyone else as wrong. Fear and insecurity destroy trust because the focus is on protecting oneself rather than genuinely assisting others.

Some people are rigid in their conformity to social standards rather than making their own observations and drawing their own conclusions. Then, in spite of all their moralities and ethics, they cannot tell the difference between when they are doing good and when they are doing evil.

I once told a cashier in a small store in Los Angeles that she had not charged me enough, and I paid her the difference. The owner of the store happened to be sitting nearby and heard this exchange. He was so impressed that we began talking. He ended up telling me the story of his life. He had been the highest ranking covert operative in the United States at the time. He had a higher security clearance than the president.

A lawyer I know represented the wife in a divorce case. The husband was so impressed by how fair the lawyer was that he ended up hiring the lawyer to run all his businesses. If someone acts with integrity and is clear and honest in a difficult situation, you know that that individual is trustworthy and would make a great friend.

Most people do not need to worry about having pure motives. They know who they are. They usually live by the standards of conduct consistent with their upbringing. But for those on a journey who wish to transform themselves and the world—these individuals will need to be clear and transparent about what motivates them. And they will be unusually careful to always be honest and fair in their interactions with others.

DREAM

The Outer Vibration of Venus
We might expect that Venus, a planet named after a goddess of love, offers dreamlike enchantments. These enchantments can be separated into outer and inner sets of effects. We can experience the outer vibration of Venus as an attractive force, almost like a tractor beam, connecting one person to another.

And with this attraction, you have a heightened awareness of your own body. You experience things you never felt before. Such feelings can be captivating and hypnotizing. At times, it is almost like being possessed by something in yourself that you never knew was there.

Overwhelming desires and shared intimacy may force everything else in your life off to the side. Your mind narrows its focus down to one individual with a possibility of gratifying your deepest needs.

There is a story of Kama—the Eastern version of Eros—with his bow. Brahma, the creator, gives Kama (erotic desire) power over all beings in heaven and Earth. No one is free of his influence or beyond his reach. "For what purpose do I exist?" Kama asks Brahma. Brahma replies, "To ensure each being has a part to play in the unfolding of the world." No one is left out. Hidden within the primal and primordial powers of erotic attraction is a force that unites us all.

The Inner Vibration of Venus

The outer vibration of Venus, then, can be overpowering. It captures and it binds. It is intoxicating—the mind hypnotized, the emotions infatuated, and the body enthralled. For what cause? Again, as Brahma explains, "To ensure each being has a part to play in the unfolding of the world."

By contrast, the inner vibration of Venus is not a whirlwind of desire. There is no tempest raging, no thunder rolling, and no lightning striking. It is not like a wave rising, cresting, and breaking, unleashing the passion of an entire sea.

The inner vibration of Venus is feeling that, without barriers or boundaries and without separation, you are one with another. The inner connection is so complete that as Psyche would assert: "Everything within you is a part of me."

The inner vibration of Venus (oneness with another) is a different way of being. We could say that such love is not of this world. But that would not be correct. Love dares to dream what can be.

The prophets of old liked to say, "It shall be so; the voice of the Lord has spoken it." But love such as this has no need to assert its power because it arises from the center of the heart. All things are derived from it and depend upon it. For those who fully experience this dream, it annihilates loneliness and is the guide and guardian who offers the keys to all mansions of the soul.

When you're around those who have an inner oneness with another, there is a feeling in the air of springtime, sacred holidays, and bliss. You feel cleansed, purified, and healed. If you relax and drink it in, you sense that beauty is everywhere.

It is a different way of being in that all parts of yourself are in harmony. The deepest inspiration within you is near at hand and ready to draw upon as you need.

Or, as Zeus said to Psyche, a woman who demands such oneness, "Until this moment love such as this did not exist. What being, mortal or divine, could ever have imagined or dreamed of a love so fine?"

There are stories about magicians who prematurely contact spirits of the sphere of Venus. In one story, the magician asked a spirit associated with the placement of Venus in his natal chart, "What can you teach me?" The spirit replied, "I can teach you about love."

Shortly after this interaction, the man fell madly in love with a woman he already knew. The relationship was wild, crazy, enthralling, and overwhelmingly passionate. But it was too much for him to handle. He wanted his life back. So he evoked the spirit again and thanked her, but said he no longer needed her assistance.

Spirits of Venus often refer those who seek to experience the mysteries of love back to the previous three spheres of Malkuth, Yesod, and Hod. There the individual can learn to meet his basic needs. He can experience peace and well-being, be grounded, and have a satisfying life. He can gain a sense of being whole and complete in himself and a part of nature. And he can gain a kind of enlightenment that frees him of illusion and false attachments.

At this point, the dream of oneness can become fully operational. Your connection to another is direct, immediate, perceptually real, and satisfying in every way possible. You have done your homework to get here.

All the same, the dream of oneness is itself a kind of spirit guide and inner teacher. It continuously reminds us of what is possible and that this oneness with another is already present within us.

INITIATION

In the initiation of Netzach, the individual's personality becomes integrated. This integration brings together and harmonizes the strengths and qualities of the three previous sephiroth.

To review, there is the feeling of being grounded and a part of nature in Malkuth. This greatly reduces social anxiety and insecurity. The individual learns to be calm and centered in Yesod so that the erratic impulses and mood swings produced by the subconscious are minimized. And there is a sense of sustaining a clear mind amid confusion found in Hod. The individual is fully responsive to circumstances while approaching problems with confidence and conviction.

In Netzach, then, the individual is caring, attractive, and poised during times of stress and conflict. Even during difficulties, this individual is able to bring out the best in others. There are situations of danger, fear, and great uncertainty that we encounter in life. This individual, however, has that charisma of someone who exudes a feeling that, on some level, we have already overcome our limitations and won the battle. He brings courage and promise to every situation.

This courage is an inner attitude. It derives, again, from mastering the three previous sephiroth. But it is also produced through acquiring a massive amount of experience.

Over and over, the individual has solved problems and had success in his endeavors in many areas of life. The individual is not just attractive and confident. He is wealthy in life experience.

A little humor might help to illustrate this. From the movie series *Mission Impossible:* "Your mission, should you accept it, is to learn to love yourself, not in a narcissistic way, but so as to know yourself in every aspect. Your mission is also to love another with all your heart, soul, mind, and strength.

"And it is to find some work in life you can also love with all your heart so that there is no end to your desire to pursue it and to perfect it. And your mission is to find and cultivate lifelong friends who are so close to each other that each of you feels he is living to some extent the other's lives along with them. And, as if crafting a plan that you seek to fulfill over the entire course of your life, you accomplish something that in a profound way enriches the world. And finally, amid all of these activities, find within yourself and identify with the dynamic powers unfolding the universe.

"This mission, should you accept and accomplish it, completes your initiation into the sphere of Netzach. At which point you will be able to look back and say, 'My life is all it was meant to be.' Good luck."

MYSTERY
Zen of Love

The Detachment Part

Romantic love comes with a strong sense of bonding. Two people have a special and usually exclusive relationship. And yet, with romance, there may also be codependence and entanglement. An individual may strive to see another in terms of what is hoped for rather than what is actually in front of him. Then again, even when there is an acceptance of the other person, there may also be a compelling desire to make him or her better.

In the long term, for love to be effective, it helps to perceive one's partner with clarity. This requires freedom from ego, from attachment, from possessiveness, and from denial. We can turn to Hod to assist us in this endeavor.

Enlightenment in the sphere of Hod/Mercury is seeing the world as it is, free of bias and presumption. To review one process relating to clarity of mind: Imagine your mind is the sky. You are surrounded by a vast, open space. Here all things appear and yet there is nothing to be attached to.

There is no envy that reaches out and tries to take something. There is no greed that would aggrandize itself by adding to its possessions. There is no jealousy that worries about something taken away. And there is no anger when something opposes its will. There is nothing to hold on to and nothing to lose.

There is no ego present and so there is no one threatening or attacking, no one here to be threatened or attacked, no attack occurring and nothing to attack with. And so there is no fear and fight/flight does not appear.

The idea is to become in one's awareness a kind of magic mirror. You want to reflect with great clarity what is before you.

The Love Part

Retaining our sense of being within a vast space of nothingness, imagine another person "in front of you." It is not like I am here and she is there. Rather, you are the space within and around this person. There is no need to refer to someone such as yourself who is observing.

Now look around in this vast, empty space. You do not see any national boundaries, no rivers to cross, no mountains to climb over. There are no fences and barriers between you and the other.

And there are no social boundaries. No rank and no class structure. No ethnicity and no language barriers. No age difference and not even a gender. "There is nothing that separates" in this space. "There is only oneness and so perfect love."

You are in a vast, empty space. This space is your awareness. And you are perfectly one with whatever appears here. Get a sense of removing the outer form, and yet merging with the inner soul and spirit of another. If you can feel a oneness, then you are creating a state of profound love.

The Zen Master of Love

What does this mystery of love feel like? We have described this before. It is cool and calming, nurturing and strengthening. It is soothing as in dissolving tension. It revives and restores. It is relaxing, as in being free of anything constraining you or weighing you down.

It is releasing, offering a refined pleasure, satisfaction, and comfort. It is accepting, banishing any hint of rejection, guilt, sorrow, sadness, or loss. It is healing, cleaning, renewing, and rejuvenating. It is endless in giving.

It is embracing, sharing, friendly, and offering a feeling of being home. It is uniting, creating intimacy and offering a noble and loving community. And it is so still, it grants visions of the past, present, and future.

Return again to visualizing another person before you. Now ask yourself, "What is missing from this person's life?" Take a few moments to sense the answer. It could be happiness, contentment, satisfaction, joy, being fulfilled, or a dream made real. It could be the individual wants a stronger sense of self-esteem, respect, or dignity. He might want to feel his actions justify having been alive. See if you get a clear picture in your mind of what a more fulfilled, more complete, and happier person would be like.

Perceiving in this way—detached and yet at the same time one with the other person—has an effect on that individual. On some level, it offers the experience of oneness free of any bias, possessiveness, or self-ish intent.

The challenge for the sphere of Venus goes like this:

> *When you love, love with your whole being—with all your heart, soul, mind, and strength.*

You will never know who you are until have this experience.

The detached empty space of our mirror-like consciousness has various qualities. It reveals the original nature of people. It generates a very high level of empathy that intuitively can sense what is inside of others and what it is like to be them. And it presents options—new ways of acting that come across are just as real as what the individual is now doing.

In the mystery of Yesod, the Moon, we ran into an amazing obstacle. Different religions do not share each other's dreams. And yet the astral plane sustains all of us as well as all paths of life. It nurtures all beings.

We could say that at this point in our unfolding of the Tree of Life, we come to a state of mind in which we embrace an individual from the position of universal love. We are accepting and supportive in every possible way. We seek the best for the other.

And yet we are not being invasive or manipulative. We are not offering remedies or solutions. We are here playing the part of the astral plane itself that sustains and nurtures. We are 100 percent present within and a part of the other person's life. This all-embracing love of the astral plane that supports all paths of life can also be called unconditional love. This is the love we are embodying during this meditation.

As I mentioned under the dream for Netzach, a feeling of oneness like this is a different way of being. Love has the power to annihilate every barrier that separates.

The mystery of love, if we embrace it, joins together a marvelous sense of transcendence with a physical, emotional, mental, and spiritual experience of being one with another. When you meditate on another person, consider practicing within this state of heart and mind. If you love feeling you are one with another, you enter a different world.

RULE 6

TIFERET/SUN

Beauty, Harmony, Uniting Opposites

Blessed are those who meet others in their darkest place and walk beside them back into the light, for there is no greater or more sacred celebration of life.

Basic Quality	Inspiration
Virtues, Vices, Negative	Humility/Pride/Domination
Challenge	Find the inspiration that guides you through life
Magical Practice	Make a book of inspirational sayings; reinforce your inspirations
Common Virtue	The better self
Magical Virtue	Stillness
Divine Virtue	The ability to heal others
Dream	Equanimity
Initiation	Make the divine world a part of yourself
Mystery	The relation of the personality and the Higher Self

Each planet in our solar system has its own themes. The Earth is oriented toward accomplishing things. In our world there is always a plan of action unfolding. If you do not have your own goals, someone will be happy to supply them for you. Failure to participate is almost the worst thing you can do.

On Earth we also have great learning opportunities—ways to grow, to serve others, or to work through some challenge in life. Nowhere will you find so many obstacles and difficulties. And nowhere else are you offered such a high learning curve.

Besides Malkuth, we pass through three other domains to reach Tiferet, the Sun. The sphere of the Moon (Yesod) emphasizes the rhythm of life and an awareness of the time and the seasons in which things manifest. Without the inner peace and a feeling of oneness with the universe of the lunar sphere, individuals have no sense of creating a "spiritual environment" through which they transform themselves. They neither understand the laws governing the spiritual realms nor do they have any sense of a path to perfection.

Without the mental concentration of Mercury (Hod), the mind is weak and clingy. And so we observe fanaticism and obsession with doctrines. Individuals convince themselves that their ideas are right, yet they lack clarity. They are busy attacking others or defending themselves instead of comprehending problems in all aspects and variations.

If we try to bypass the realm of Venus (Netzach), we lack empathy—how to connect directly to the person in front of us. There is a lack of an appreciation of art, of personal harmony, and of the ways in which the attraction between opposites express beauty.

Yet the sun is different from all other realms in our solar system. Each spiritual being has its own inner source of inspiration. Those under the influence of the solar sphere are not just inspired by Divine Providence. Within themselves, the fifth element of Akasha becomes a mirror so pure and deep that aspects of the Creator are reflected directly through them. If you hold up a mirror to reflect the sun, then the light you see is the actual photons that the sun is emitting. With solar spirits, their inspiration is a direct reflection of divine being.

For this reason, there is something wildly creative and cosmic, and a nearly incomprehensible harmony radiating from them. They have the abilities to heal, to restore, to protect, to reveal, and to empower all paths of life.

BASIC QUALITY
Inspiration

From the Earthzone spirit Pigios: "Inspiration is within everyone's reach. You only need to ask yourself what is missing from your life. Imagine desires satisfied, needs fulfilled, and visions attained. Enter the dream. Make it part of yourself."

VIRTUE, VICES, NEGATIVE

Virtues: Humility, charisma, mediation, peacemaking, conflict resolution, service, dynamic integration of all aspects of oneself, purity, inner union with the divine.

Vices: Pride, arrogance, malice, enmity, harboring grudges, vulnerability, manipulation, hazing, retaliation, blind devotion, darkness that thrives in the shadow of the light.

Negative: Domination—desire to control others; enslaving the world, disintegration, accursed, without conscience, psychic vampires, false prophets, cults and oppressive secret societies, dystopia, dictators.

CHALLENGE

Find the inspiration that can guide you through life and enable you to become the person you wish to be.

MAGICAL PRACTICE
Reinforce Your Inspirations

Tony Robbins emphasizes that it is our own responsibility to live life with gratitude and to be highly motivated in accomplishing our goals. Franz Bardon emphasizes the power of autosuggestion. A magician, using the powers of a trained concentration, can transform first himself and then the world.

Here in the sephirah of Tiferet, the domain of the heart, we undertake the Great Work. This is creating and maintaining the inspiration within our souls that unites all opposites so that the light within us becomes brilliant like the sun in the sky.

✳ Exercises: Two Practices for Inspiration

✳ Part I. Make a Book of Inspirational Sayings

Philip Carr-Gomm, the head of the Order of Bards, Ovates, and Druids, told me that he made for himself a book of his favorite inspirational sayings. He mentioned this because a poem of mine was among them.

The practice is to make a book of your own favorite writings that inspire you. Review it on a regular basis. Use it to sustain the light within you.

Also include personal experiences that you find inspiring and worth recalling. Consider special moments when you experienced beauty, wonder, and awe; when you felt saturated with love or peace; when you felt fully alive; when you had one of the desires of your heart fulfilled.

What dreams, visions, ecstasies, or spiritual experiences have you had that you felt were sacred? When did the divine speak to you, move you, or touch your life? When were you thankful just to survive and be alive?

When did you act with courage, great confidence, or conviction? When was someone kind to you when you needed it most or was there for you when no one else was?

In a relaxed state of peace and serenity, recall the various things that inspire you. Allow them to pass before your mind as if you are in a stream of consciousness.

Sometimes just reading inspirational words and visualizing certain images will trigger your memories and bring back deep feelings. Sometimes the words evoke feelings that are like portals that take you into other realms that can be endlessly explored. Or the words create a vibration like a lucid dream, or they unite you to an entire universe of love, wisdom, purpose, and missions to accomplish.

Free associate. Move freely between one thing and another without evaluating or labeling. Enter a zone of pure feeling. Open yourself up so the light can touch you.

A few examples of sentences that affect me deeply:

1. From the book *Pumpkin Seed Point,* by Frank Waters, "Adrift on a sea of motionless time, I come to see there are worlds enough for becoming myself."

   I easily fall into a semitrance whenever I read those words. I relive what Frank Waters felt when he wrote them.

2. "Blessed are those who meet others in their darkest place and walk beside them back into the light, for there is no greater or more sacred celebration of life."

   I appreciate the sentiment because I have gone through some dark times and no one was there with me.

3. "There is an absolute contentment in which the inner self is at peace with the universe."

4. "Blessed are those whose minds are as open and clear as the sky, for their peace shall be as a sea that has no shores and as a stream that flows from the dawn of time to the ends of eternity."

5. "The universe is on the verge of exploding because of the joy it contains." —Cargoste, a sylph

6. "In regard to love (if you want the full experience), you would not be getting your money's worth, would you, unless you feel you are within your lover living her life as if it is your own." —Hagiel, a Venus spirit

7. "The prime directive for all souls incarnating on Earth: Become your own creation."

And examples of personal experience:

I had a special sense of well-being when I was age three. My two brothers and I had life preservers on as my mother, along with my father, sailed her twenty-two-square-meter sailboat on Lake St. Clair. The wind was very light as we slowly sailed through a flock of Canada geese who were not disturbed by our presence.

When I was twelve I was riding along in my father's Cessna 180 seaplane as we were flying up into Canada toward Flack Lake from Detroit. My father casually turned to me and told me to keep the plane at a certain altitude and compass reading with the wings level. And then he climbed into the back seat and went to sleep for three hours. For me, this was an initiation—his generation, having discovered flight, was handing that power down to me.

You can also review some of your all-time favorite songs or other forms of art.

✳ Part II. Reinforce Your Inspirations

Next, select two or three inspirations from your list. Briefly focus on one and then move to the next one and go back and forth until you have a feeling for each of them. Then bring them all into your mind at the same time.

Again, from a heart of stillness that embraces all things, sense what underlies and unites them. See if you find how they interact, blend and join, rising them to a new level.

Over the last month, I have recalled a great many experiences that I would never have revisited except for this exercise. Each in its own way is special for me. Many do not "fit" the idea of inspiration, though in one way or another they are charged with power and feeling.

Here are examples of three experiences that I meditated on.

1. A few minutes from my house is Hanauma Bay on Oahu. I have gone there many times to snorkel and see a vast variety of fish.

   This time I was a few feet offshore and I put my hands down into the water. Immediately I felt the water was alive, as if it was a living being.

   I have interviewed something like fifty of what I call "mermaid women." These are women who feel an unusual connection to water and who are extremely empathic. They often say that entering the ocean is like "returning home" or "being embraced by their mother."

   This time at Hanauma Bay I felt something similar. It was like being a fetus in the womb, where you are part of another person's life and vitality. Oceanography is a study of the ocean including life forms, ecosystem dynamics, currents, waves, plate tectonics, geology of the sea floor, and chemistry. But oceanography does not study or know of the soul of the ocean or that, for those who are perceptive, the ocean is a conscious being. In this experience of mine, the barriers that separate human from nature vanished.

2. I woke up a friend when I called her on my phone. She was in a very receptive state of mind. Spontaneously I had the experience of being one with her.

Franz Bardon warns not to become enticed by mermaids because their beauty is such that you do not long for any further spiritual experience. For the next three hours after we spoke, it was as if I looked inside of myself and all I could see or feel was her presence. I understood why Bardon gave that warning.

Also, one time I asked Swami Rama for a taste of what he experienced when he asked his master for *shaktipat*—a transmission of the master's inner spirit to the student. For a few minutes I experienced what the masters of that lineage pass down to their students—it was a feeling of a fully conscious woman being inside of you and one with you.

As I already mentioned in Netzach, the attainment of oneness is a different way of being. You are suddenly inside of the mystery of life rather than outside looking in. There is no more searching or quest. You are complete in yourself.

3. A third experience comes to me spontaneously from time to time. It is often triggered by drinking a cup of coffee or by a sugar rush like eating chocolate chip ice cream (though I have stopped eating ice cream). In it, the world is perceived from a state of great harmony—problems are solved, conflicts resolved, realizations attained, and all personal limitations are transcended. Even the problem of suffering is addressed, for the answer to suffering is not intellectual, but an action: become healed or heal others.

During this experience I find myself saying, "Life is so incredibly beautiful." This is the ecstasy of the Air element that offers an outrageous feeling of joy. Again, as the sylph Cargoste states: "The universe is on the verge of exploding because of the joy it contains."

It is a truly dazzling, radiant experience. And yet it often appears from nowhere and during the worst times in my life. In this experience, I am perceiving the world from the point of view of Divine Providence as it operates in the solar sphere.

I now reenter these three experiences, letting them flow through my mind without editing or evaluating. And then I ask myself, "What underlies each experience?"

With the Hanauma Bay experience, I feel a sense of being one with the sea. Society is not intervening. Instead, it is me in a direct connection to nature. With my friend, I have the experience of oneness with another person. And with the solar vision of beauty, there is a feeling of briefly becoming radiant with light.

At this point, I am ready for the next step. I ask myself, "What underlies all three of these experiences so that I sense the one source from which they all arise?" What comes to me is a sense of sharing with another person what is sacred, the wonders of creation.

The source is the sephirah of Tiferet, an eternal, unending radiance within which all opposites are united and all opposition overcome. This exercise takes part of your list of personally inspiring experiences to the next level. It refines, purifies, and distills. It takes you into the pure flame of inspiration that is at the center of life from which all experience arises.

Religions by definition are the custodians of various sacred experiences. In which case the sacred serves as a guide to how to live one's life. But each of us also have our own encounters with the sacred.

You may notice in practicing an exercise such as this that you are moving freely between personal and transpersonal and between human and divine. Here the emphasis is on your life, your inspiration, and your own experience with transformation.

As one spirit puts it, "Make it a lifelong habit to gather into one place every memory of what inspires you in life. Hold these things before your mind and relive them so they continue to be fully alive.

"And now take the final step—make a space inside yourself big enough so that all these things that inspire you can reveal a source of inner light that has the power, the love, the wisdom, and the freedom to transform you into the person you are meant to become."

COMMON VIRTUE
The Better Self

Every soul desires to transform the world through love.

SUFI SAYING

I have mentioned how a few of the individuals that I interview "see" not just the person in front of them; they also "see" the person's future self or the "better self" that the individual can become.

Put simply, you look at someone and you imagine what this person would be like if his problems were solved, his conflicts resolved, and his purposes clear. You imagine his motivation and inspiration fully operational so he is self-assured, free of doubt, and has made the best choices. In other words, you see the individual as being highly successful in every way appropriate for him or her.

Often when you look at someone in this way, there is an observable effect on the other person. For one, the other person may get the feeling that you are in touch with what is deep inside of him. And it is clearer to the other person when he is choosing his best course of action. You are being supportive and also reminding someone that he or she can be better.

Some who can see others in this way often see the other person in the present and in the future in the same moment. If you imagine yourself to be in the future talking right now with someone's future self, then when you suggest to the person what he may become, your words have more force. You are not speaking hypothetically but rather of something that is 100 percent real to you.

I use the phrase "graphic imagination" to describe this visual ability of imaginatively stepping into the future and seeing what is there (or what is possible). You are not using just your mind. You are imagining with your whole being that you are in the future situation.

You can take this further. You can see the other's better self as if that self is more real than the person who is in front of you right now. In this case, you help bring through the traits of his evolved self.

✳ Exercises: Visualization

✳ Part I: Visualize Someone Else's Better Self

Try this. Visualize someone you know as being in front of you. The individual is so real you can reach out and touch him.

Review this person's strengths and weaknesses, the individual's advantages and disadvantages, and the best and the worst moments in his life.

Now see the individual change into his better self—everything good and positive that he can become. Desires are satisfied, purposes accomplished, and dreams fulfilled. Put together a feeling, a thought, and a picture of what this might be like for the individual.

To heighten the sense of reality, you can have a conversation with this future self of the person. You can ask, for example, "How does this feel for you?" "What did you have to do to get here?" and "What helped you the most in making changes in yourself?"

You may also notice things about the other's better self—there is more clarity, more energy, more peace, contentment, happiness, self-confidence, strength, and courage.

Meditating on someone in this way, even when he is not present, has an effect on that person. It heightens the individual's awareness of his freedom to make new choices and to change. It makes real what may otherwise not enter the other's thoughts or feelings.

Here is an example. I wrote one woman after I imagined her future self: "Obviously, you become very successful in your acting. But you already embodied the inner feeling of success before the outer world success appeared. And the particular charisma you have internalized is being able to bring together all parts of someone so that they have the energy to move forward in their lives past whatever is holding them back.

"It is not the Tony Robbins' attaining your personal goals. Rather, it is becoming a different person. Goals will not get you there. New goals proceed from being here.

"And if I ask your future self, 'What did you do to get here?' your future self replies, 'I see people as being free, completely harmonious, having found their own best source of inspiration. I do not have to say anything to them. They just spontaneously start talking about themselves and their plans in a way they never thought about before.'

"The 'trigger' from having this vibration is that when casting or a director or producer look at you or thinks about you, it is easy for them to visualize you as part of their next project."

A poem on seeing another's better self.

I love your eyes
So quiet and peaceful

A place to let go and forget who I am
Until I awaken to the sound of waves breaking
And the scent of the sea
I see the man I am meant to be
Walking toward me
Your eyes dream him into being

✳ Part II: Visualize Your Own Better Self

We can also visualize our own better self. Imagine you are looking into a mirror and seeing this other self that is you, or else simply visualize this person in front of you. Again, this is you when you are fully inspired, highly motivated, fulfilled, content, at peace, and successful in whatever endeavors you are focused on. Practice until this image is easy to call before your mind.

It may be the case that if you describe to someone the traits of his future self, he will object. He may point out, "I am not ready to become this person. I have too many traumas from the past I have not worked through. There are things inside of me that I still repress, which I am certainly not ready to transform into something positive.

"I have issues. I am jealous and angry. I have impulses I can't control. And there are things about myself that baffle me and are totally beyond my understanding. Perhaps in time I will become what you say. But right now, I cannot even imagine some of these things you say about me."

These objections have to be taken seriously. You can't just sprinkle fairy dust on someone and say, "Believe and trust. Now you are changed." But then again, we are in Tiferet, the realm of the heart. Recall the nature of love. It completely accepts the world as it is and at the same time it dares to imagine what the world can be. The heart is capable of embracing past, present, and future from a state of deep love and divine grace.

MAGICAL VIRTUE
Stillness

In stillness, things become calm, quiet, relaxed, and at peace. There is a sense that motion, movements in time, cease and then you perceive with great clarity.

Take a relationship with someone that is important to you. Review briefly the entire history of that relationship from the first moment you met, until the last moment you have experienced thus far. And then look again as if each moment is still alive, is still happening. See all of it before your eyes.

Very briefly, review your entire life from the moment you were born. Step back and look at it again as if each moment is equally alive and still happening. Quiet, calm, relaxed, at peace, and clear—see all of it arrayed before your eyes.

People sometimes ask, "Can you change the past?" If you change the way you look at the past, then it becomes different.

Here are a few comments on stillness by Zhevekiyev, the head of the twenty-fourth lunar mansion:

> Stillness is the center of the wheel of time, that upon which all things turn. It is the perfection of psychological equilibrium—in and through you every imbalance seeks balance, every discord seeks harmony, every weakness strength, and everything negative transforms into positive. Every journey, ideal, and quest finds fulfillment, manifestation, and attainment. Every desire finds satisfaction, every craving gratification, every sign of the zodiac unites with its opposite and then together they all unite and return to the center.
>
> Stillness is a history of nations in which every king or man of power in attaining absolute sovereignty also is completely humble, seeking only to enrich and fulfill the lives of his people.
>
> Stillness is a world in which every lover makes an absolute commitment to another to ensure and to guarantee that the other's life is fulfilled in every conceivable way.
>
> Stillness is a world in which any person in quiet meditation can easily perceive any other person's life on Earth in its complete history as in a drama or a stage play unfolding amid conflicts and resolution, tension and release, with supporting cast, with dynamic and dazzling subplots about to be written. And yet there is this also: nearly infinite treasures of life are just offstage at the edge of our consciousness waiting to enter and bless the individual's life.
>
> Stillness is a world in which if you sit down to meditate, and if

you so desire, there is always someone sitting there with you, and together you dream the deepest dreams at the core of each other's being.

And there is an inner stillness that is in harmony with the universe that slowly, gradually, and imperceptibly takes the person that is you and makes all things new.

In stillness, time halts. The experience of every human being on Earth, past, present, and future, appears before you. And you perceive each moment of these experiences as if they are still happening.

If you pursue stillness, you discover that the fiery light of creation is all around you. It is a great harmony underlying and embracing all things. It is filled with joy, infinite love; everywhere and in everything, it holds the world within its heart.

DIVINE VIRTUE
The Ability to Heal Others

A good story captures people's attention. To this end, it has conflict, character development, and resolution. The incarnation of a world teacher by necessity takes the shape of a story. He descends from the sphere of the sun, a realm of pure light. He puts on human form, cloaking himself and accepting human limitations. His life then unfolds like a drama that is so convincing that it speaks to us, and we feel we are a part of it.

But the story is not just about a hero. It is not a drama that takes place "out there and performed by another." The story is about the possibilities of light unfolding within you. The teacher comes not when life is bright. He appears when things are dark, where there are suffering and loss.

He meets us in our darkest place. Extending his hand as a friend and guide, he offers to lead us out of the darkness and back into the light.

The darkness in life is sometimes very great. But a spirit of the sun can say, "There is no darkness I have not been within; there is no loss that I have not felt." The empathy here is perfect—you realize he feels exactly what you feel.

Tiferet harmonizes all the sephiroth. When it does this on a divine level, it restores the harmony within anything. If this divine virtue were embodied in a human being, he would be able to heal anyone of any illness and restore any soul to wholeness so that at last one feels fully alive. Those who embody this virtue are very rare in human history.

DREAM

The dream of Tiferet is to be united to a world of light. The result is that you can then look out on our world with its suffering, confusion, and injustice and maintain a calm equipoise and clear perception. In this equipoise, there is no separation between the spiritual and the human sides of oneself. The human and divine live within and are a part of each other maintaining complete harmony and balance.

I know a few individuals who live part of this dream. One woman says, "I am already in heaven." She has a down-to-earth job as a real estate agent. She also does healing massage. And yet part of her is completely transcendent—that is, it is independent of this world.

Both she and another woman I know often intervene in other's lives. If someone is angry and out of control, they can transmit to them part of their own experience. It is like giving someone a time-out. For a little while, the individual feels his conflict has vanished. He then has a chance to calmly look around himself and decide what is important.

INITIATION

In this initiation, we sense that there is a divine world and we also sense that we are not a part of it. Slowly, like a tree that sprouts from a seed, we find a way for this radiant, spiritual light to take on substance and life within us.

If we rush the process, we risk becoming shallow, self-righteousness, fanatical, manipulative, and arrogant. If we fail to be sufficiently diligent and committed, our focus is overridden by distractions and consuming passions that take us in other directions.

If we are wise, we will first undertake the initiation of Malkuth in which we gain a solid and enduring connection to nature with its sense of inner silence. And we will undergo the initiation of Yesod where we integrate our conscious and subconscious. We learn to give our full attention to our instincts and emotions.

With the Hod initiation, we put aside any need to control other people in order to feel secure. Instead, we develop an enduring commitment to truth and clarity. And in Netzach, we gain empathy and emotional integration so we are effective in the world.

And then finally, here in Tiferet, we enter a state of deep receptivity to the divine. This requires that we become so empty, clear, and still that the divine world can appear within us without distortion or weakness.

Those who succeed in this endeavor have moved beyond the expectations of society and the doctrines of religion. With real skill, they have made their own observations and pursued their own development over a lifetime. Step-by-step and systematically, they internalized within themselves something wonderful and amazing. Inspiration, ecstasy, and divine perception become a permanent part of their lives.

MYSTERY

The Relation of the Personality
and the Higher Self

In meditation, you in your personality and you as a divine being come together, join hands, and create new dreams.

The mystery in Tiferet is the relationship between our conscious self and our higher self. In place of higher self, we could say your true self, your better self, or the person you are meant to be. Or, to be more adventurous, we can simply refer to God, the Creator, your guardian angel, or even Divine Providence, Akasha, and so on.

Your personality that you present to other people in your daily life and the spiritual part of yourself may be quite separate. You do what you need to do to get through the day. And then, when you meditate, your consciousness is on an entirely different level.

Most people will not experience any conflict here. Their spiritual practices enrich their daily life. They feel calmer, more integrated, and insightful. On the other hand, what I am referring to as the higher self exists outside of space and time. It possesses amazing insight and unusual powers. And it has no attachments.

However, if we connect too quickly to our higher self, there may be serious side effects. Our false ideas, and things we repress or deny in ourselves, are suddenly exposed to the light. Selfishness and attachments dissolve. Our beliefs about ourselves, society, religion, and the spiritual world are revealed to some extent to be pure fiction.

We are suddenly stripped of narcissism, inflation of ego, psychological complexes, fear, and obsessions. These artificial supports, which seemed so essential, vanish. The contact with the spiritual part of ourselves can be devasting to our ego, our social identity, and our personality.

In the realm of spirit, there is no social self or ego to get inflated. There is no power to be possessed. There is only an awareness penetrating through or outside of space and time. All things arise from it. It is a part of and within all things. And it is so magnanimous that it oversees, guides, inspires, and fulfills all things.

It is possible, then, while meditating, to activate to some degree this transcendent self. But then the part of ourself that is here in incarnation has the job of figuring out how to fit such elevated insights into our daily lives while also dealing with the side effects of the contact.

There is a great price to be paid if you are going to make contact with the divine in a serious way. You have to confront the darkness in yourself. And this is where the otherwise really brilliant and talented students will fail—they cannot pass through the emptiness, the void, and the abysses that exist within the human heart. Opening the gates to spiritual realms requires that we make a monumental effort to align our conscious selves not with human ideals or man-made doctrines, but with the actual purposes of Divine Providence.

The Franz Bardon version of sending energy to the higher self is that you place your consciousness in Akasha—a state of trance that penetrates through space and time. In other words, you practice being your higher self rather than imagining it separate from you.

And then you place a "cause" here. This cause is usually a combination of a picture and energy. The energy can be vitality, an electromagnetic volt, or a cosmic letter (which Bardon describes in his third book).

To summarize, there is—first of all—a pure mental or symbolic image that is used in contacting one's higher self, God, Creator, Divine Providence. And second there is an energy component. Why is energy necessary? Shouldn't the universe supply all our needs?

Part of growing up is making a contribution to society. And this is accomplished through work. Work produces and also requires energy. Your body, soul, and mind also use and produce energy. To participate in the unfolding of the universe, you decide on what part you wish to play. You make contributions toward that end. Otherwise, you remain in the position of a child dependent on others' efforts, energy, and work. You are taking rather than giving.

You can, of course, simply pray or engage in devotional activities. But though satisfying and wholesome, this is neither acting as a creator yourself, nor is it taking responsibility for your actions.

And, as I mentioned, contacting one's higher self or spirit can set off devasting side effects. Before "contacting" one's spirit in a magical way, it may help to meditate on the kind of spirit connection you want. And energy itself can be a problem. Similar to any electrical system, you need insulation, transformers, circuits, and so on; otherwise you may overload or short out your nervous system.

This is analogous to taking a high school student and placing him in college. He may be academically ready but still unprepared for how impersonal and large the classes are. He may not be mature enough to make friends and maintain a social life. And he may not be ready for the independence and responsibility necessary to deal with the free time, the parties, and distractions, for example. Premature contact with the higher self can also trigger confrontations with the dark aspects of yourself that you are not aware of.

What dark aspects? When you contact something "higher," you are opening yourself to truth and light. This opens the door to what is hidden or repressed in yourself. Your father, grandfather, or great-grandfather did or felt terrible things. Just as they passed down to you their DNA, something of that blind desire or horrific emotions may live within your psyche.

Or the person you were in a past life reawakens for good or for evil. You are now not what you were before. But you are still presented with a choice, a temptation to take a shortcut to achieve your goals or to satisfy a desire you never knew you had.

And there is a confusion that arises from adding a higher level of consciousness to your life, from having a multiple dimensional awareness. You may enter a dreamlike state of mind in which this world feels unreal. This may distract you from being fully present so others find it difficult to relate to you.

The relation between the personality and the higher self is a balancing act. If you prioritize your spiritual activities, you may diminish your personality. In a sense, you have become a slave to an invisible master. If you pursue the affairs of daily life and your career without paying attention to your higher self, then you may easily fail to seize the opportunities your spirit offers you. You had fun. You were happy. But you totally missed out on the chance to change the world in a dynamic way for the better.

Dialogues between the Personality and the Higher Self— Krishna and Arjuna

In the *Mahabharata,* two great armies wait for Arjuna to give the command to commence a battle. But Arjuna's resolve fails. He drops his bow.

Krishna, the avatar of Vishnu, is Arjuna's chariot driver. He steps down from the chariot and expounds to Arjuna on what becomes the *Bhagavad Gita.* Krishna urges Arjuna to be totally detached and yet to be like himself who "is never without action."

Krishna says, "In the heart of action, you must remain free from all attachment, for there is another intelligence beyond the mind."

In response, Arjuna asks Krishna to reveal himself as the higher being that he is, "Show me your universal form."

Krishna transforms as he describes himself, "I am the infinite, eternal, and the immortal Self—no fire can burn, no water dissolve, no air dry, and no sword pierce . . . Before such glory, space melts away into nothingness, time vanishes into nonexistence, and causation dwindles into emptiness.

"Ranging beyond names and forms, passing free into woods and forests, mountains and rivers, into day and night, clouds and stars, passing free into men and women, animals and angels, as the Self of each and all am I.

"Truth flows from me just as light radiates from the sun and fragrance emanates from a flower . . . I am the transcendental bliss, the absolute intelligence, the supreme synthesis of consciousness that shines in the shrine of every heart."

Arjuna then says, "My illusion is disowned. My error destroyed. By your grace now I am firm. My doubts have dispersed."

Problems in Connecting to the Higher Self

> *If your heart becomes bitter, dry, cold, or hard, then the light on Earth is lost.*
>
> KRISHNA

The Conversion Experience and Vishnu's Knot

Vishnu's knot is a blockage in the heart chakra that prevents energy and feelings from flowing through the heart. Typically, when someone has a strong and even genuine conversion experience, such as being "born again," or, as some initiation ceremonies call it, "twice born," his entire life may be changed by this event. It changes his values, his motivations, his ethics, and most often he now feels part of a loving community.

Unfortunately, individuals are unable to reproduce in themselves the depth of love, inspiration, illumination, and acceptance that they experienced during their conversion. Like a drug addict, then, there is a craving that arises to relive that initial contact with inspiration. One temporary remedy is to renew the initial experience vicariously through converting others to one's beliefs or cause.

The desire to guide others to see the truth can become the act of an emotional vampire. Hungry to taste again the feelings of unconditional love, the individual attempts to feed off of the emotional vulnerability and trusting receptivity in others. An actual remedy may require a serious quest to find an original source of inspiration.

Opposed to such a search is the instant gratification offered by indulging in group dynamics guided by the hypnotic, charismatic individuals on the hunt to capture new souls for their cause.

Imagine a heart chakra that is "open." The individual is warm, loving, and caring. He accepts and affirms other people. He is like an old friend to everyone he meets, and he seeks to bring the best out in them. And he is highly empathic. The Vishnu's Knot, by contrast, is everything that blocks a person from reaching this level of love and caring.

The Vishnu's Knot is best summarized in the phrase "special interests." You are a member of a specific religion, nation, ethnic group, minority, or hold to a specific set of ideological doctrines. Consequently, there is your group and then there are others. Members of your group are what count, and other groups are a threat, the enemy, or the competition.

This outlook may be great for success, for survival, or for community membership, but it is not good for the heart. Once you put a label on other people, your empathy crashes to zero. If the survival instinct is dominant in an individual, then other people are either for you or against you. If the desire for power is dominant, then other people are a means to an end. You use them and discard them.

You can also meet individuals who consistently present themselves as being warm, loving, caring, and highly empathic. Your first impression is that here is someone you can trust completely. But in actuality the individual is running some sort of con. And the most dangerous ones are where he believes his own lies to be true.

For example, Bernie Madoff ran a Ponzi scheme. He could do this because he had all the right credentials, all the right connections, and was highly successful in his own right. But, due perhaps to some high caliber Shakespearean character flaw, he chose to do something that would destroy the lives of thousands of people.

Bernie Madoff was living a life in which "all your dreams come true." Except on the seventeenth floor of his office building, there was a secret back room printing out fake financial statements so these dreams could be sustained.

Balance between the Third and Fourth Chakras

The dynamics of the third chakra (solar plexus) and fourth chakra (the heart) are straightforward. In the third chakra (Hod and Netzach), you assert and express yourself. You take care of your own needs and interact with others in a fair and balanced manner. You love and are loved in return.

In the fourth chakra (Tiferet), your motivation becomes more expansive and your focus is on assisting others. You care for them as if they are yourself.

In the third chakra you solve problems and meet your personal needs. In the heart chakra, you harmonize not only all your conflicting needs, for needs invariably conflict with each other, but you harmonize the needs of the world around you.

With a weak heart and strong third chakra, you may be a bully. Or you may be direct, honest, and straightforward, but you never really get around to understanding those around you even if you have known them for years. You just do not have the kind of empathy and curiosity that requires.

With a strong heart chakra and weak third chakra, you have great empathy and understanding of what others want and need, but nothing really comes of it. You support others, but where is the tough love? And why have you been so oversensitive and vulnerable? And why do you feel your efforts on behalf of others go unrecognized and unappreciated? You do not present yourself with enough force of personality that your presence alone changes people.

Those with a combination of strong third and fourth chakras know what is going on with others and have actually done a great variety of things with other people. Over the years they have acquired extensive experience.

You want to develop empathy and communicate effectively? Start with yourself and the people around you. Ask countless questions and do not stop asking. Several Eastern masters taught me things they had not taught anyone else. Why? I demonstrated to them that I could sense the spirit within them. And then I was also the only one who ever asked them to.

Put the third and fourth chakras together and you get a man or woman with a great heart who also has great power and is cordial and friendly. You cannot fool them or put something over on them because they know you too well and will not let you get away with it. And their presence is a persuasion all of its own. They have gone through places in the soul where others have been unwilling to go.

RULE 5

GEVURAH/MARS
Self-Mastery

Basic Quality	Daily practice in arts of self-mastery
Virtues, Vices, Negative	Strength/Fear/Terror
Challenge	Find an ideal or purpose that inspires you to master yourself
Magical Practice	Develop balance between your personality traits
Common Virtue	A quiet exuberance
Magical Virtue	Astral Immortality
Divine Virtue	Embodying the energies of nature
Dream	Having the power you need to accomplish your purposes
Initiation	The process of acquiring power
Mystery	The four elements unite to become one energy field comprising two opposites of masculine and feminine

In Tiferet, we bring together all aspects of ourselves by uniting with a level of inspiration that transforms us into what we wish to become. This enables us to live life with harmony, beauty, and enhanced creativity.

In Gevurah, it is no longer about just us—our goals, our needs, our desires, and our self-transformation. We come to this sephirah seeking to master ourselves in order to serve. Self-mastery is important for succeeding in a career and vocation. But now we are seeking to master ourselves by uniting with the creative powers unfolding the universe.

Gevurah/Mars, then, follows Tiferet/Sun because our wills must match the forces we encounter in life. The essence of Mars is to be relaxed and yet to have the totality of your being ready in any moment to act—this is an immense accomplishment and a divine virtue. To transmit this capacity, the planet of Mars has been placed within our solar system.

When I project my mind into the red aura of the sphere of Mars, I am surrounded by visions of how to make myself into a vehicle through which universal forces of nature can be channeled so any obstacle is overcome. This power stands ready to engage the world and to accept any mission. And yet this ability to act is balanced with an inner grace and peace that belong only to those great warriors who have attained self-mastery.

The outer vibration of the sphere of Mars is seen in martial art training and professional training. The inner vibration of Mars is about overcoming our weaknesses and attaining balance in our journey toward self-mastery.

BASIC QUALITY
Daily Practice in Arts of Self-Mastery

The basic quality of this sephirah is that one must practice self-mastery in some aspect daily. What form that self-mastery takes is for the individual to discover.

VIRTUES, VICES, NEGATIVE

Virtues: Strength, resolve, determination, concentration, vigilance, self-defense, survival instinct, stamina, daring, decisive, protecting, persevering, and self-mastery. Seizing opportunities as they arise.

Vices: Fear, unwilling to take risks and/or taking excessive risks, procrastination, hesitation, indecision, uncertainty, whining, complaining, blaming, anger, rage, hazing, abuse, hatred, rigid and arbitrary authority, rigidity, wasting energy, lack of commitment, failure to act, no plan of action, no plan B, despair.

Negative: Terror, violence, domination, bondage, cruelty, brutality, revenge, war, gangs, mob rule, dictators, monstrous actions, concentration camps, genocide.

CHALLENGE

Find a cause, an ideal, something to commit yourself to that is so noble and commanding, so captivating, that you are motivated to master yourself and unleash the full power of your will to protect and transform the world.

The difference between the "unleash the giant within" in Netzach/ Venus and this commitment is that in Gevurah/Mars we train on a professional and a magical level. This is no longer personal. Self-mastery becomes a divine art.

MAGICAL PRACTICE
Develop Balance between Your Personality Traits

In Malkuth, the magical practice is to observe your daily routines. Ask yourself every day, "Is there another way I can use my time and energy so I am more effective and satisfied?"

In Gevurah, the question is slightly different. It is "In what ways can I develop and balance the different sides of my nature so I am more effective and accomplished?"

To review, human nature has five aspects: with the Air element, we consider our mental clarity, strength of concentration, ability to work with ideas, and our internal sense of freedom.

With the Water element we develop our empathy—our ability to understand and to feel exactly what is going on in other people. And we develop our own sense of contentment, happiness, and feeling at peace with the universe.

With the Earth element, we learn to be practical, attending to our responsibilities and taking care of our physical needs. We are grounded and feel at home in this world.

With Fire, the question is "Am I able to achieve my goals in the time frames that I desire? Do I have the courage, daring, and commitment to move forward against all obstacles?"

And with the fifth element of Akasha the question is, "How strong is my conscience? Do I have a reliable inner guide to prompt me with suggestions and offer insights into the most difficult decisions and problems in my life?" And, "Do I have a connection to the higher spirit within myself such that power, wisdom, love, and purpose are all fully active within me?"

The magical practice in Gevurah is mastering ourselves in terms of attaining a balance between all five elements. In developing feeling and empathy, we do not want to diminish our survival instinct, our willpower, or our demand for justice. In gaining clarity of mind, detachment, and intellectual depth, we do not want to lose our practicality and feeling grounded.

The balance between the elements is called magical equilibrium. We are pursuing a psychological balance, but it is sufficiently difficult that attaining it is a magical action in this way: we are making our own soul our spiritual training ground. Emotional health and well-being become a lifelong quest.

Study yourself the way the Wright brothers studied wing design, the way Thomas Edison experimented to find the right filament for a light bulb, or Mendeleev systematically and tenaciously assembled the periodic table. Finding the right emotional balance in yourself is an amazing accomplishment.

Note: As I worked Gevurah, I ended up writing a book on the four elements. See *The Four Elements,* published by Falcon Books Publishing.

COMMON VIRTUE
A Quiet Exuberance

What is the feeling that best inspires you to attain your objectives and accomplish your mission? We can sense this in great martial artists.

They have a daily practice that continues over the course of their lives.

Think of doing what they do. You set aside minutes or hours each day for a practice related to mastering some aspect of yourself. And in that space of time, you engage in endless repetition of your exercises. But this is not mindless behavior. You are constantly observing, monitoring, testing, checking, modifying, and perfecting those exercises.

We observe the results of how well people are practicing their sports or arts in competition. One prevails over another. And then the sport or combat is rescheduled and the ordeal is repeated.

But the arts of Mars are not just measured in terms of how well we are doing in comparison to other people. The challenge of the Mars sphere is to master some aspect of the dynamic forces unfolding the universe. If this is used as the measure, then comparison to other competitors is irrelevant. You are uniting with nature, not triumphing over other human beings.

With Mars, there is an inner focus in which you prepare yourself so you have the energy, the enthusiasm, and the drive you need. The greater the challenge, the greater you must open yourself from within to build the reserves of energy you will need to move forward without distraction.

To build this emotional charge takes calmness and stillness. At the same time, there also has to be the emotional will to unleash all that you have gathered to whatever extent you require to deal with external circumstances. We could call this courage, passion, exhilaration, resolve, determination, and so on.

Or, to state it simply, for the warrior, nothing exists but this moment in which he is ever ready to focus his total being. And yet to attain this level of focus he must love with equal passion the years that go into his training and the constant readiness, which are in themselves his supreme accomplishment.

The spirits of the sphere of Mars seek to unite themselves to the powers of the greater universe so they can become the vehicle through which the universe accomplishes its will. This is not just being passionate about what you are doing. They exist in a state of quiet, ecstatic exuberance, for when they look within, they see the universe unfolding.

MAGICAL VIRTUE
....
Astral Immortality

Astral immortality is feeling you are united to one or more of the five elements from within. This is not just a psychological appreciation of the part the element plays in your personality. Far beyond your social identity, you feel you are a part of nature.

✳ *Exercise: Union with the Five Elements*

Relax. Inhale and exhale. Focus on your breath. Now focus on the Air surrounding you in the atmosphere. With continued practice, the Air of the sky is the only thing in your awareness. And yet you can switch with ease back and forth between focusing on your breath and feeling you are the sky.

The psychology of the Air element enables you to feel clear in your mind, objective, and detached like the vast, open expanse of the sky. And like wind rising, circling, and moving the clouds, or a gentle breeze stirring the leaves of trees, you feel free, playful, uplifted, and cheerful.

As this connection deepens, you feel you are the atmosphere. You are no longer perceiving from the point of view of a human being. Instead, you are pure consciousness operating within the vibration of the Air element.

Do the same with the Water element. Focus or imagine that the blood flowing through your body is Water with properties of nurturing, healing, soothing, purifying, renewal, and innocence. It makes things feel alive.

Add to this a sense that you are surrounded by a sea of cool, blue-green watery energy and that this sea is love. Imagine that you are floating in Water and that another person has her arms beneath you holding you up. And that this individual creates in you and in that Water the feeling that she loves you with all her heart and soul and that she is one with you. If you practice being immersed in this sea of love, you become that sea of love. Then it becomes easy in any moment to shift your consciousness so it is united to this love.

Fire is in the metabolism of your body as you break food down and convert it into heat and energy. Take a few moments and sense the temperature of your body as compared to your surroundings.

You can extend this. Imagine the room you are in is filled with brilliant sunlight. Then imagine it is filled with purple-red light that generates an electrical charge. Energy can be intensified and amplified through concentration and converted into willpower, conviction, and dynamic visions of what you wish to be.

With the element of Earth, you can focus on your feet. Or perhaps do some gentle stretching and yoga. Keep your mind focused on tension and release in the muscles during the stretching and relaxing. Here your awareness is immersed completely in your physical being. You eat solids and drink liquids to maintain your health and strength.

The other three elements are present in the Earth element as well. Your breathing exchanges carbon dioxide for oxygen in sync with the trees that reverse the process. You drink liquids and are purified and nourished. And your metabolism producing heat and energy enables you to act and take charge of your circumstances.

The fifth element of Akasha is also present. With each element we are aware of how that element extends in space. The Air element surrounds us in the atmosphere. We can imagine floating in a lake or sea. Using our imagination, we can fill our room with sunlight or various qualities of fiery energy. And with the Earth element we can feel a part of the trees, mountains, and the Earth as well as sense its internal quality of silence.

In each case, space itself can be filled with an element and then that element can dissolve again into nothing. Empty space is detached and yet extremely creative.

Similar to a mind free of thoughts or a space free of objects, here we have a state of awareness free of form or image that nonetheless supports and encompasses everything that exists. Stop thoughts from rising in your mind for a few moments and you find Akasha is beside you and within you.

Here in Gevurah, we are embodying the magical virtue of the previous spheres. As we deepen our practice with the elements, we unite with them from within. Gradually, we feel nature is at the core of our being, and that the innermost energies of life are fully alive within us.

DIVINE VIRTUE
·······································
Embodying the Energies of Nature

With the divine virtue, we embody an element on a higher level. Here we deepen and master our connection to an element in order to produce specific results. We develop this power to whatever extent we need to accomplish our purposes and to fulfill our missions.

Some people rule over other people using a negative version of an element. It is not courage and electrifying enthusiasm they use to inspire others. Instead, they incite rage, hatred, or fear, intensifying those emotions until they can motivate people to do what they want.

The negative element is easier to access. The positive takes more work, but the results are stable, creative, and enduring.

As we have seen with the Water element, you can immerse yourself in its vibration to feel a loving, healing, nurturing, and soothing energy flowing through your body. But this control of the element can be dramatically increased. You take the same energy field, but now you imagine it filling whatever space you are in. If you deepen and strengthen this experience, you can extend this watery, healing energy anywhere to assist anyone in their healing process.

In this case, we are mastering the Water element far beyond our personal and psychological sphere. And we are moving beyond a feeling of inner union with Water. We are now operating with a direct connection to nature as part of the dynamic forces unfolding the universe.

Similarly, we can use the Air element to develop our sense of detachment, clarity of mind, optimism, cheerfulness, and so on. And we can acquire the Air element's depth of wisdom from identifying with the vast expanse of the sky.

With a greater connection to Air, we can expand our awareness to comprehend the thoughts in other's minds. And some individuals will find it easy to penetrate actual weather formations like thunderstorms and hurricanes and direct them according to their will. Weather control is practiced in Buddhism and various indigenous traditions.

With Fire we can learn to amplify our will and power in order to manifest what we desire more quickly. We can perceive with greater clarity and move forward in life with great conviction and faith. There are divine purposes that can only be fulfilled by those who have joined their personal will to the purposes of Divine Providence. In which case, our connection to Fire will produce far greater power than we are accustomed to seeing in great leaders.

With Earth, we will find again the requirement that we embody the patience and endurance of Divine Providence. There are purposes that require a lifetime of preparation before they can manifest. The Earth element grants us the internal silence and commitment that we will need to be free of distractions and remain focused on our work.

And finally, with the fifth element of Akasha we can learn to use it to dissolve negativity in our own personal space. But through deepening our connection to it we can certainly become active participants on the world stage and influence global events so as to produce more harmonious outcomes. The fifth element steps in to reduce suffering and to act as the conscience to keep others focused on their best courses of action.

The inner vibration of Mars entails feeling joined from within to the dynamic powers unfolding the universe. There is no ego here and no sense of competing with others to see who is better. The test of your purposes is cosmic in scope—have you mastered yourself to the extent that you need to channel the creative powers that shape history in order to manifest your ideals and to fulfill your purposes?

To do this, your inner union with the five elements—Air, Water, Fire, Earth, and Akasha—reaches a level of ecstasy. You are now part of something far greater than yourself. Like an agent of Divine Providence, you are its servant, its voice, and the vehicle through which it manifests.

DREAM

In the dream of Gevurah, you exude power. It is not power over others or being strong as a form of vanity. Rather, you experience yourself as having whatever power you need to accomplish your goals and objectives in life.

As an exercise, you might try making a picture of yourself having whatever power you need to fulfill your purposes. Since this is your imagination, you do not have to limit your dream in any way.

If I ask myself as I appear in such a vision, "How do I become what you are?" my response is relaxed, reassuring, and certain, "The power is already within you. Just let it come out."

INITIATION

All the great battles in life are first fought within the heart.

This is straightforward though quite difficult. We are surrounded by institutions and people with power. This power is governmental, religious, educational, financial, economic, societal, and so on.

Power is proprietary—people treat it as a personal possession rather than a gift to be put to its highest purpose. They are not willingly going to give it up or share it. Furthermore, power by its nature keeps secret how it operates. It takes its goals, purposes, and activities for granted. They are not to be interfered with or reformed.

The naive think that if justice and truth are on your side, then all you need to do is speak out, and actions will be taken to make things right. How easy it is to crush such naivety.

Consequently, to work with power you will need to proceed with great stealth, secrecy, persistence, and training. And you will need to acquire knowledge, experience, and wisdom until you become a player in society and on the world stage.

Some who wish things were simpler complain that a postindustrial, pluralistic, and capitalistic society is so diabolical that it co-opts its strongest critics. It gives them forums to speak on. It offers them wealth, recognition, and success. It brings them on board.

As soon as they become famous, like any other celebrity, in no time their image is being used to sell something. They have appeal to a specific audience. Why not cash in on your fame? It does not have to be about money. You can simply get the recognition you have always craved. And so their idealistic vision of a just society is briefly honored and then quickly forgotten.

A lawyer once told me that the first ten years after he started work, his practice was extremely difficult. The second ten years things were more manageable. But the third ten years his law practice became quite easy. There was synergy. He had luck. But more important, the judges all knew him and tended to rule in his favor.

For others, when they reach the top, they do not encounter what they expected. Things are more difficult. The stress and competition have taken their toll. They feel numb or dead inside.

And so the voice of Mars: Motivate and master yourself. Deal with your own flaws. Exude a dream of power that, in a quiet, unassuming way, contains absolute confidence. In which case, you will discover that many of your worst battles in life you have already won.

MYSTERY

The Four Elements Unite to Become One Energy Field Comprising Two Opposites of Masculine and Feminine

So far, we have taken two steps in exploring magical equilibrium. Under magical practice, we have sought to develop a healthy and balanced personality. This produces a mature and responsible individual who functions well in society.

In terms of self-mastery, we take personality traits that are weak and make them strong. And we take negative personality traits and make them positive. It is clear enough what this entails on a personal level. If you get angry in an inappropriate way, take that low-grade, fiery energy and make it bright and clear. In a tense situation, relax, put aside ego and distractions, and focus on the bottom line. Become the solution to a problem rather than part of the problem itself. That is Fire strong, pure, and clear.

If you get confused, overly attached to ideas, and argumentative such that your mind operates like hot and cold, wet and dry, like clashing storm fronts, develop your mind so it is free of attachments to ideas. Learn, study, investigate, analyze, and contemplate. Withhold judgment until you weigh the strengths and weaknesses of ideas and consider both sides of any position before forming a conclusion.

And under magical virtue we have exercises for embodying the four elemental energies of nature in ourselves. We described this possibility as attaining astral immortality. These elemental energies have their own psychology, feelings, and perceptions. In many ways, this level of awareness is well beyond the personality traits and character qualities we exhibit in daily life.

Since we are moving beyond the expression of the personality in society, we are exploring spiritual anthropology that asks these age-old questions: What is it to be a human being? What is human nature? What is it to be and to feel fully alive? And what are we capable of becoming?

We can develop the mind beyond what we need in our social life and career. We can seek a mind that is clear, open, luminous, and vast as the sky. This is not easy to do, but after all it is your mind. There is no limit placed upon what you can accomplish.

Are your feelings numb or injured, drawing you inward and away from engaging others and the world? Find a stillness and peace in yourself like a calm and serene lake. Here the flash flood, the whirlpool, rogue wave, and riptide dissolve. Water and love are everywhere—in us, around us, sustaining us, creating us, and inviting us to attain the highest that life offers.

Does life on Earth with its limitations, restrictions, inertia, and inequality weigh you down, making you depressed and oppressed? What must you do to take the life handed to you at birth and make it into a story worth telling? In what way can you unite your will, your thoughts, and your feelings to produce works of genuine value that enrich the world?

What inspiration lies hidden within you? What are your deepest values, and what commitment must you make so that those values shape what you do, enabling you to become the person you were always meant to be?

Under the Mystery section of the first sephirah of Malkuth, I described how the four elements in nature and society are often in conflict with each other. Too much fiery will, and feeling is destroyed. Too much Air, emphasis on the mind and intellect, and the individual may lose a sense of being practical and down-to-earth. He fails to comprehend that will is as important as knowledge and wisdom.

And similarly, too much Earth, emphasis on material wealth and success, and the individual may lose his objectivity. He relies upon traditions to guide him, and he accepts the prearranged goals of society as his own standard. And, though successful, he may miss seizing a vast range of opportunities that present themselves to him.

Too much Water and the individual may lose his survival instinct. With too much empathy and feeling you lose the wisdom of tough love and empowering others to solve their own problems. And, with that excessive feeling, you may feel vulnerable because you are not fully engaging others and asserting that your needs and goals are as important as theirs.

The mystery of Gevurah is that when harmoniously integrated, the four elements become one energy field combining two opposite polarities of masculine/electric and feminine/magnetic. You have the Air element present in this dynamic matrix representing insulation, design, and control. Without the detachment of the Air element, it is easy to become enthralled and obsessed with the creative power you have at your disposal.

The Earth element keeps things down-to-earth, realistic, and practical. The Fire is present in the intense, concentrated, and explosive heat. And the Water element is in the magnetic field that fully contains the electric, amplifying it through its opposite polarity.

This dynamic energy field, however, can become very imbalanced. If the electric/Fire is too strong, there is the risk of psychological hazing, domination, and manipulation. Fire needs fuel to burn. Without the support and feelings of happiness, bliss, and well-being that Fire needs to thrive, Fire tries to take these things from others by force, coercion, and violence.

If the Water is too strong, the magnetic energy is short on light, clarity, and management of the Fire principle. It is weak on solving problems. And it lacks objective observations and strong purposes. In which case it can be overly protective, smothering, bitter, resentful, and tied to the past.

And yet at any point if there are strong side effects, you can enter an Akashic state of mind. Akasha, formless awareness, independent of space and time, is the source from which the four elements arise and also that which dissolves when their work is complete.

Too much Fire? Overcome by Fire's intensity and explosive power? Feel anger and rage rising up inside of you when you work with Fire and will? Akasha takes that Fire and reduces or removes it.

There are of course dictators with massive armies and weapons of mass destruction at their disposal. Yet with enough practice working with Akasha, you become the dictator's conscience. You weigh in on his karma saying, "This is permitted and this is not permitted." We have a responsibility to make this application of Akasha our own.

On the other hand, when harmoniously aligned, the Fire element with its concentrated will acts to manifest its visions and fulfill its responsibilities with great empathy and regard for the needs of others. Its immense and heightened power no longer seeks to take control of the entire world—as someone is always trying to do in every century. Instead, it seeks to fill the Earth with love. The reason this vision of universal love has never been proclaimed in human history is that the magnetic, yin principle has never been equal to and in command of the yang, electric principle.

This model of the feminine embracing, containing, and transforming the masculine comes from the magical practice called "volting." You create a ball of hot and condensed electrical energy and surround it with a ball of cool, magnetic energy. In this image, the masculine electric principle is always contained by the feminine magnetic energy. This relationship of masculine and feminine is the opposite of what we normally see in society.

At the same time, a "volt" is not unleashed upon the world, overwhelming others with its power. It is placed within Akasha, which again is a timeless and spaceless state and plane of awareness. From that controlled state it exerts an influence on the world, manifesting whatever purpose you have placed within it. This image is more clearly recognizable in the Hindu and Tibetan tantra in which a male and female are joined in a state of peaceful meditation.

This practice of uniting the electric and magnetic energies leads us in the direction of harmony and balance. Knowing the positive versions of masculine and feminine enables us to overcome the negative versions. If you find yourself wanting to exploit and dominate others to achieve success, then do not identify yourself with the negative yin with its extreme insecurity, fragility, and rigidity in order to balance yourself. Rather, seek the positive version—well-being, happiness, contentment, and oneness with nature that are self-sustaining and not dependent on being recognized and validated by others.

If you find yourself victimized, hopeless, manipulated, and used, do not identify yourself with the negative yang with its blind devotion, shallow ideologies, and demand for conformity. Seek rather the positive yang in yourself—certainty and conviction about your purposes, clarity of mind, and fearless resolve. These are character traits you can cultivate independent of your social role and personal history. The idea in magical equilibrium is to produce in yourself both the full masculine and the full feminine opposites that are positive and not negative.

✱ Exercise: Experiencing Masculine and Feminine Energies

We can move beyond ideological, metaphysical, and psychological terminology in describing masculine and feminine. Rather than using words, we can experience these energies inside of ourselves. Then, after engaging these energies and directly acquiring firsthand experience, we can carefully choose which words best describe our own, unique experiences.

Recall our exercise with imagining Water flowing through our bodies instead of blood. Flowing Water has the qualities of being soothing, releasing, calming, nurturing, and healing. Stay with this focus and gradually add to it the sensations and feelings of being surrounded by a blue-green sea of cool, watery energy. Here we can explore deeper feelings of happiness, serenity, peace, and contentment.

At this point, we are joined to the extreme feminine that is part of nature. As a primary energy unfolding the universe, the yin is inherently receptive, without form identification, and it is all-embracing. It is everywhere and within everything, offering support and love. It has the power, still unknown in our world, of being able to unite with, contain, and transform the soul of any person.

Through practice, we can deepen this vibration of energy for as long as we wish. There is no end to its exploration.

Now slowly shift your focus from the cool sensations of Water to the sensation of heat in your body. Pursue this until this sensation of heat is the only thing present in your awareness.

Pause for a moment and compare this feeling and sensation of heat with the cool, watery sensations we were working with at the beginning.

The heat is more intense, assertive, and acutely aware of survival, for again Fire requires fuel in order to exist. There is also a force and strength present in the heat. It is ready to confront and to overcome obstacles in its way.

If you stay with the sensation of heat, you may sense it becoming more intense and even explosive. Now we are reaching the opposite of the magnetic, cool, flowing, and receptive Water. We are creating the yang version of power in ourselves.

This power inherently takes command and seeks to control. And, again, it can do this in a very positive or a very negative way. It can defend and protect. It can offer stability and acquire whatever resources are needed to survive. It can act with complete self-mastery, courage, and vision. Or it can haze, manipulate, and dominate, furthering only its own interests while destroying the freedom and well-being of others.

Now join this dynamic and highly charged yang power in yourself with the yin principle of cool, magnetic, receptive, all-embracing Water. In other words, imagine your body is surrounded by and penetrated with love. You are "held in the arms of love," or you feel love saturating every cell of your body, or love is one with you, with all that you are in every aspect and vibration.

We are taking the extremely intense and highly charged fiery energy and penetrating it through and through with love so that love and power are fully united. As Psyche would say referring to Eros, "I want to be one with him such that everything he is is a part of me." Or simply say "I love you with all my heart, soul, mind, and strength" as you create in yourself a state of perfect love.

In society there are a lot of issues and conflicts regarding gender in terms of psychology, social roles, and hormones. But in magic, the two opposite principles of masculine and feminine as they operate in the universe are perfectly clear. They are one with each other and they are never separate.

Unfold this mystery in yourself and attain freedom.

RULE 4

CHESED/JUPITER

Wealth in All Aspects

Basic Quality	Participation in groups
Virtues, Vices, Negative	Leadership/Hypocrisy/Dystopia
Challenge	Imagine you possess the material and spiritual wealth that enables you to enrich others' lives
Magical Practice	Consider practicing a high-level spiritual or magical training system to get the most out of life
Common Virtue	Universal love
Magical Virtue	Transformation
Divine Virtue	Magical Blessing
Dream	Imagine belonging to an ideal community committed to assisting mankind
Initiation	Work at making the world a better place
Mystery	Spiritual community/A genuine cosmic religion

The aura of Jupiter embodies wealth on all planes of existence. Here we find excellence in literature, philosophy, art, architecture, music, city planning, festivals, education, job opportunities, science, advisory councils, judicial systems, government, economics, health, and hospitals.

When it comes to changes in the life of an individual or of a community, Jupiter represents continuity and smooth transitions. It values the best of tradition. And it loves the idealism, enthusiasm, and sacrifice that have produced the great accomplishments of past ages.

Jupiter expands our horizons in life. It increases our opportunities to experience life on all levels of our being. It is the embodiment of group interaction, leadership, and high purposes and ideals. Through Jupiter we find our greatest avenue for service and community participation.

If I place my mind in the spiritual aura of Jupiter, I feel surrounded by wonderful resources and all sorts of support, friendship, and fulfilling activities. There is a vast increase in educational opportunities and means for learning.

What is the best way to work through your karma and learn your deepest lessons in life? Jupiter has the answer. It will find you a place in life where you feel you belong, are needed, are loved, and your skills are incredibly useful to others. Over the decades you will acquire great wisdom, extraordinary depths of experience, judgment, and discerning intuition.

The vibration of this sphere demands that you think in terms of being wealthy within yourself. And this wealth means having such an expansive spirit that you seek to enhance every situation you are in, making it better because your interaction adds something of value.

You can tell when Chesed has touched your life. As the years pass, you feel that wisdom that has placed you where you could acquire those experiences through which you could grow the most and be of the greatest service to others.

Just as with Netzach/Venus, we can also discuss an inner and outer vibration of this planetary sphere. The outer vibration of Chesed/Jupiter represents physical and social mobility. You are able to go where you want to go, live where and how you want to live, meet the people you want to meet, and pursue the projects you want to pursue.

With wealth in the outer world, you have access to the best doctors, lawyers, professors, psychologists, coaches, and brokers. You belong to the best social and yacht clubs. You probably know famous producers, directors, and actors. You have the best cars and boats, and you probably own your own airplane. Free of debt, the physical world offers you countless opportunities and avenues for action.

You also understand the incredible amount of work that goes into producing wealth. You understand how that wealth can be used to safeguard and enrich the lives of individuals as well as of society. You do not have to be selfish and enthralled with the American Dream of owning a ten-million-dollar house and having a garage full of expensive cars. You can do things with that wealth that are of enduring value.

The inner vibration of Chesed represents mobility in the spiritual worlds. When you want an answer to a spiritual question, you get the answer you need. When you want to work through some difficult karmic issue, you have the wisdom you need to do so.

You understand the original purposes being fulfilled in any religion. You understand the deepest purposes guiding anyone's life. You understand the original purposes of creation and how to align with and fulfill them. You are not just a philanthropist. You are an agent of Divine Providence here on Earth to accomplish a divine mission if you so choose.

With wealth in the inner world, you understand the inner workings of the soul. You have access to divine beings who specialize in the great issues of life and how to guide not just individuals but entire societies and nations on their highest path. You do not merely have a highly evolved guru assisting you in your development. You are able to experience the entire array of spiritual realizations and perceptions that are available to mankind.

Inner peace with the universe? Close your eyes. In a moment, you feel the universe inside yourself radiant with glory, dazzling with beauty, magnificent, and holy. What about love? With personal love, you feel in this moment that you are one with your lover who shares with you the deepest concerns within your heart. With a wider ranging love, you feel you are joined to a community of world servers who are inspired by the highest light and whose dedication is transforming the world.

And as far as a guru goes, you feel you are connected to a spiritual being who clarifies exactly what your gifts in life are and the best way you can use them to grow and to benefit others. Human gurus know about how to introduce you to the realizations of their lineage.

They do not know about how to set you on the mysterious paths of life that lie before you. With the inner wisdom of Chesed, the divine has taken hold of your life and transformed you so that the world is greatly enriched by your presence.

Some individuals are among the wealthiest people on Earth. Everything that can be purchased with money is available to them. At the same time, we can equally consider that almost all of them are impoverished when it comes to the inner wealth—the wisdom—of Chesed.

They live in the most expensive homes, own sports teams, entire islands, are the largest shareholder in different corporations, and are among the biggest philanthropists on Earth. But in terms of wisdom, they are homeless, bankrupt, forsaken, and alone. It does not need to be this way. The inner and outer wealth of Chesed is meant to complement and fulfill each other.

BASIC QUALITY
Participation in Groups

Whereas the sphere of Venus holds the enchantments of two falling in love, Jupiter encompasses the charisma and spirit of celebration and connection that create and sustain communities. There is pageantry, respect, and honor. And there is a direct and immediate awareness of how your life is fulfilled by participating with others in producing works that benefit the world.

VIRTUES, VICES, NEGATIVE

Virtue: Leadership, altruism, generosity, philanthropy, nobility, character, compassion, wealth of knowledge, wisdom, sacred traditions, pursuit of excellence, mentoring.

Vices: Hypocrisy, malfeasance, political correctness, conformity, complacency, negligence, denial, inaction, stagnation, social rigidity, collective superego, ideology, group hysteria, bigotry, discrimination, character flaws.

Negative: Dystopia, social upheaval, anarchy, corruption, racism, injustice, mob rule, urban decay.

CHALLENGE

Life is short. And yet every individual is given opportunities to be of benefit to others. Leave the world a better place than the one you entered. If you can, design for yourself a life that allows you to accumulate the experiences that makes you wealthy in body, soul, mind, and/or spirit. Then offer this wealth to others in a way that is beneficial and practical.

Find your own unique path that, on the one hand, accepts and works with the world as it is and, on the other hand, in realistic, feasible, and enduring ways, makes the world a better place.

MAGICAL PRACTICE

Consider Practicing a High-Level
Spiritual or Magical Training System
to Get the Most Out of Life

I think of magical practice as accelerating your learning curve. It heightens your five senses and your imagination so that you have the perception of an artist. You learn not just to be emotionally balanced and stable. You make a study of the full range of what human beings can feel on personal and collective levels. You also vastly increase the quality of your interactions with other people and bring a high level of concentration and enthusiasm to whatever you undertake.

Magical practice, then, is condensed life. You are accumulating, refining, and transforming life experience. Such training requires a great deal of work, discipline, and effort. And yet, looking back over the decades, you can see clearly how you have not just lived a full life. You have acquired perhaps two or three lifetimes of experience instead of just one.

The downside to such practice is that it brings to the surface psychological and spiritual difficulties that you may not otherwise encounter. If you open yourself in meditation, exploring what is hidden in your soul, what horrors and insatiable cravings suddenly awakened that you would not normally encounter?

And when you open yourself from within, it is not just your own personal demons you have to confront. There are collective "monsters of the id," as Freud would say, and conflicts between the archetypes that demand resolution.

Yet I often hear myself telling someone, "You do not need to practice magic. Life itself is magical. We have direct computer-to-brain communication. We have instant investing online that involves all nations. You can communicate with anyone on Earth for free using Skype. You have the videotaped lectures with all the class notes from places like Harvard and Stanford. There are young people who today are writing programs that will make them billionaires in a decade."

Why on earth would anyone study magic? We are in a golden age of learning, discovery, knowledge, and even human nature is transforming.

Preparation for training in magic? I recommend for people new to magic that they first consider Dale Carnegie's class on public speaking for developing communication skills. And I recommend first a careful study of free videos by life coaches, for example Tony Robbins. He is using magic made simple for the masses in a very effective way.

The only reason I study magic, other than to try to find out the truth about the outlandish claims of religions, is to solve a problem that has no other solution than magic—namely, establishing justice between nations and eliminating war. Perhaps only in magical training can an individual come to hold immense power and in the same moment be free of all ego.

And that is the nature of magic—to be aware of how all things arise from nothingness (consciousness without form or image); and in the same moment, to perceive the origins and the highest paths of life belonging to each person and nation.

Put another way, magic is a study of how to make the best choices in life. It is a serious attempt to answer the question "What is the best use of my time and energy while I am here on Earth?" And this is a Chesed/Jupiter question: "What work of value can I pursue that will enrich the world?"

To this end, find and practice a universal magical/spiritual training system. An example is the system of self-initiation offered by Franz Bardon drawn from the Western Hermetic tradition.

Franz Bardon's Self-Initiation System

All spiritual paths begin with the maiden, for she gives all
of herself to the thing she loves without holding back.

For me, Franz Bardon seeks to train individuals so that while still in incarnation they acquire the abilities of a higher spirit of the Earth who oversees some aspect of human evolution. Each day, 360 of these spirits exert a benevolent influence on the entire planet.*

This is an astonishing level of development for any individual to imagine, much less to achieve. Here is my summary of some of the abilities a Bardon student might develop in himself.

You make your mind completely empty of thoughts. An empty mind has many applications. It is reflective like a mirror, being both detached and perfectly clear. It is receptive like the ocean and flowing like a stream able both to embrace and to nurture life. It is open and vast like the sky filled with a near-infinite variety of light.

Being empty like a void, it penetrates through and also stands outside of space and time. It is serene like moonlight and imaginative as a dream—in this state of mind, anything is possible and you can revise, reverse engineer, and redream any event in life.

It is enduring like a mountain, and solid like steel, embodying the silence of the realm of gnomes. And it is intense and electrifying as when polar energies reach their height in the moment before lightning strikes.

With such a mind, when you think about someone or some being or spirit, there is an automatic connection between the two of you. Your mind is then able to detect very faint sensations and amplify them, producing clairvoyance, telepathy, and clairsentience.

Using a trained imagination and power of concentration, you visualize the thing you wish to manifest as if it is real right now in this

---

*From *The Practice of Magical Evocation* by Franz Bardon. The 360 heads of the zone girdling the Earth hold in constant harmony all actions and conditions of the planet. They can inform the individual about the past, the present, and the future of our physical world, and each head, by force of the Akasha-principle, can affect our Earth. Each head is endowed with certain special assignments and areas of responsibility.

moment. You do this designing your action so it is aligned with a divine purpose.

Add energy to your picture, imbuing it with feelings so it is fully alive. And you take into consideration the forces, situations, resistance, and obstacles that must be overcome to make your vision reality.

The mastery of the four elements (Earth, Air, Fire, and Water) is practiced on all four planes—Akasha, mental, astral, and physical levels. With extended practice, you are learning to create each element from out of nothing and also dissolve it again.

Practicing over many years, your mastery of the four elements frees you of the bonds of karma, for now you are fully conscious of the hidden forces that underlie the motivations, desires, and will within yourself, other people, communities, traditions, nations, cultures, and religions.

When I consider the entire spectrum of methods in Bardon's three books, with over five hundred different spirits and twenty-seven cosmic letters, this summary is what I come back to in order to understand what I am doing. Self-transformation, self-mastery, self-empowerment, and integration—aligning oneself with the forces, the laws, and the harmony of the universe—are at the heart of the process from beginning to end.

I imagine that any serious system of initiation will present a cosmology—a summary of the active energies that underlie the unfolding of the universe. And then it will ask the student to experience and to harmonize these energies within himself.

Somewhere out there in the future, everything I describe will become a part of standard education. For now, magic is simply an intense and systematic training of body, soul, mind, and spirit that conventional educational institutions do not comprehend. But education will catch up, and society will offer enlightenment along with knowledge, justice along with successful careers, and new forms of self-awareness such as graphic imagination, multidimensional awareness, a professional level of empathy, and an inner attunement with nature.

If you "listen" to the planet Earth, this attainment is one of her dreams. In addition to the Earth, Saturn has a spiritual plane in which reside forty-nine Judges. These spirits oversee the karma of all beings, planets, and spheres in our solar system. Both positive and negative spirits are under their command. For these spirits, establishing justice on Earth is not optional. Manifesting this ideal is part of the rent we must pay if we wish to remain on Earth.

COMMON VIRTUE
Universal Love

In Tiferet/Sun, we have an embracing, uplifting, and transforming love. The love in Chesed/Jupiter is more proactive. It brings people together and offers them unique opportunities. The love in Tiferet is brilliant in intensity. The love in Chesed is more practical. It creates communities and traditions that express Tiferet's inspiration.

Tiferet's love unites the individual to the source of life. Chesed's love lays the foundations and provides the physical and spiritual wealth that empower people so that with greater ease they become fulfilled and live complete and satisfying lives.

An essential aspect of universal love is its depth of feeling, which expresses itself through empathy. This is not Venus, where the goal is to produce two individuals who feel everything inside of each other at the same time and who have the desire to love, to nurture, and to fulfill each other. In Jupiter, the empathy feels what everyone feels. In bringing people together, everyone assists everyone else.

It is not just an action as in saying, "I have helped you. Could you now go and help others?" It is magical in nature. It creates the sense that to help another is like helping oneself at the same time. It is not the "Do unto others as you would have them do unto you" as a moral obligation. Instead, to help others expresses the real you.

This is the aura and vibration of Jupiter when you look up at it in the night sky. Its light shines with universal benevolence and kindness.

You can tell when universal love is operating within you. With ease you can recall numerous examples when you helped other people without any benefit to yourself. You acted as a good Samaritan when there was no one else there to assist someone in need.

MAGICAL VIRTUE
....
Transformation

You participate in, support, and—if necessary—invent programs that transform people. Now this is tricky. Every revolutionary wants to change human nature in order to transform society. But that is not what they do. Instead, they say to themselves, "If we could only take control of society and reshape its institutions, then we would have a better world." And they fail in this endeavor because they lack the wisdom that brings the individual in harmony with the dynamic forces unfolding the universe.

The magical virtue, then, is to be an astute observer of human behavior and of human nature. No one system as of yet can grasp the complexity and potential of what human beings are and can become. What motivates human beings? What ideals capture their imagination and their loyalty?

When you observe someone change for the better, what just happened? Is there a way of taking an individual with his personal history, his family of origin, and all of his unresolved needs, desires, and conflicts and empowering him to become his better self, to realize his full potential once his issues are addressed?

Imagine what someone would be like who embodies this virtue. You would be with someone who listens to the story of your life without imposing his values and solutions on you. He would be completely accepting and supportive. He would sense the best in you. He would feel what you feel and see the world through your eyes.

Your pain and confusion would not disturb his serenity or reduce his receptivity, because he perceives you from within a world of love and light. He possesses a deep stillness that accepts and comprehends conflict without being disturbed by it.

He is practical, down-to-earth, and a no-nonsense kind of guy. But in his presence, you feel an uplifting reassurance that convinces you that from the deepest levels inside of yourself, you are beginning to become transformed. For such individuals, life is inexhaustibly rich. There is always a means to take hold of the situations of life and make something better from them.

In effect, we bring together the inner silence and quiet ecstasy of

Malkuth, the contentment and serenity of Yesod, the mental openness and clarity of Hod, the empathy and magnetic love of Netzach, and the stillness and inspiration of Tiferet. In doing so, we give people the resources they need to better themselves.

The revolutionary requires a quick solution because he is impatient with intolerable conditions. A person with universal love, by contrast, possesses a timeless wisdom. He speaks to all ages of the world. And he offers light, insight, and the means to those who wish to be transformed from the very depths of themselves.

DIVINE VIRTUE
Magical Blessing

In the Zen of Love section under Netzach/Venus, we combined complete detachment with deep empathy—the feeling of being one with another person. Again, just the meditation practice exerts an influence on another person that produces feelings of being connected and loved.

In blessing another's life with the vibration of Jupiter, our contemplation of the other's life extends far beyond our own mental and emotional influence on another. In the "I bless you," we are speaking with the voice of the divine world. Connected to the universe from within, we are also connecting the other person to a wealth of opportunity and good fortune that is the vibration of Jupiter.

✦ *Meditation: Consider the Four Elements* ✦

For the Water element: See the individual as loving and deeply loved by others.

For Earth: See the individual as solid, stable, practical, and possessing a marvelous ability to succeed in his line of work.

For Air: See the individual as having an understanding mind, highly receptive and skilled at accessing and solving problems.

For Fire: See the individual as determined, preserving, and possessing a high level of commitment.

Of course, these things vary for each individual. The basic idea is to imagine that the individual possesses those abilities and attitudes that enable him to get the most out of life and to give the most to others to enrich their lives.

> *May the sun shine upon all your paths*
> *May friends always walk beside you*
> *May love always guide you*
> *And reach the inner recesses of your heart*
> *May every task you seek be made complete*
> *May you be the sun and the moon to others' lives*
> *May you be as the light of dawn to others in the darkest*
>   *night*
> *May you taste the happiness that comes only to a few in*
>   *every century*
> *May you find another who brings you comfort*
> *And is always there to share all your cares*
> *As we travel the path of life seeking to fulfill a dream*
> *The gift you give of yourself is all I want or need*
> *Peace to you*
> *May the peace of the sun and moon, the sky and seas*
> *Always flow through your dreams*
> *And in the end may you look back and see*
> *That your life was all it was meant to be*

✳ Exercise: Chesed/Jupiter Blessing

How do you see another person's life through the eyes of Chesed/Jupiter? There is synergy: spontaneously, the best connections arise that enhance and fulfill the individual's life. The individual finds himself in situations where he can learn the most, give the most to others, and feel the most love. He has respect and appreciation. He is at his most creative. He is given the means and insight to deal with his greatest problems. And he has the resolve and determination to use these opportunities to their best advantage.

Visualize an individual in front of you and step-by-step put all of the above together so you see his life enriched and fulfilled.

The idea of blessing another individual comes in part from practicing the cosmic letter *G* on the mental level in Franz Bardon's book *The*

Key to the True Kabbalah, Bardon says that this cosmic letter grants the ability to bless an individual in all four aspects of Divine Providence.

In Bardon's approach, you meditate on to the Akashic plane of awareness. There you identify with Divine Providence, which, in this case, seeks to fulfill life in every conceivable way. But this state of mind also unites Jupiter and Saturn because it requires that an individual learn whatever it is he needs to learn in order to be fulfilled.

Then you bring the meditation down to the mental plane where you consider an individual's life circumstances. There you visualize clearly the individual being fulfilled, loved, and creative within his historical circumstances. The mental plane applies the expansive divine awareness to actual situations in life.

Of course, we can always ask, "Do you really want to intervene in someone else's life in this way? Perhaps an individual, with all his stress and difficulties, is exactly in the situation where he needs to be to learn whatever he is meant to learn."

And that may be. If you go around offering opportunities and granting new insights and abilities, some individuals will immediately take whatever free time or new energy you give them and use it to abuse other people, seeking revenge, or indulging in narcissistic cravings. I have seen exactly that happen so I know it is true.

Some individuals are on a downward spiral and they will simply not be satisfied or learn anything until they reach the bottom. Some individuals will never learn the value of wealth until they actually make money for themselves rather than having the government or others give it to them.

On the other hand, the planet Jupiter exerts a benevolent influence on the Earth. For one, its gravity attracts asteroids to itself that would otherwise hit us and end life on our planet. The aura of Jupiter can accurately state, "It is my nature to offer opportunities that fulfill life in every conceivable way. This is who I am. I create order and stability and then I fill the world with wonder and beauty."

And, as with the idea of ending wars, people sometimes say that we need wars to learn. But I can imagine someone else saying, "You know, where I am from, we have ended wars because we have put forth the time and energy to make that happen. You have not yet learned to do this for yourselves. Instead of investing in diplomacy and negotiation, you spend roughly 1.3 trillion dollars a year on your armies and military research. If you want to live in peace, you will have to commit to different priorities."

DREAM

The dream is seeing yourself as part of a community that is filled with inspiration, pursues noble causes, and whose members are united from within through their shared values and visions. This is like the law of polarity in which attraction brings about what you desire. Here, when you imagine a spiritual community, you vibrate with all others who share the same vision.

With such a community present in your life, there is a palpable life force and aura that flows through you. It is uplifting. It is energizing and inspiring. "Membership" brings with it access to the vast array of physical, emotional, mental, and spiritual resources that such a community provides. There are effortless and spontaneous interactions with others who have a commitment to assuring that each person has the opportunities needed to accomplish his or her goals.

There is not just honor and nobility. There is a divine presence as well that guides and assists the community members so that they attain the best in life. It is a community committed to service, which also offers the means for its members to become enlightened in order to accomplish that service.

INITIATION

The challenge in Chesed is to design for yourself a life that allows you to accumulate the experiences that makes you wealthy in body, soul, mind, and/or spirit. Then offer this wealth to others in a way that is beneficial and practical.

The initiation in Chesed is your personal journey toward this end. Put another way, you acquire the qualities of character, the inner purity of spirit, and the nobility of purpose such that when opportunities arise, you are able to fully respond to them. You do not end up paranoid, narcissistic, with an inflated ego, or obsessed with power. Instead, you use the opportunities given to you in the best way possible.

I have had interesting conversations with one of those religious people who go door to door. He had a world-class level of active listening. He not only heard what I was saying and caught the feelings behind it, it was like he was in the future experiencing the various outcomes and possibilities of what I was talking about.

I told him, "You are overqualified for what you are doing. With your communication skills, you should be helping to resolve conflicts in the Middle East or between Russia and other nations."

But he did not understand what he possessed. He was still wrapped up in the concerns of Yesod—family, psychological and spiritual security, and involvement in his local church. The idea of putting his talents to their best use never entered his mind.

He was not a servant of the divine world, which he could have been. He was insecure, a creature of tradition, and unwilling to do his own thinking.

The initiate of Chesed is always asking himself, "How do I make this world a better place? What can I do that makes a difference?"

Another way of describing the initiation of Chesed is to recall the idea in Hod of imagining what you want as if it is already real right now. And then you make a point of living and feeling as if that is true.

In Netzach, we reviewed how Tony Robbins teaches seminars that empower individuals to meet their personal goals. In Chesed, we take those methods of Hod and Netzach and apply them to community. In other words, we create and maintain a dream inside of us in which we are already a part of a spiritual community, and in which we possess the skills, material wealth, and spiritual wisdom we need to fulfill the tasks we have set before us.

We all know individuals who are stingy, or else whose psychological wounds have made them slaves to the past. We also know individuals who have crazy and unrealistic dreams, or who are enamored with themselves. They are narcissists who constantly crave attention and never really consider other's needs.

In Chesed, we meet the kind of person who spontaneously takes the deepest dreams inside of you and offers ways for them to become fulfilled. He is expansive, opening new horizons in life for you to explore. And he possesses great wealth of experience from which he draws the knowledge that enables you to succeed.

Some dreams will bring you love. Some dreams will result in a garage full of very expensive cars and perhaps a private jet to boot. Some dreams will bring you honor and success. But here in Chesed we create dreams that transform the world, enriching life in new and wonderful ways.

MYSTERY

Spiritual Community/ A Genuine Cosmic Religion

The mystery of Chesed is a "spiritual" community operating in our world. There are no temples or churches, no buildings, no initiations, no degrees or rank, no doctrines, and no rituals.

The idea of a "genuine cosmic religion" comes from Franz Bardon's description of the fifty-fifth spirit of the sphere of Mercury called Mebaiah. Bardon says, "He is an original initiator into genuine cosmic religion and a loyal assistant on the way to perfection."

Mebaiah's vision of a genuine cosmic religion is something wonderful—space, time, history, past, present, future, matter, and all spiritual realms are reflected inside of you. Such a vision spontaneously produces a divine sense of peace, since you are united from within with the universe.

To do this, you live the best life you can. And as you meditate, there is an "automatic" connection—an "invisible" influence—that occurs between you and others of a like mind. You resonate with each other. You inspire and uplift each other.

To some extent, this kind of spiritual community is analogous to the astral plane of the planet Earth. The astral plane offers support to all races of beings, all spiritual lineages, all religions, and all paths of life. The astral plane is all-embracing, affirming, nurturing, energizing, and offering a vast range of resources for everyone to draw upon. A spiritual community, in a similar way, creates and maintains an energy field that surrounds, animates, energizes, and provides insight to those who are connected to it.

If I pause from my writing, I can sense the spiritual community that influences me. There are, of course, many students of spirituality. But this community also includes many races of beings. The mermaid queens gave me a five-year project to study incarnated mermaids so that I might better understand their race. They introduced me to the magnetic field to which they are united that surrounds the entire planet.

I have sat and meditated with incarnated gnomes to try to get a better grasp of what it means to sink your mind down into the dense solidity of the Earth element. I have been inspired by the wild, outrageous cheerfulness and joy of incarnated sylphs as well as by the sylph Cargoste, who has an expansive understanding of the enlightened mind. And there has always been an incarnated Fire spirit present in my life, insisting I unite with the power of its element.

From time to time, a higher spirit of the Earth or other spheres offers me suggestions to consider about possible courses of action. Even the forty-nine Judges of Saturn weigh in on me, demanding with absolute authority that I write a manual for eliminating wars on Earth. You could say that my conscience has been shaped by the inner world.

On the other hand, I have puzzled over this idea of a "genuine cosmic religion" as Franz Bardon puts it. How do you take a Hermetic training system like Bardon's and turn it into something that has a social life? How do you build community with it? What values would that community share? What kind of people would it contain, and what would motivate them to work together?

Many religions claim to be universal, but they are saturated with hatred, sustained by fear, and inherently imperialistic. Their core doctrines are formulated and designed to destroy opposing ideas, and, at best, minimize the contributions of other spiritual paths.

Sometimes the practitioners of these religions are insanely insecure. How do you find people who are compassionate, who strive for balance and virtue, and whose purpose is to serve without that service being contaminated by selfishness or guided by a narrow range of beliefs or ideas?

Chesed/Jupiter establishes communities. A spiritual community is not just a set of friends and a well-connected organization. It is a community that has become a family. Its members are inspired by the heart of life and are committed to accomplishing the highest and greatest work that can benefit others.

Though this community exists to serve, it is so balanced that it continuously probes all aspects of wisdom to discover what grants the deepest fulfillment. Its members do not view themselves as being special, elite, or only allowing the qualified to participate. Its members do not enjoy special privileges or fringe benefits due to rank, loyalty, and seniority. They certainly do not define themselves by what they believe or by the ceremonies of a sacred tradition.

Instead, this community defines its success by the wealth it is able to offer to others. There are problems solved, conflicts resolved, inspiration granted, healing provided, broken hearts mended, despair banished, doors opened, work and new life achieved. The connection between its members is inner: heart-to-heart and soul-to-soul with love and energy continuously flowing between them.

A Few Characteristics of Such a Community

Unlike spiritual seekers who are primarily focused on their own development, this community celebrates all four elements on all planes as well as their divine aspects. For example, the will among some of its members, like spirits of the Earthzone, is focused on eliminating corruption in governments. There are practical and effective ways for dissolving malice and hate, for overcoming those who make a career of subjugating and dominating others. To protect the needy, the helpless, and the vulnerable is an ideal that they are able to pursue because they possess the power to do so.

It offers a place of refuge in the soul—a place of peace and serenity where every human being can go. Here the feeling of sanctuary and temple atmosphere are sufficiently strong that peace flows like a stream from the dawn of time to the end of eternity. Such peace is not a belief. It is more like this: relax, exhale, and find a place in your soul in this moment so that you feel an absolute contentment or an inner peace with the universe.

The community establishes astral immortality in the soul. Again, one or more elements in the individual are so strong, so complete in the identification with nature, that the soul no longer deteriorates when the individual dies—neither in this life nor another nor during any age of life does the individual possess less emotional force inside. The individual's emotions are forever new in and through their strength of vibration and inner life.

The community teaches formless consciousness. We see people using all sorts of group affiliation for support and growth. They pledge allegiance, seek liberty, fraternity, equality, and brotherhood. They rely at times on monasteries, ashrams, churches, cathedrals, groves, and stone circles.

But there is nothing that can bind or limit the freedom of the human spirit. Freedom is the nature of consciousness itself. In other words, your cosmic religion will empower you to be fully engaged, acting creatively in history, and at the same time be fully and totally transcendent and independent.

The mind is like the sky—open, pure, clear, luminous—identifying with absolute freedom and attaining an inner union with cosmic harmony, perceiving directly from within oneself the laws that govern the universe. A genuine spiritual community finds a way to embody that oneness and clarity within its members.

It teaches individuals to sense each other directly from within so there is a soul-to-soul and heart-to-heart connection that each is free to establish with any other. And it teaches individuals to perceive love as a direct exchange of energy from one to another.

Historical religions all have ceremonies, rituals, pageantry, and festivals. A genuine cosmic religion takes all of human history, the journey itself toward attaining full awareness, toward ascending and becoming pure spiritual being, as its celebration, festival, and pageantry.

Therefore, the story of each individual's life, his or her experience with each life transition, the passage into and through each desire and need, is celebrated.

There is the attainment of an inner experience of being saturated with love in every cell of your body and overflowing with love from the core of your being. And the discovery through personal searching of the divine purpose arising from one's heart? The Earth itself and life with all its conditions and restrictions are our training ground for attaining completion in all things.

A genuine cosmic religion has taught its practitioners how to listen, to listen so well they can sense another's life experience as if it is their own, to listen so well that Divine Providence considers them part of itself.

To summarize, for me the prime directive of all souls incarnating on Earth is "to become your own creation." A genuine cosmic religion embodies and empowers this declaration of spiritual freedom. It supports each individual's endeavor to decide what you want to become and then to become it.

✱ Three Exercises: Spiritual Community

First, evaluate a spiritual or religious community that you have participated in. Note its history and the part charismatic individuals play in enriching and guiding its development. Notice what members of this community do, what their stated goals are, and the actual transformation that occurs through their practices.

Note the great value a viable community offers. It grants emotional stability to its members. It offers comfort, encouragement, and inspiration. And it establishes in the individual a sense of historical continuity—the human world is participating with the divine world as presented in its stories, sacred texts, and the key moments in history through which it forged its identity.

Our second step is to imagine what a spiritual community could be if the full potential for human development is present in it. Consider the ecstasies and transformations of the five elements.

In the Air element is a feeling of absolute freedom, of a clear and enlightened mind, of great joy and cheerfulness, an artistic temperament, and a sense of harmony that pervades the universe.

In the Earth element is a practical and realistic feeling of belonging and being home in this world. There is a timeless sense of peace and well-being. There is an internal solidity that comes from feeling joined to nature. And there is a quiet bliss in feeling you are working at what you love and that those things that you care about most are always close to your heart.

In the Water element is a sense of being joined to an endless love that pervades the universe. As Christ prophesized, "Out of their bellies shall flow streams of living water." Here you find the means for fulfilling this prophecy.

Establish yourself in this element, and you annihilate loneliness; healing others is a natural consequence; and there is a sense of innocence—you are free of the traumas of the past because in each moment your sense love is overflowing from you like an inexhaustible aquifer.

And consider the Fire element that gives birth to light. Take a moment and for a few seconds imagine the room you are in is filled with light as brilliant and dazzling as the sun. Do this for a minute each day for forty or fifty years. Now you understand the nature of divine authority and power. For light reveals everything hidden, and it provides the energy to accomplish any mission.

And there is the fifth element of Psalm 90, the Heart Sutra, the Bhagavad Gita, and the Prajnaparamita. Awareness without form or image, fully conscious, aware of the origins from which all things arise, the vast expanse encompassing all things and that accompanies them through all their journeys of change and transformation. Here is the power to dissolve all malice and to return anything to its original nature and divine destiny.

Perhaps you get together once a week or two in a small group to practice the silence meditations of the Earth element or the active listening of the Air element. You can get together and focus on Water flowing through your bodies and of being joined to a sea of love that grants you to some extent the ability to heal others.

Together you can visualize things you wish to be by using the power of imagination and light. And you can practice formless meditation wherein the mysteries of space and time lift their veils and unite you to all things from within.

And finally, sense that inner connection to others. When I do this, I sense that sitting here meditating with me are all those I feel close to in life, all those who have inspired me, and all of those who assist me in fulfilling my work. Space and time no longer separate us. And we are embraced and sustained by an endless sea of love.

RULE 3

BINAH/SATURN

Limitation and Enlightenment

Basic Quality	Appreciation
Virtues, Vices, Negative	Judicial temperament/ Negligence/Treachery
Challenge	Overcome your limitations
Magical Practice	Master your deepest lessons in life
Common Virtue	Appreciation of the gifts of the past
Magical Virtue	Identifying with the void
Divine Virtue	Dissolving negativity, malice
Dream	Placing causes in Akasha
Initiation	The feeling of how precious life is
Mystery	The final test of enlightenment: creating love where love does not exist

Outer energy: Saturn is sometimes viewed as a nightmare. There is sadness, sorrow, grief, loss, disgrace, shame, failure, suffering, and pain. Saturn's voice speaks not of Jupiter's opportunities, good fortune, adventures, and new horizons. Instead, the energy is dense, heavy, and filled with the spirit of oppression.

Saturn is a time when you are held back from moving forward—when getting what you want is confronted by overwhelming opposition. You are beset by darkness, and you cannot find a path to follow.

Nothing around you seems to express or reflect the desires of your heart. All opportunities for gaining experience, for feeling alive, and getting the most out of life come crashing down. Your hopes are dashed to pieces, dreams shattered, your life shipwrecked.

Saturn's vibration destroys false attachment, eliminates waste, removes inefficiency, and dissolves inertia. It basically says, "Do not be distracted or compromised. Remain focused. Stay the course. Accomplish the work set before you."

Yet amid Saturn's demands is a knowledge of equilibrium and balance. Its serenity is so refined it can restore harmony to anyone who has lost his path or any soul that has fallen into darkness.

You will know when you have made a good start working with Saturn. You will find in your heart (quite separate from the events in the outer world) inner strength, inner peace, and complete freedom.

Saturn's inner energy simply asks, "Did you learn what you were meant to learn, and did you do what you were meant to do?" Your status in regard to these two questions determines how Saturn views you.

We can look back briefly on other sephiroth. Take Netzach/Venus. Its outer vibration is very familiar. It is overwhelming attraction and desire. The five senses are continuously bombarded with pleasure, bliss, and ecstasy. Every unfilled longing rises up saying, "Here. With this person, you can find complete satisfaction and fulfillment." And the intellect concurs, saying, "With this person, you will find a lifelong friend, companion, and lover with whom you can feel one."

But in spite of that whirlwind of sensations and feelings, even with the high learning curve that accompanies knowing another person, erotic attraction offers no path that leads to mutual understanding. To get to oneness you are going to need maturity, real skills in relating to another person, profound empathy, and unselfishness. There is a time of decision with Venus in which you must decide—Do you seek gratification or do you want to learn the divine arts of love?

Saturn offers a similar process. When Saturn in its full force enters our lives, something of great value has been taken from us. And it is never to be found again. And so there follows sorrow, grief, and loss.

Saturn also requires a decision. The inner vibration of Saturn says, "We exist here in this world under great limitations. Yet in our souls we are divine beings, and in our minds we are free. You are not here by accident. You have things to accomplish—create love, establish justice, assist others in their time of need, and transform yourself. Do not fail in this endeavor."

BASIC QUALITY
Appreciation

Saturn is understanding the sacrifices others have made so that we are alive and enjoy the freedom and opportunities that we have.

VIRTUES, VICES, NEGATIVE

Virtues: A judicial temperament, superhuman patience, diligence, implacable will, equanimity, equilibrium, recollection, contemplation, discipline, unshakable self-esteem, humility, conscience, protector of all spiritual paths, mentor, thankfulness, accomplishment—producing works of enduring value, establishing justice.

Vices: Negligence, fixation, rigidity, failure to take responsibility, inattentive, preoccupied, lack of conscience, anguish, degradation, oppression, conspiracy, feeling abandoned, alienated, estranged, lack of self-reflection, ungrateful.

Negative: Treachery, betrayal, corruption, criminal enterprise, a lost soul. Feel as if you are among the dead. A wasted life. Incarcerated. Obsessive. No opportunities. Stuck. Groundhog Day. Madness.

CHALLENGE

Traditions are very important. They are the custodians of experience. They offer direction and guidance. But no tradition defines who you are. You are free to make your own choices.

Take hold of your limitations. Learn from them and overcome them.

MAGICAL PRACTICE

Master Your Deepest Lessons in Life

The voice of Saturn says, "Experience life to whatever extent you can. Discover what makes you happy and brings you satisfaction. Find some things worth doing that are right for you and totally captivating.

"Yet also discover your deepest lessons in life and then take the time and make the effort to learn them."

These lessons are whatever holds you back, whatever limitations you are to overcome, and whatever interferes with your attaining harmony within yourself. Make the study of love, wisdom, will, and consciousness your passion, your daily meditation, and a permanent endeavor.

What keeps you from being happy? What family karma has been passed down to you from previous generations—prejudice, false assumptions, bias, selfishness, greed, arrogance, abuse, fear, hostility, domination, vulnerability, ignorance, and so forth?

What stands in your way preventing you from attaining something great or pursuing your dreams or attaining your destiny? What is missing from life that no one else sees or seems able to address?

For Saturn, life is a school, a college. You signed up for the human experience. You would not be getting your money's worth if you do not make your best effort.

Consider the basic components of life in terms of the Hermetic tradition:

The element of Fire is willpower. But for Saturn, divine purpose is essential, otherwise willpower falters and produces disasters.

The element of Air is wisdom. But for Saturn, your mind must be as open as the sky and as clear as a mirror. All boundaries and limitations must be left behind, otherwise you live as if you are blind.

The element of Water is love. For Saturn, you must become one with another without a trace of attachment, possession, or grasping. Fail in this endeavor, and you are like a sailor on the open ocean without a home port.

The element of Earth is consciousness. Do you have something to accomplish? For Saturn, the work that we do in life must be of such value that that it endures through all ages of the world.

✳ **Biographical Note** ✳
PART I: MAGICAL EQUILIBRIUM

My deepest lessons in life originally presented themselves to me quite differently from what I sense now. Initially, my primary concern was the threat of nuclear war. It was beyond my understanding how people like Bill Gates and Warren Buffett could amass their fortunes knowing that in thirty minutes the world as we know it could end. But when I look inside their minds, I can see that this question never occurred to them.

On a personal level, I needed to free myself of a fiery will that had been implanted in me. At times, I was incredibly angry.

I also had a gradual realization that Christianity had for two thousand years engaged in a cover-up. For political and psychological reasons, it denied the possibility of spiritual training and spiritual perception. I had to work through and beyond that tradition. I did so in part by studying spiritual anthropology—a detailed firsthand examination of the training exercises in various religious traditions and the results they achieved.

I also had tremendous mental tension. My mind was far more developed than my emotional life and I had no internal practices involving being aware of my body other than sports activities. I was also overzealous in trying to learn new things. And I had no sense of a profession or career.

Rather than focus on investment counseling, something I might have excelled at, I went all in on spiritual quests. It would have made more sense to succeed first in business, which would then have enabled me to pursue my spiritual interests from a position of freedom. It then would have been easy to set up organizations that assisted me in my research.

But the lessons I needed to learn most involved mastering the five elements inside myself. In the end, I had to change myself before trying to change the world. The element of Water, for example, with its superhuman empathy and healing power, is completely missing from Western culture. I had to do original research and quite a few interviews with astral mermaids and incarnated mermaids to discover how Water operates in the soul. And then I had to figure out how to adapt what I learned so it was helpful to me.

The Water element by itself can destroy your survival instincts and place you in a narcissistic state of bliss where you lose interest in the external world. The love that mermaids experience in their astral kingdom is for the most part worthless in our world. It has too much enchantment along with a kind of cocaine high and not the kind of practical application that changes people.

And the fifth element of Akasha remains an incredible challenge. In Tibetan Buddhism there are practices identical to what Franz Bardon calls in his Kabbalah the cosmic letter U or the void. I had to take that pure meditation and work on the applications to geopolitical issues around the world.

But I was not supposed to just get the sense of void as being a second "home." I am meant to master it as if I am an incarnated Earthzone spirit, a being authorized to use Akasha in overseeing human evolution.

It made perfect sense that early on I would find myself living in a Buddhist monastery where I was initiated by the head of the oldest order of Tibetan Buddhists. These lamas had what I needed to learn. But due to their culture and feudal outlook on society they had absolutely no sense of how to apply their wisdom so it is useful for individuals living in a postindustrial, pluralistic, and democratic society. And they have false assumptions that the external world is unreal, which diminishes their curiosity and learning curve.

It would take me twenty years of magical practice before I understood the importance of first mastering the five elements. Bardon himself once appeared to me in a dream and demanded that I stop studying the auras of spirits and focus on the elements. My journey has resulted in books such as The Four Elements; Undines: Lessons from the Realm of the Water Spirits; and Mermaids, Sylphs, Gnomes, and Salamanders.

PART II: NORTH AND SOUTH NODES OF THE MOON

A perspective on your deepest life lessons can be found in your natal chart's North and South lunar nodes. You can use an online program to cast a free natal chart on one of many internet sites. This will usually include your north and south node locations. You can then *find a simple interpretation by searching, for example, "north node Sagittarius south node Gemini."*

The South node represents areas of experience from past lives in which you have excelled. It is something you are good at or take for granted. In the movie Lord of War, *Nicolas Cage plays a weapons dealer named Yuri Oriov. He is very good at what he does, and so he keeps doing it even though he ends up losing his brother, his wife and child, and his parents. You could say his South node involves making deals with terrible people and succeeding at it. His North node would be the opposite—helping disadvantaged people survive and start new lives. Often the excessive experience you have in your South node position is utilized in a positive way by redirecting it through the North node position.*

With my South node in Sagittarius, to say the least I have an excessive amount of conviction and certainty about what justice is and a flair for searching out the truth of the universe. But it would be a disaster if I were to spend my life engaged in these same pursuits. All the same, by focusing on communicating what I know inside myself, I can open up paths for others and enrich their lives. In this case, it is about communicating with others rather than seeking an ideal or a vision.

COMMON VIRTUE
Appreciation of the Gifts of the Past

The common virtue in Binah is gratitude, thankfulness, appreciation, and celebration of the gifts of the past. To be able to look back and say, "My life was all it was meant to be." In which case, we can also say, "Saturn was my spirit guide. She was tough at times, even incredibly hard. But she did what she had to do to produce something wonderful."

For some people, the past is like a warehouse. There are crates and boxes lying about, misplaced, or lining long rows of shelves. The air is dusty. The place is downright boring.

For others, the past is like an old museum filled with relics and exhibits that have no relevance to today. You do not enter here to renew yourself or seek knowledge of what shall come to be. It is not a happy place.

And for some each moment in the past continues to live on. The discovery of fire, domestication of animals, agriculture, architecture, trains, cars, flight, computers, art, and jurisprudence are still filled with wonder.

For some, the past is as real as the present moment. And the future is here too, for the past and future are well-connected, each defining and fulfilling the other.

If you want the feeling that best enhances our experience with Saturn, be thankful, appreciative, and grateful for what you have been given. Take nothing for granted.

MAGICAL VIRTUE
Identifying with the Void

The magical virtue of Binah is to take "the void," a vast, empty state of mind, and meditate on it until it feels like home.

Buddha

The newborn infant who would later become Buddha (roughly 563 BCE to 480 BCE) was given the name Siddhartha (Pāli: Siddhattha), meaning "he who achieves his aim." Buddha attained complete enlightenment solely through his own efforts. He had no gurus or spirit guides to assist him because there was no one within Hinduism or in India that possessed the degree of enlightenment he attained.

Buddha's mind is like a clear mirror—it perfectly reflects without distortion or blur anything that appears before it. Consequently, Buddha's mind also embodies perfect empathy. With this mirror-like awareness, it is easy to know another's experience as if it is your own. With Buddha mind, you can think, act, evaluate, perceive, and make decisions without using thoughts or images. You can feel, but there is no need to direct, shape, contain, or define those feelings. Feelings too are another kind of energy that you can be fully aware of from beginning to end.

For Buddha, an enlightened mind is identical to absolute freedom. You perceive in each moment a path of action that is free of obstacles or hindrances. If you meditate in the vibration of Buddha's mind, you feel completely relaxed and yet fully awake, clear and detached yet fully engaged.

What Buddha has done is make the void his identity. He never loses that sense of perfect, mirror-like clarity and an awareness that anything being experienced is itself part of the void.

A little humor, from *Stories of Magic and Enchantment*.

And the Creator asks, "Did I not create the sky by night filled with countless stars?"

And the angel replies, "Yes."

And the Creator asks, "Why did I do so?"

And the angel replies, "So that in one single glance men might perceive that the mind is infinite."

The Creator says, "And?"

The angel replies, "And if they persist in contemplation, perceiving without thoughts intervening, they shall sense a great stillness embracing the universe in which the beginnings and ends of all things are united in peace and harmony."

✦ Quantum Reality Meditation ✦
A Brief Introduction to Another
Aspect of the Enlightened Mind

Take a breath. Now imagine a void, a vast space without light, no day or night, no form, no substance, no matter of any kind, no electronic or magnetic vibrations, and no gravity.

It is like a very big room filled with shiny black light, a room with nothing in it. And because there is nothing in it, there is no time or space, because time and space require form and movement as a reference.

We can refer to this void as quantum reality. It contains all possibilities. It is the source of all things that can appear from nothing and take on being. So rich and vast, the entire universe as well as an individual's life arise from out of it.

You might actually go outside at night and take a look at the night sky. Hold that image in your mind—the vast space that contains all those stars. Then remove the stars and the light. Keep that sense of open, empty space. Then remove the Earth as well, so that what lies on all sides of you is an infinite emptiness or just a very big, empty space. Then think of this clear space as something you "own" and that you are able to use anytime you wish.

If you practice this, then you get good at it. It is quiet. It is peaceful. There is no disturbance of any kind. There are no interruptions or distractions. It is the nature of mind itself when it is still—it has the ability to be perfectly receptive, reflective, and clear like a mirror. And it offers this fabulous gift. It can dissolve into nothing anything that is negative.

There is another unusual quality that belongs to this state of mind. Since there are no boundaries and no definitions of any kind, there is no separation. In this space of awareness, only oneness exists. You can still recall or enter memories from your personal history. You can relive all the experiences of your own or someone else's individual identity. And yet, in this state of mind, anything that separates one from another dissolves.

And there is also this: the void embodies absolute freedom to be and to become whatever you wish. There are no restrictions that exist within the void regarding what can be imagined, felt, or conceived of as a possible course of action.

It is a mental clarity that can think and perceive without having to use ideas or thoughts to think. It is the perfect response of the mind to any situation that appears in time. It is so rich and deep that a "cause" no longer produces an "effect" and so karma, compulsions, and obsessions dissolve in its presence.

If you stop the mind from thinking, no mental activity at all, then only the original purposes of creation—wisdom itself—can express itself. All other thoughts, ideas, ideologies, psychologies, theologies, and philosophies fade away.

This is because there is no one here to feed ideas that require desire, need, ego, selfishness, insecurity, or greed to survive. In effect, you learn to observe without thoughts intervening. I have mentioned this before. Stop your mind from thinking and look around yourself—you find yourself in a different world.

Put simply, if your mind embodies nothingness, you have stepped outside of the stream of history and of the flow of linear time that we reply upon so much to get through the day.

Ten Useful Aspects of the Void

To review the different aspects of the void:

10. The void is your space. There is nothing to weigh you down. There is no one telling you what to do. There are no limitations. No obstacles. No barriers and nothing to overcome.

9. In the void is infinite peace. We are surrounded by hundreds of billions of galaxies. The void embraces and supports everything.

8. The void is where you can create and dissolve any feeling. Try it. Imagine anger and hatred. Now imagine a very hot, burning ball of Fire in front of you. The heat is radiating in all directions.

Now imagine this ball of Fire gone. It has vanished. It has dissolved into nothing. Anger and hatred are energies and, like a ball of Fire you have conjured up through imagination, they can cease to exist if that is what you wish.

Imagine depression, sorrow, and sadness. Now imagine a very heavy, dense ball in front of you as if it is made out of lead. Imagine that ball gone. The weight has vanished. You can do the same with the feelings that weigh you down. The void amplifies your imagination.

Recall or sense anxiety or obsession. Now imagine a ball in front of you like a sphere filled with the blue sky. Except this sphere has dark clouds like a hurricane or tornado inside. Now imagine the turbulence dissolving into nothing. No more disturbances in the atmosphere. No more feelings of anxiety.

Imagine greed, jealousy, and possession. Imagine a ball of Water in front of you that is sticky, impure, or contaminated. Now imagine the ball gone. The same meditative action applies to greed, possessiveness, or jealousy. They are gone. They are no more. There is nothing here in the void to grab or to be attached to.

Emotions and feelings are energies in your body. You can reflect on them and process them. You can get to know them in every nuance and aspect. But, in the end, they arise and appear in the void—the vast open space of your awareness. You are free to guide, transform, or dissolve them according to your purposes and volition.

7. The void is wisdom and understanding. You can capture in one gaze the past, present, and future of what you are looking at. You can experience things from the other's point of view. You can imagine likely outcomes and opportunities that can be seized upon. You can comprehend the way the world is and also the way it is meant to be.

6. The void specializes in modifying and changing karma. Again, think of sitting in a dark theater where a play is being performed on stage. That play is your life and there was a script written for you to act out before you were born.

   Every time you have been angry, depressed, lonely, sorrowful, needy, or hurt—all those feelings were waiting for you to experience as you walked into different scenes and spoke the dialogue written in the script.

   But you can decide if you want to continue playing your assigned role with its predetermined feelings, thoughts, and self-image.

   Imagine sitting there in the theater and calling out to yourself up there on the stage: "You already did that too many times. Try a different response." And the you on the stage hears this shout from the dark theater as the voice of his own conscience speaking to him from inside.

5. The void allows you to identify with the original source of anything that has come into being so that you develop insight into why things exist as they do.

4. The void is omnipresent. If you think of someone, then that person is right here, now, and present with you in the void. There is only you and that person.

   To be aware of another from within the void is to be one with that person, since nothing else exists in your awareness.

3. The void is silence. As silence, here is where you can cherish and nourish in your heart your highest dreams and ideals. Your dreams and ideals are always near to you and a part of you.

2. The void is a divine workshop. If you wish to create a future, to manifest a dream, here is where you see it, envision it, enter

it, and live it, so it is so real that you embody its vibration and feeling. This is because there are no barriers to imagination in the void. Nothing prevents you from experiencing "here and now" as being completely real, whatever it is that you seek to fulfill.

Creative artists and genuine prophets make the void a second home because they enjoy the freedom and the stimulation to their imaginations to which the void gives rise.

1. And of course the void is the experience of perfect enlightenment. Free of all attachment because here there is nothing to which one need be attached. There is no assigned identity or set of predetermined responses because you yourself are the original source of perception and experience.

You see the world as it is because your mind is reflective as a perfect mirror that sees without bias, blur, or distortion. Whatever occurs, you perceive in your awareness according to what it is without the mind imposing a meaning or interpretation on it.

DIVINE VIRTUE
Dissolving Negativity, Malice

Whenever righteousness becomes lax and injustice arises, then I send myself forth to protect the good and bring evildoers to destruction. For the secure establishment of the laws of the universe, I come into being age after age . . . I was born to destroy the destroyers.

KRISHNA

A representative government of the people, by the people, and for the people puts in place laws, police, judges, bailiffs, courts, prisons, and so on. The executive branch, on a national, state, and local level, hires police, probation officers, lawyers, and so on to ensure that laws are enforced and citizens protected. In general, those who are a threat to others find their rights are increasingly restricted until they are removed from society.

And yet there is always a trade-off. Too much freedom and lack of regulation and some individuals harm and take advantage of other individuals without any recourse. On the other hand, if society exercises too much control over individuals, then freedom is lost and the society becomes oppressive.

The divine virtue for Binah is a spiritual judicial system. Perhaps it is activated when negative people overwhelm positive people. All the same, issues concerning fairness and justice are usually left to societies to address. As governments evolve, we can see judicial systems becoming more effective.

Perhaps it is more accurate to say that the spiritual world takes an interest in human affairs when spiritual development itself is in danger of being compromised. We might imagine that magic itself can become so abusive that it is possible to close down all paths of spiritual development in a society.

In this case, the spiritual world might intervene directly and place severe restrictions on a society or else simply eliminate a nation, a religion, or even an entire civilization. In other words, Saturn's method of education is primarily associated with restricting or taking away. When something is gone, then finally its true value can appear.

If you want kindness, mercy, generosity, good fortune, benevolence, and inspiration, then look to Jupiter or the Sun. If an individual or nation shows up in the court of Saturn, things have already gone far enough that only the most severe remedies are available.

This issue of a spiritual judicial system is seen most clearly in regard to wars. Human beings are permitted to have wars. A strong leader says to himself, as many corporate CEOs also say to themselves, "If I can stretch out my hand and take something, then that is exactly what I am going to do." And so we have Enron, WorldCom, and Bernie Madoff in the corporate world taking everything they can from others.

And in history, we have Alexander the Great, Julius Caesar, Genghis Khan, Napoleon, Hitler, Stalin, and Mao looking around and saying to themselves, "Let me see. I can easily take this and that. But I wonder how much more can I take? Perhaps the entire world. Let me try."

"All power is given from above," says the prophet. So where is "the above" when it comes to the barbarian cruelty and the hideous suffering of wars? Obviously, the spiritual world leaves issues concerning justice in the hands of humanity, in our hands. If you do not like something, then fix it. Do not sit around like a baby whining and complaining.

We might suppose that in religions the saints, sages, and holy men would address this issue. But they do not. They leave issues concerning justice and power in the hands of evil men to decide. The uses and abuses of political power have never been part of any spiritual training curriculum. Perhaps at this point in history we should seriously study how power "given from above" so often ends up in the hands of dictators and evil men.

In perspective, then, this divine virtue of Saturn—of dissolving malice, hatred, ill will, and negativity—is relevant. We are at a point in history where a few individuals can damage the entire planet. Let us consider this matter of dealing with the negative first on a personal level.

I have already described the enlightened state of mind and the void. You imagine a big empty space with nothing in it. Call it the void. You put off to the side everything personal about yourself. Your role in society, your feelings, your thoughts and opinions, your biography, your religion, and your social identity. Put it all in the closet, so to speak, and close the door. Now here we are. We are in a psychological and spiritual state of mind where even space and time are not present.

The void dissolves negativity because the negative principle requires something present to attack, to possess, or to flee from. But these things are not present in the void.

You can do this when you are with a negative person or else imagine a person in front of you. He or she is in your void. Nothing else exists than you and this person.

Now imagine that the negative energy in the other person dissolves. You can actually sense the hatred, malice, and desire to dominate draining out of the other's body until it is completely gone. If you can imagine a vast void around and inside of others when you talk to them, then you may notice that they tend to be calm and reasonable when you do this.

This may work on a personal level with people who you know who are negative. But highly dynamic and powerful individuals have often made a lifelong study of how to control, dominate, and exploit others.

The meditation that you have worked on for five hours over a few weeks does not compare to the decades in which they have refined, tested, and perfected their negativity. To be effective on a geopolitical scale, like them, you have to make dissolving negativity a lifelong commitment.

Of course, people remain free. But if you succeed in dissolving the negative energy in an individual, the negative principle no longer leads to success. A person remains negative, but the influence of their negativity is greatly reduced. In effect, you have saturated another's aura with the void that diminishes the influence of negative actions. The power another holds through fear, domination, and manipulation dissolves.

The Voice of the Void

There is no vice I cannot twist and bend
And turn again into its opposite virtue.
There is no compulsion or obsession I cannot
So fill with light it becomes kind and bright.
There is no ill will or malice I cannot
Convert into chivalry or true nobility.
There is no crunch or karmic bind, no evil intent or
  design
I cannot refine within my mind
Into contentment and absolute satisfaction.
There is no suffering
I cannot so enfold within my palms
Spit on, blow upon,
And recreate as beauty hidden in the heart of life.
Such are my power and might;
Such are the depths and the heights
Where my wings fly.

DREAM

Akasha is a spiritual plane and also a state of awareness. What happens tomorrow—where the stock market opens, the speech the president will make, a war that flares up, a mass shooting, a scientific breakthrough, an asteroid shooting past the Earth, or a volcano erupting—the events of our physical world are already registered in Akasha.

If you are sensitive and still your mind, you may be able to sense something of the future. Once a year I have a lucid dream in which I wake up in the future. I look around and try to memorize everything I see. I take notes when I awake because I have just seen what will come to be.

Such things as sitting at a desk surrounded by electronic devices that allow you to communicate with others around the planet; big mechanical machines that are programmed to water farm land; a Starbucks latte that has a different taste with each sip; and a war between two nations that must not be allowed to happen. Things like that.

These "causes" in Akasha—events that are to be—have their own shape, activity, and emotional force built into them. They are as yet immaterial and invisible but, like gravity, they already weigh upon our world. When the pandemic began, I could see in advance that people would be rioting in the streets, but I did not know why. In the future, the stock market will fall 30 percent or more. That is certain. But the question is when and why, and how quickly will it recover?

Causes in Akasha take time before they manifest in our world. An individual has a biography. He rises in power. He is then in a position where he makes a decision that affects millions of people and the history of his nation.

Another individual is torn and twisted inside. He searches for remedies. In a moment of clarity, he forges for himself a path of healing that frees him from the torments of his past and enables him to be a healthy and creative individual within society.

History is shaped by three things: necessity, desire, and dreams. Some things are beyond our control. At least until science and technology give us power over nature.

Some desires motivate individuals, driving them to seek satisfaction. They approach the future as an extension of the self they already know. And with some luck, and if they work hard, they may well succeed in getting what they want.

And some events in the world are brought about through what we dream. In a dream you can remake yourself into something wonderful that is completely beyond the limitations of your present desires and wants. This is a divine mode of dreaming.

The future is malleable, open to suggestion, and totally receptive. For any conflict, you can dream a future in which the conflict is fully addressed, resolved, in a state of harmony, and where lasting peace exists between all parties involved.

In Akasha, nothing prevents you from experiencing "here and now" as being completely real, whatever it is that you seek to fulfill. If you want to place a "cause" in Akasha, your dream needs to be compelling, persuasive, and relevant. Your vision must become like a living being, something that is fully alive. This vision then overrides and reshapes others' dreams, desires, and images that also are seeking to manifest.

The dream for Binah is of being able to place a cause in Akasha, within these spiritual realms surrounding us. This cause is so dynamic that, in spite of all opposition and all limitations, it manifests.

In magical terms, you enter a deep meditation or state of trance. You imagine you are in Akasha, such as the void that I frequently describe— a state of awareness outside of, or prior to, space and time. And then you envision exactly what you wish to become real, as if it is already real right now in every way.

You are providing a clear and very refined vision of the future. And you are imbuing it with energy—the emotional force, a mental plan of action, a spiritual purpose to be fulfilled, and an entire visualized network of supporting cast to assist it manifesting.

I could be one of the richest billionaires on Earth, or a very powerful diplomat. In which case, I might be able to present a persuasive plan that would get the prime ministers of Israel and Gaza to sign on to an enduring peace plan. All of this accomplished independent of the U.S. State Department, which never seems to grasp the reality of opposing states.

On the other hand, what if I were more skilled in placing causes in Akasha? I could synchronize the vibration in the minds of these opposing leaders such that they themselves then possess an unshakable and electrifying vision of peace that overwhelms all opposition. That would be placing a cause in Akasha. If sufficiently powerful, that cause then operates independent of me and does not stop until the vision within it becomes real.

The takeaway from the dream of Binah is that, with the help of our imagination and concentration, we can enter the divine workshop in order to alter reality and remake the world.

"Without a vision, the people perish," says Solomon in his book of Proverbs. The dream in each sephirah offers hope. It makes the sephirah feel alive. In a dream, you can experience now what you wish the future to be.

Saturn offers the vision that your mind and imagination are not pathetic or superfluous when confronted with a hostile world. They help shape reality.

INITIATION

Every separation, loss, farewell, and goodbye is a sacred rite in my eyes.

THE CHIEF JUDGE OF SATURN

The play *Our Town* by Thornton Wilder won the Pulitzer Prize for Drama in 1938. Edward Albee describes it as "the greatest American play ever written." The play tells the story of Emily Webb, who dies giving birth to her second child.

After her funeral, Emily finds herself among other dead people. Although she is warned not to fixate on her past life, Emily decides to go back and relive her twelfth birthday. She can see, but not interact with, the living. And she knows what will happen next in the sequence of events.

Realizing how unaware the living are of how special it is to be alive, she turns to the stage manager and asks,

"Do any human beings ever realize life while they live it?—every, every minute?"

The stage manager replies, "No. Saints and poets maybe . . . they do some."

When we lose something that we cherish or depend on, then the loss and grief hit us. But Saturn does not go away and then return after thirty years for what is called a "Saturn return."* Saturn is with us every moment.

The initiation of Saturn is not some abstract, metaphysical realization of a sage, saint, or Bodhisattva. It is an artistic sensitivity like the experience of Emily in Thornton Wilder's play.

Can you seek to be fully alive in every moment while also being aware of life as if you have already died and are looking back at it from the other side?

Is there an inner peace and serenity that embraces equally both life and death? Can you embrace life with tenderness knowing that joy and sorrow, love and hate, and wonder and horror walk side by side in our journey through life?

Can you be touched by evil, broken, abandoned, and alone and yet be so open and receptive that in each moment you are ready to let go of the past and enter the light?

Do you have the purity of will to make the best of any situation you enter regardless of the extent of the unknown that looks you in the face?

Have you been anointed by divine grace in the depths of your heart such that you have unshakable faith that love will triumph over separation, darkness, and loss?

Saturn has given you this sacred gift if you can sense how special, precious, and beautiful each moment is.

MYSTERY

The Final Test of Enlightenment:
Creating Love Where Love Does Not Exist

Blessed are those who create love where love does not exist, for they have passed the final test and have attained cosmic freedom.

---

*The "Saturn return" (roughly every thirty years) in astrology is a time when Saturn upsets our world and asks us, "Are the choices you are making in accord with your deepest values? Because if they are not, then what you depend on will fail."

Saturn would like us to learn all we can about life here in the physical world. There are tests, difficulties, ordeals, and many things to accomplish. But if you want to reduce all that Saturn requires down to one test, then this is it: When you are placed in a situation where there is no love present, where there is no support or backup, can you create love where love does not exist?

A Christmas Carol is a novella by Charles Dickens. It tells the story of Ebenezer Scrooge, an elderly miser. On Christmas Eve, Scrooge encounters his old business partner, Jacob Marley, who has previously died. Marley tells Scrooge he is to be visited by the spirits of Christmas past, present, and future.

Without his consent, and as if in a lucid dream, three spirits take control of Scrooge's dreams for one night. Scrooge experiences his own past, present, and future, as if he is actually present witnessing the events as they unfold. Finally, with the Spirit of Christmas Future, Scrooge realizes that his life is without significance. Through this life review, Scrooge is transformed—"'Spirit!' he cried, tight clutching at its robe, 'hear me! I am not the man I was. I will not be the man I must have been but for this intercourse. Why show me this, if I am past all hope!'"

The spirits did not put these words into Scrooge's mouth. Scrooge, on his own initiative, adopts their point of view. The implication is that if you give someone enough one-on-one attention, you can have a remarkable influence on them. When done right, there is a blending of minds. The spirits perceive what Scrooge experiences. At the same time, Scrooge experiences what each of the spirits perceive.

This process entails a very high level of empathy. In *A Christmas Carol,* the spirits control what Scrooge experiences without interfering with his free will. In the process, they manage to imbue Scrooge with a different spirit. We could say that in a matter of hours, Scrooge relived the major events of his life. He saw the choices he made. And he was able to sense how things might have turned out if he had made different choices.

Under the Zen of Love section in Netzach, we learned to do something similar to what occurs in *A Christmas Carol.* You sit with a person and meditate on the other, so to speak. You put on the other's body and wear it as if it is your own. You feel what the other feels. You think the other's thoughts. Your review the other's life as if his experiences and memories are your own. And you do all of this while retaining a very high level of mental clarity and detachment.

After all, as a Venus spirit might ask, "What is love and friendship if you do not feel you are within the other person living that person's life as if it is your own?"

The outer life of Venus carries with it all sorts of crazy—and many times, overwhelming—attractions. The inner spirit of Venus is simply attaining a state of oneness with another person. There is the mad dance, and then there is the calm, nearly divine feeling and perception of being one with another.

The Zen of Love section can be used with friends, lovers, and people of significance in your personal life. The level of empathy is such that you know others' lives equal to or better they know themselves. Saturn's approach, on the other hand, is more universal in scope and power.

The Judges of Saturn can say, "We create limitations so that in overcoming them, you can attain cosmic freedom." There is an authority and finality present. "If you want to attain cosmic freedom, then there is a final test."

Here is the difference between the Zen of Love and the Saturn approach. With Saturn, you bring realizations, feelings, insights, and experiences of all ten sephiroth to the meditation you share with the other person.

If he needs inspiration, then you are the inspiration of the sun. If he needs self-mastery, then you are the will and power of Mars. If he needs faith and conviction, then you are the electrifying certainty of Mercury, a voice of thunder, awakening the truth in the core of his being. If he needs serenity and inner peace, then you embody an inner peace with the universe of Yesod that is inexhaustible and without end.

On an astral and mental level, you are so close and so connected that you experience what he experiences, and he experiences what you experience. Without interfering with the other's will, you are

100 percent there for the other person, with the other person, and in a sense, a part of the other person.

To conclude, Saturn might turn to anyone and ask, "How can you say you have learned all there is to learn about the physical world unless you can pass this simple test—to create love where love does not exist?"

RULE 2

CHOKMAH/URANUS

Wisdom, Destiny

Basic Quality	Revealing new things
Virtues, Vices, Negative	Creativity/Failure to prepare/False prophets
Challenge	Work with the divine world in fulfilling a task
Magical Practice	Dialoguing
Common Virtue	Appreciation for the gifts of the future
Magical Virtue	Role-playing the future
Divine Virtue	Revealing new magic to the world
Dream	The dream of magic
Initiation	Listening
Mystery	Divine missions

In the earlier sephirah of Chesed/Jupiter, we offer others gifts and opportunities. Here in Chokmah/Uranus we also offer gifts, but these are new and previously unknown. And they are so astonishing that they often appear to be magical in nature.

In Yesod/Moon, we listen to and we work with the subconscious, using its language—graphic imagery and feelings—to manifest the future. In Chokmah/Uranus, we listen to the divine world or some aspect of Divine Providence. We seek, among other things, a transmission or *shaktipat.* Later on we will seek to transmit to others the essence of who we are, what we have learned from life, and our inner spirit.

The future—fusion reactors, wireless and free electricity, the cure for cancer, longevity bordering on immortality, genetic engineering and pharmaceutical advances, new economic theories and practices, the way to feed the hungry, heal the sick, help the unfortunate, resolve conflicts, establish justice between nations, probe the mysteries of matter, and reveal the paths of spirit—these are some of the gifts of Uranus.

Those who are adept in this sphere often have gained everything they could want or dream. And so they look beyond themselves, seeking to acquire gifts that fulfill other's lives. They remain gentle and kind even though mysterious powers operate within them.

BASIC QUALITY
Revealing New Things

The Basic Quality in Uranus is offering the world new things that you create or invent. Like the Wright brothers, Edison, Henry Ford, Tesla, Einstein, and so on, it is working with the divine world to manifest something in real time.

VIRTUES, VICES, NEGATIVE

Virtues: Creativity, invention, experimentation, foresight, vision, clairvoyance, faith, conviction, adaptability, a divine partnership, a divine mission, pursuit of a quest, good listening skills, joining two worlds.

Vices: Failure to prepare, poor commitment, false assumptions, attachment to the past, lack of vision, no imagination, absence of a plan B, the Shakespearean/tragic flaw that ruins or diminishes your accomplishments.

Negative: False prophets, destruction, fall of empires, end of a way of life, breakdown of society, man-made megadisasters, exhaustion, havoc, dehumanization. It is your end of the world supervolcano or Carrington Event, George Orwell's dystopian novel *Nineteen Eighty-Four.*

In the 1956 movie *Forbidden Planet,* an advanced, alien civilization creates a machine that enables them to physically manifest whatever they wish just by thinking. But the unknown desires buried deep in the collective unconscious of that race—the monsters of the id—awaken and gain access to the advanced technology. The Krell are destroyed in one night from the primordial rage hidden within them.

Beware the side effects of magic as well as new technology. They can bring out the best and the worst within you.

CHALLENGE

The challenge is to reach beyond yourself and utilize the resources of the divine world in accomplishing missions on Earth.

King Solomon: "There is a time for everything, and a season for every activity under the heavens . . . He has made everything beautiful in its time."

Here in Chokmah/Uranus, there is a time to work with the divine world as a partner. Through an act of will, you choose to reduce suffering on Earth and to reveal new gifts to mankind that change the world.

MAGICAL PRACTICE
Dialoguing

In romantic love, we have an exclusive relationship with another person. We share special moments. And there is an inner connection. You can ask a couple, "How did the two of you first meet?" The partners briefly become alive as they answer. All of the above makes the relationship something worth sacrificing for.

There is flirting, courtship, falling in love, a marriage proposal, vows, a wedding ceremony, a honeymoon, anniversary, renewal, and many more milestones. And yet these things are almost all captured in the simple act of giving another person your full, undivided attention. This brings into play your subconscious, your feelings, your mind, and your spirit.

This special kind of connection is seen in dialoguing. We give our full, undivided attention to the other. We can do this with an individual as well as with God, with Divine Providence, a higher spirit, or even an ideal. We recall and celebrate the past. We envision and prepare for the future. And we unite together in the present moment in whatever way is appropriate.

There are psychological practices that use dialoguing to process your feelings. In your imagination, you can have a conversation with another person. Talk to the individual as if he or she is actually sitting in front of you. This can be a parent, relative, friend, lover, teacher, coach, mentor, minister, and so on. Review your experiences together—when you first met, what occurred, what you share in common, the things you have done for each other—and continue from there.

Simply by imagining the presence of the other person, an interaction has already begun on some level. There is a faint exchange of energy. This interaction does not need to be verbal. An exchange can occur of feelings, visual images, or any combination of sensory stimuli. It can be a stream of consciousness like zoning, which I describe earlier in the book.

You can also have a conversation that begins with the mind but then brings up deep emotions. For example, you can have a conversation with an institution such as your college, the army, a sports team, a club, a church, or a religion. And you can have a conversation with nature—with the sea, the sky, the sun or moon, the Grand Canyon, Yosemite, Sedona, and so on. And, similarly, you can converse with a tree, your subconscious, with the past, with the future.

Dynamics of Dialoguing

In dialoguing, it is necessary to maintain the full tension of two different people, spirits, or things bringing their whole being into relationship with each other. If one side of the relationship becomes either dominant or passive, depth and connection are lost.

If individuals rely too heavily on their own imagination, instead of maintaining a focus on the other, the dialogue turns into fantasy. This fantasy can be exciting or nightmarish, but it is not transforming. And alternately, if the dialogue is focused solely on facts and history and leaves out imagination and consideration of possibilities, it loses opportunities. When both sides of the dialogue are equally active, there is a newness and unpredictability.

In all cases, you must remain directly focused on your own sensations, feelings, and perceptions. If you sustain a sense of wonder, beauty, light, life, and love, and if there is something you feel deeply about being expressed, then you have entered into a state of dialogue.

Someone asked, "What is the difference between dialoguing with a real mermaid and an imagined mermaid?" This can be compared to a dialogue with a real woman and with a fantasy. The fantasy can be amazing and enticing, but it makes no demands. A real woman, no matter how submissive, makes demands. Give and take are required for a connection to be real.

In Chokmah, we enter a dialogue with the divine world. This dialogue is ongoing. We bring the totality of ourselves to the conversation. We recall the entire history of our relationship, including what we have given to each other and learned from each other. And we consider possibilities—what we can do for each other or accomplish if we work together.

In such a dialogue, we create a "listening space"—or perhaps more accurately we could say we create a sacred space in which we are fully present with each other. This act of listening enables an exchange to occur on the deepest levels.

In Netzach, friendship and love are described as feeling you are within and living the other's life along with that person. In Chokmah, we can say that there is a conversation in which others' inspiration and light are within us and become our own. This level of interaction is basic for evoking the magic of Chokmah/Uranus.

The difference between this dialogue and the many kinds of prayer is that here we move halfway toward meeting the divine world. One way to do this is to imagine that you are the other side of the conversation. If you dialogue with another person in your mind, you will need to imagine that you are the other person when you respond.

Similarly, as a preliminary for dialoguing with the divine world, you imagine that you are the divine world when you respond. At least make an effort to assume its point of view, its knowledge, its wisdom, its will, and its love. Now, when you speak and listen for a response, your mind and heart are open so that the interaction is effective.

COMMON VIRTUE
....
Appreciation for the Gifts of the Future

Gratitude, thankfulness, appreciation, and celebration of the gifts of the future.

The two of cups tarot card depicts an exchange of feeling and love. An energy bond is created celebrating the moment and extending indefinitely into the future through an implied pledge and mutual commitment. What is within one is now also within the other. The two are now more than they would be on their own.

In Binah, without appreciating the sacrifices and gifts of the past, you cannot understand the present world. As Warren Buffett likes to tell his company managers, "Be grateful for all you have. You have more wealth than any king in history."

In the same way, without understanding something of how the future unfolds you are living an illusion. Your present understanding of yourself and the world just might be a complete illusion considering how things can radically shift in meaning due to future events. This translates as "be ready in any moment for monumental changes so you can move with them, seizing opportunities as they arise."

Two people can connect to each other in such a way that they describe their relationship as "we share the same soul." It is not just a flow of feeling going on between the two of them. It is more like a beam of light, which includes passion and even telepathic thoughts, connects them.

When Uranus is behind a relationship, it is not about falling suddenly, unexpectedly, and intensely in love, though that may be present. Instead, it is more like standing before a gate and through it you can see impossible and unimaginable things.

If you have paid your dues to Saturn, and are free of those attachments and faults that otherwise would bind you to the past, you can pass through this gate, take hold of some of those treasures, and bring them back to share with others in our world.

The lessons of Saturn grant you freedom. Uranus grants the magical keys that unfold and re-create the universe.

You will know when you are in the presence of someone adept with the two of cups of Uranus. It is easy to talk about the future in this person's presence. You may be sitting across from him at a table, but it is like he is already there in the future seeing what can be, as he speaks to you now about fulfilling your dreams.

An interesting exercise related to the two of cups is to imagine a friend in front of you. You each hold a cup filled with liquid. Now look into the other's cup and see what is there. Imagine tasting it and discover its qualities. Is it water, wine, or juice? Is it the taste of a vision? Do you go inside of a shared dream? What is the feeling?

And the same for your own cup. What are you giving to the other? What part is heart and love? What part is dream and vision? What part is desire and longing?

Now imagine the gift you might prefer to give to the other, and also what the other might be able to give to you. Friendship and love have depths, and these depths can change and be transformed by bringing your love and imagination into play.

With one friend, the cup she gives me tastes like white wine. The taste is of cool, soothing release. And my cup for her is the taste of supreme success in life.

If I were to ask for more, the cup she gives me would fill me with a sense of love saturating every cell in my body. And the cup I give to her would be success but also that same love—of feeling saturated with love in every cell of her body.

MAGICAL VIRTUE
Role-Playing the Future

Once again, in Chesed/Jupiter we bestow gifts that enrich other's lives, offering them new opportunities and horizons to explore. In Chokmah/Uranus, you are manifesting something that changes the world. The effects are much wider in scope.

The philanthropic foundations, the Ford, Carnegie, Rockefeller, and Bill and Melinda Gates Foundations, offer many benefits to others. But Henry Ford, the Wright Brothers, Tesla, and Edison changed civilization. Their activities are more like Uranus than Jupiter.

For Warren Buffett, one of the richest men in the world, you do not need to make a massive effort to succeed. You just need to do a few things really well and not make too many mistakes. That is very Jupiter. Uranian gifts to the world usually require a massive amount of research and preparation to reveal something new.

The difference between the dream we worked on manifesting in previous sephiroth and the dream in Chokmah is that our concentration is about ten times greater. You can see individuals act in an analogous way in daily life. You ask someone who is a master in his field to solve a problem, and he brings a great amount of experience to the effort. When he focuses his mind on the problem, he is in an altered state of consciousness. He is running through all possibilities, searching out the best solution. When I say he brings a great amount of experience to the problem he wishes to solve, he has already worked extensively on how the world can be engineered so it is more efficient and better.

Masters have made what they wish to manifest easy because they have put into it in advance an immense amount of work and research. Again, the Wright brothers researched the aerodynamics of the wings and turning mechanism on their plane. They built their own wind tunnel as they studied different designs. Edison experimented with thousands of materials before coming up with the right light bulb filament.

Marie Curie spent thousands of hours refining her elements to produce radium. The Manhattan project brought together a vast array of scientists and ran three separate industrial projects at the same time to acquire the fissionable material they needed for a bomb.

They were working to produce something that did not exist yet. Tesla had an actual picture in his mind of an alternating current engine. But it took years to produce a prototype.

To do these things, part of your imagination is in the future looking at what will be. And then you ask yourself, "What do I have to do so that this vision can become real?" And then you continue to work until the vision manifests.

In Yesod/Moon, we practiced dreaming what we wish to be as if it is real right now. In Binah/Saturn, we talked about placing causes (dreams to manifest) in Akasha. Here we take this act of dreaming further. We include in our dream all the experiences, virtues, and realizations of the previous eight sephiroth.

We are role-playing, in detail, the future. The focus, concentration, and force of personality carry with them a greater degree of conviction, clarity, and certainty. There is the motivational speaker with a ten-million-dollar house, and twenty cars in his garage—he dreamed a dream in Yesod of being happy, satisfied, successful, and experiencing "massive pleasure." But he has not yet made it to Chokmah/Uranus.

Again, compare the man who pursues the American Dream to Tesla, with a clear picture in his mind of an invention that would shape the next century. Tesla dreamed on behalf of the human race, as did Newton, Einstein, the Wright brothers, and Henry Ford.

In Chokmah/Uranus, our dreams bring through what is missing in life, not particularly for ourselves, but for the world. Consider a few such dreams:

> *That government of the people, by the people, for the people, shall not perish from the earth.*
>
> GETTYSBURG ADDRESS

> *I have a dream that one day this nation will rise up and live out the true meaning of its creed: "We hold these truths to be self-evident: that all men are created equal."*
>
> MARTIN LUTHER KING, JR.

I had a dream in which I heard the new anthem of a united North and South Korea. This is something I visualize. But at night when I slept, the song appeared to me from out of the future. I have dreamed of a spiritual community whose members are free of insecurity and fear. Through an inner union with each other, they serve not themselves or some narrowminded set of doctrines, but rather they oversee, as do the Earthzone spirits, the protection of the Earth and the evolution of the human race.

I have dreamed of women coming into their full spiritual power. I often speak of this in terms of an ancient time in Atlantis when such a magical group of women once existed.

> *There was an ancient order of women*
> *Whose magical beauty was so great*

> *They could dissolve all malice and hate.*
> *Every being was their friend.*
> *The broken heart they could mend*
> *And the lost soul was found again.*
> *For 5,000 years they ruled in complete secrecy*
> *Being free of the desire for fame and all vanity*
> *Until in the end*
> *Men sought knowledge instead of harmony*
> *And power instead of beauty.*
>
> FROM *STORIES OF MAGIC AND ENCHANTMENT*

And like that order of women, I have dreamed of a world in which a wisdom is present that can dissolve all malice and hate and restore those who are obsessed with power to a path that leads to the enlightenment of the world. In such a world, justice shall fill the Earth as water covers the seas.

QUESTION: When shall war be no more?

ISAPHIL: When there shall appear on Earth four or five in whom there is no fear; and whose souls are so clear that when malice, evil, or ill will draws near, these things dissolve as if they were never there.

When four or five shall remain in each generation, then your race shall awaken. The beauty of the stars and the seas and the mysteries shall appear within your dreams. These treasures of soul shall overflow, filling your world with light and healing.

I dream of a world in which human beings embody in themselves full consciousness of the four elemental realms hidden in nature. And in this dream and consciousness, the planet Earth itself fulfills one of its dreams—a race shall appear that shares the feelings in the heart of the Earth—for she feels one with the universe.

Conclusion

In Chesed/Jupiter, we acquire wealth that enables us to enrich the world. This is material wealth that provides connections and mobility in the outer world. And, equally, there is wealth of wisdom that grants us mobility in the inner, spiritual worlds. Such wealth gives us the ability to live life with grace, equilibrium, and nobility.

The wealth in Uranus is more magical. It shifts paradigms and designs new civilizations. We create multidimensional awareness. "In my father's house are many mansions." We not only visit these mansions. We make them available for others to visit.

Previously I have mentioned graphic imagination. With it, we experience as real whatever we are imagining. With the magical virtue of Chokmah, we use this graphic imagination to envision the future. We explore that future in great detail, making it a part of ourselves. And then we work until the future becomes a stable and enduring reality.

Any weakness, and the process can fail: Your imagination may not be clear and focused. You may not believe with 100 percent certainty in what you envision. Or you lack the adaptability, commitment, hard work, and resourcefulness needed to manifest it.

Henry Ford, having put into play a manufacturing process that would soon create more cars than horses in the United States, envisioned the same application for small planes. He had the idea of flying cars. But his timing was over a hundred years too soon.

DIVINE VIRTUE
Revealing New Magic to the World

I have mentioned that every revolutionary dreams of changing human nature. They all fail. This is because they lack the patience and wisdom to bring about such transformation. So they settle for controlling people by changing institutions in a way that keeps them in power.

The divine virtue in Chokmah reveals magic to the world in ways that change human nature. In the past, teaching magic has been strictly regulated. You find it in magical lodges who swear their members to secrecy on pain of death. Such groups have rank and authority that they use to exert strict control over members.

You find it in ritualized religions like the Hopi and ancient Hebrews. The Hopi would literally kill someone who made a mistake in performing one of their sacred rituals. And the Levites, the priests among the Jews for over three thousand years, still have genetic markers separating them from other Jews. In Tibetan, Hindu, and Taoist traditions, there are lineages of masters who carefully screen and prepare a small number of disciples to carry on their esoteric traditions.

The problem is that if someone makes contact with the vast inner dimensions of the magical world, or is touched by its immense power, they can literally go crazy. Or they suffer inflation of ego. They think they are already a divine being like a god, because of a few psychic feats they can perform. Or once introduced to other dimensions of awareness, they lose their ability to function in this world.

If you give magic to some people, they want to use it to be first in line to win the lottery. Or they use it to get people to buy whatever they are selling. Or they use it to take revenge on their enemies.

Obviously, people need to pay their bills. They want to be guided in their career choices. They would like to be blessed with love and good fortune. They would like to be inspired to be all that they can be. All the same, magic is a sacred power that should be used with great humility.

In this book, I present exercises relating to the four elements. Some of these can be safely practiced for a lifetime. And if you master them, they change human nature. But there are dangers to be faced and a price to be paid. Consider the meditation we did with the Water element.

Part I: Imagine that your blood is Water, since it is already around 82 percent water. Sense or imagine the sensation of that Water flowing through your body doing what Water does. It purifies, soothes, heals, and renews.

If you get very good at this meditation, you will discover that you can calm, soothe, and heal others, the way you do with yourself.

Part II: Imagine cold Water. For example, you can start by simply imagining your feet are immersed in icy, cold Water. Gradually you can extend this sensation through your whole body.

In my mind, these two exercises enable students to fulfill the prophecy of Christ, which has remained unfulfilled for two thousand years. Christ said, "Out of their bellies shall flow streams of living water." Every Christian church should designate one or more members to master the Water element until they are able to heal others. This is an application of the magical virtue of Chokmah.

Studying the Water element changes an individual. The bodies of men are too hot. Taking a cold shower or taking an ice bath does not do the trick. Having the best sex in the world will not change a man. The cold-water sensation and the receptivity of Water have to be internalized. At that point, the male has balanced himself with his female counterpart. He has acquired calmness, serenity, and a healing power that relationships themselves do not produce to this extent.

All the same, the Water element carries with it certain difficulties. It needs to be balanced with Earth, Air, Fire, and Akasha to be stable. The feelings in Water are so blissful and innocent it is very easy to lose one's survival instinct. As the song goes, "There is no sickness, no toil, or danger in that bright land to which I go."

For example, you cannot take your mind off of driving a car for more than a few seconds without risking an accident. Experiencing bliss and letting go into the flow do not harmonize well with being vigilant and fully aware of one's environment.

Experiencing bliss also puts an individual at risk of becoming narcissistic. Being enraptured with one's own feelings and sensations, an individual may ignore being empathic and caring. Though bliss can make an individual more confident and charismatic, it can also lead to becoming self-possessed.

The Water element, in its pure love, is very much at odds with the lower brain. Forged over hundreds of thousands of years, the lower brain demands that we be tenacious in defending boundaries, constantly in competition with others over acquiring resources, and that we seize whatever power we can, so that our weakness does not result in death. Consequently, the balance between feeling and pursuing necessities essential for survival are left to each individual to discover.

To give a gift of magic to the world, an individual will need the personal willpower of Mars, the mental clarity of Mercury, the awareness of one's subconscious of the Moon, and the practicality and stability of the Earth. And Saturn will weigh in with its demands that we take full responsibility for ourselves so that we are free inside, and not the plaything of obsessions and illusions.

A second magical exercise this book pursues is an empty mind. This "magical" state of awareness is taught in religions, but it is done in a proprietary and compartmentalized manner. You study Zen and the master may say, "It is impossible to have a mind free of thoughts for ten minutes." And so students do not try to develop such a mind.

Alternately, in some Hermetic traditions, the master will say, "Take a few weeks to practice having a mind free of thoughts for ten minutes." Sometimes if you tell someone they can do the improbable or the impossible, they will actually do it.

Or an empty mind can be taught, but its applications will be severely limited if this gift is approached in a narrow-minded way. In some traditions, they develop a superb mind free of distractions. But they add the assumption that the external world is not real. This is an extremely introverted approach to life.

The external world is very real. It has its own history, and it unfolds with momentum in a dynamic way. A new invention or discovery can affect everyone on Earth so their lives are fundamentally different. Make assumptions about your spiritual superiority, and you can end up losing your nation because you fail to notice someone is planning an invasion.

Or an empty mind is taught in a devotional context, such as opening your heart to experience divine grace. The emphasis is on purity, with the assumption that you are weak and need someone to save you from your own mistakes.

Or it is taught as one step in a series of exercises training the mind, so the individual becomes a master in a lineage, or else a supreme martial artist, able to defeat all opponents. Again, individuals can develop a masterful clarity of mind, but then it is only applied to maintaining the integrity of the individual's religion, lineage, or tradition.

An empty mind is far more than all of the above: an empty mind enables you to transfer your mind into—and experience—another person's consciousness. An empty mind is able to dissolve negativity. Negativity cannot survive a state of awareness that is unattached, due to being free of all form identification.

An empty mind is extremely receptive. As such, it is able to receive impressions from any spirit. Your mind creates a "listening space" in which the mind of others can be heard.

An empty mind is able to create and dissolve the four elements at will. This enables you to experience the mental aspect of the elements—will, love, intellect, and inner silence—and the feeling side—electrifying enthusiasm, oneness, joy, freedom, and rugged endurance.

It enables you to experience Akasha, in which you perceive life from other levels of awareness, such as experiencing the afterlife. An empty mind creates a judicial temperament. It is able to work with ambiguity and is free of insecurity. It is able to understand and to modify your own—and others'—karma.

It enables you to create heightened states of ecstasy and rapture—an inner peace with the universe, a love that has no end, a sense of oneness with all living beings, an appreciation of the wonder and beauty in each moment of time, a spaceless and timeless state of awareness from which all things arise, and a great harmony that governs the unfolding of the universe.

We might imagine Saturn and Uranus giving an interview to those who intend to practice magic. Saturn asks, "Have you taken responsibility for all the decisions you have made and for all aspects of your life?

"If so, then let me introduce you to my friend Uranus. He will show you that you are a divine being and that you possess magical powers that you will find very useful for transforming yourself and the world.

"But if you touch these magical powers before you are ready, you will find yourself back in one of the previous sephiroth, which you will then experience in its negative aspects. This is not a judgment or failure. It is simply an indication that you need more experience with life before you take into your hands the powers of a creator."

In Binah, the task is to discover your deepest lessons in life and then take the time and make the effort to learn them. My deepest lessons related to mastering several elements. By contrast, in Chokmah, my task has been to uncover the magic in each of the five elements and then to use that power to re-create myself. Every conflict I have had in life dissolves as I master the five elements. You can create harmony and peace in the outer world because you have learned first to create harmony and peace within yourself.

The Hero's Journey

The divine virtue of Chokmah is revealing new magic to the world. But there is a story that often accompanies this. Joseph Campbell, the mythologist, refers to it as the hero's journey.

For Joseph Campbell, one story is told throughout the world in a thousand different ways: Though living in safe, secure, and familiar circumstances, the hero is called, accidentally stumbles, or else is tricked into crossing the boundary demarcating the familiar world and the unknown.

He leaves behind the setting of family and protective community. In doing so, he bypasses the shadowy figures or culturally sanctioned guardians who watch over the boundaries leading into the unknown.

Because he travels beyond the safe limits of conventional knowledge, he acquires unusual companions—animal, human, or divine—who aid him in his journey. Along the way, he overcomes dangers, traps, and monsters.

Finally, after undergoing a supreme ordeal, he discovers various kinds of treasures. But the journey is not yet complete. These treasures must be brought back and shared with others, for the value of what he finds is not known to him or us until it is established within the human community.

"Though living in safe, secure, and familiar circumstances . . . "
You probably already had your own life laid out before you. For example, go to college. Get a job. Marry. Raise a family. Participate in social institutions such as attending church. Retire. Grow old. Die.

"The hero is called, accidentally stumbles, or else is tricked into crossing the boundary demarcating the familiar world and the unknown."
There is more: He wanders due to intense curiosity or restlessness, is caught up in or swept away, *called,* invited, conned, set up, fooled, hired, bribed, ordered, conscripted, coerced, enticed, or seduced.

I like to say, magic is so dangerous that you need to be:

1. Called, as in having an angel appear to you, God speak to you, or a vision presented to you.
2. Have a problem that requires magic as the only solution.
3. Possess superhuman patience.

"Follow your bliss" will not take you on this journey. For example, there are the ecstasies of the four elements that are beginning to well up inside of you: an outrageous, otherworldly sense of freedom and celebration, an innocence that draws upon a love that embraces the universe, an indestructible sense of will, or an inner silence that is so complete you can hear the voice of any being speak.

In the dynamics of storytelling as outlined by Robert McKee, a story begins with the "inciting incident." The inciting incident propels you to take some sort of action in pursuit of an object of desire, conscious or even unconscious, that will restore harmony to your life: zombies run riot, a beautiful princess needs to be rescued, your plane/train/building is hijacked, your country invaded, you witness a murder, you are recruited as a spy, bad things begin happening to you, you inherit a castle, you are fired from your job, your spouse divorces you, and so on.

My life's inciting incident is my practicing in third grade "duck and cover." Get under your desk in school because in thirty minutes a nuclear war could send the human race back to the stone age, and/or destroy the ozone layer that would make life extremely difficult. At least five times we have been minutes, if not seconds, away from an all-out nuclear exchange.

And as if this vision of nuclear fire consuming entire cities was not enough, the church ministers enjoyed an adrenaline rush as they talked about hellfire and damnation of the soul. I found such visions intolerable. There was human or spiritual power but there was absolutely nothing comparable in terms of wisdom being presented.

And then we have Chernobyl and Fukushima reactors in full meltdown, but our nuclear physics programs taught in universities around the world have developed no plan B for dealing with this crisis. How stupid is that?

"He leaves behind the setting of family and protective community. In doing so, he bypasses the shadowy figures or culturally sanctioned guardians who watch over the boundaries leading into the unknown."

"The shadowy figures or culturally sanctioned guardians": Like the Dean of students who kicked out thirty students in my class of '69 during the summer before our senior year. I talked him into putting me on probation. Like the president of the college who called me into his office and said my sensibilities were questionable because of a movie review I did for the school newspaper. Like the ministers and preachers who insisted they and they alone knew the absolute truth regarding life, death, salvation, and how to live a good life. After all, some of them had glanced into the unknown and realized in that moment that only terror lurked there, and darkness, and devilish woes. No, for them, all spiritual realms are off-limits. Spiritual perception should never be pursued.

Like the professors whose focus was on the past, and not the present or future. Like the other students and friends who occasionally might sense a gate leading to the astral plane but quickly turned back. To obliterate the memory of what they saw, they attached themselves to a strict set of theological doctrines. Like the girl whose face turned white when she stepped inside the Theosophical Society bookstore. I realized in that moment I could never marry a Christian. My curiosity requires me to study all world religions, and all genuine paths of spirit.

What defines a boundary? On the other side is the unknown landscape of the soul that is tremendously time-and energy-consuming. This is because there are no reference points, no maps, no paths to follow, no paradigms, no doctrines, no creeds, no religions—all of the above no longer apply.

And then too there is the immense isolation. Franz Bardon evoked hundreds of spirits during the late hours of night in a graveyard. During their quests, all the great world teachers passed through this separation from other people. In the stories of their lives, this is impossible to miss.

After all, a vision quest is your vision. Once enlightened, Buddha said that enlightenment cannot be taught. But, as the story goes, Indra, king of the gods, persuaded him to teach so that the gods themselves could overcome their karma.

Solomon had no one he could talk to who could possibly understand his wisdom. He could see that instantly when he spoke to others.

And John the Baptist, the foremost promoter of Jesus, was genuinely perplexed and confused. So he sent his disciples to ask Jesus, "Are you he that should come? Or should we look for another?" And Jesus himself pointed out that it was a Roman centurion, not even a Jew, who had the greatest faith of anyone in Israel.

You journey beyond the conventional boundaries of society intent on completing your life's work, and no one understands who you are or what you are doing. That is psychological isolation.

"Because he travels beyond the safe limits of conventional knowledge, he acquires unusual companions—animal, human, or divine—who aid him in his journey."
In college, I began to meet women who I called "door people." I did not know how to define what I was describing. But later on, I realized these individuals felt unusual things that were beyond anything I had ever encountered before. Like an inner sense of well-being, an inner peace, or they could perceive the astral plane. This meant, for example, that they could accept who I was. I have never run into anyone who could accept me as I am. You have to act normal, otherwise people experienced acute anxiety being around you.

Decades later I would sense that some of these "door people" did not have human souls. They were incarnated mermaids, sylphs, Fire elementals, gnomes, starseeds, and more. Such beings have a vast range of feelings and intuitions as well as psychic and spiritual powers. Some of them could do things that rivaled even the great world teachers.

Why did the Brothers Grimm in Germany not notice such people as they went around collecting fairy tales? The Brothers Grimm were focused on establishing a body of literature. They were not trained in ethnography, in which you carefully listen to the experiences of an individual, rather than a story handed down from generation to generation.

Why did Carl Jung not write about door people? Jung was

focused on the dynamics of the archetypes in the collective unconscious, like the great mother, the father, the child, the maiden, the
hero, the trickster, and so on. If Jung met an incarnated mermaid, he
would only notice that she was remarkably vivacious and unusually
attractive in a way he could not define. And this is because incarnated elementals are not a part of the collective unconscious of the
human race.

They are identical with nature (have nature at the core of their
being). When they relax, their aura vibrates directly as a lake, a river, an
ocean bay, or the entire ocean. In their natural state, they have no ego,
no social identification, and no human causes that they feel compelled
to embrace. Jung would have to study Hermetic psychology—to find
the universe reflected inside of yourself—if he wanted to understand
such women.

From time to time, the divine offers you gifts. There is the clairsen-
tience that enables you to read the aura of any human being or spirit.
It also enables you to study how the mind of these beings work as well.
You can literally think their thoughts.

This clairsentience is part of the basic training manual for Hermetic
students—*Initiation into Hermetics*. But the manual does not explain
all the applications and the range of what you are given.

And from time to time, divine beings offer you gifts. One brings
back a muse you had in another lifetime. Another refers you to spirits
who serve as consultants on your quest. Some make suggestions that it
takes you decades to understand. Finally, you "get it," grasping what was
so obvious to the spirit.

And some offer you joint projects to fulfill—act as an ambassador
for their realm. Describe in detail exactly what is required to move back
and forth between their realm on the astral plane, and the world in
which we exist.

"Along the way, he overcomes dangers, traps, and monsters."
Like what? Like be willing to pass through the darkness in yourself. Nearly all brilliant students of the spiritual realms fail in
this task.

There is recapturing projection. Some women are so beautiful, so enchanting, that it is best to forget that you ever met them. Or else you have to go on a quest and make the realm from which she came your home as well.

Or there is again that problem no one seems able to solve. Once touched by power, people become obsessed with acquiring more. This problem is not particularly your problem, though it stares you in the face every single day. It is a problem between the archetypes in the collective and global unconscious.

And why is that a problem? Let's look at it. In this moment I can sense a love that embraces the universe. It is everywhere. It is within everything. It is a sovereign queen that oversees the unfolding of every life and is within and nurturing the soul of every being.

And equally in this moment, I can sense a sovereign and absolute power that can take any vision and make it real. There is no limit on its authority or range of actions.

But this all-embracing love and sovereign, absolute power do not work together, at least not in human history. To study this, look at a relationship between a man and a woman. Find a man who is strong, certain, possesses absolute conviction, and is 100 percent committed to his purposes. (I am using male/female out of convenience. These abilities are not limited to gender.)

And find a woman who can fully embrace all that this man is— understanding every aspect of his thoughts, every feeling he feels, every sensation in his body. And not only that.

When he thinks about what he wishes to accomplish, she makes that vision fully alive as if it is already real. She brings it to life not only for him but everyone whom he contacts. She is his muse, his spirit guide, and his guardian angel. They share the same soul.

Now to complete our exercise, imagine that she can do the same that she does for her lover with any other man or woman on Earth. Take the absolute worst of humanity—like those dictators that each year right now are responsible for killings tens of thousands of people through their actions. She can also transform them as well, turning them from darkness to the light. This benevolent influence within the global archetypes does not yet exist on Earth.

"Finally, after undergoing a supreme ordeal, he discovers various kinds of treasures. But the journey is not yet complete. These treasures must be brought back and shared with others, for the value of what he finds is not known to him or us until it is established within the human community."

It is far more difficult to share with another what you experience so that he makes it his own, than it is to go on a quest and acquire whatever realization, enlightenment, or wisdom that you were seeking. And this is where all of our world teachers have failed us. They did not find a way to effectively teach so that they could hand down to others the spirit that was inside of themselves.

In a sense, the goal from the first moment you are "called" or begin a quest is to figure out how you are going to share with others what you find. One partial answer is to create a spiritual university. Enable the student to study with all the great masters of the Earth. Present wisdom that is universal and cosmic in depth.

And then do what Joseph Campbell says mythology itself does. Stimulate students' curiosity. Offer them new and unknown places to explore. Speak to their restlessness. Challenge them to dream. Capture their attention with wonders and visions. Call them. Invite them. Write screenplays and produce movies. Give seminars, whatever it takes, so they experience something of the beauty and wonder of the universe that radiates from within them and is them.

DREAM

The dream in Chokmah is of being magical. And this is as it should be, for the magical side of life contains many upgrades and enhancements. If you can tap onto them, then you are living a different life in a different world.

You can overturn the weight of karma and fate. You can manifest dreams and visions that are improbable or near impossible. You can reveal things that otherwise remain unknown.

In magic, you have multidimensional awareness. You discover you now have the keys to many mansions of the soul.

You unite from within to the dynamic powers unfolding the universe. You find nature at the core of your being.

You are able to evoke and converse with spirits that oversee and guide human and spiritual evolution. And you can reach the point where you are acting as a higher spirit who is also fully active in incarnation as a human being.

The "dark" side of magic, like the dark side of the American Dream, is that you imagine you can get something for nothing, like "The world owes me" or "If you can reach out and take something, then it is yours to possess."

In the bad dream of magic, as in the dream of all dictators, you control the world with your will. You are never held accountable, and you never have to change, develop, or grow.

In the "good" dream of magic, you have a sense of awe and appreciation for the beauty of the universe. For you, life is sacred and every moment is filled with wonder. And though you may have powers and abilities beyond what others can imagine or dream, everything you do is characterized by harmony, fairness, and justice. The "you" never gets in the way of the purposes you pursue.

INITIATION

In the psychological practice of focusing taught by Eugene Gendlin, you focus on a problem from a clear space inside yourself. You next find a "felt sense" for the sensations in your body that appear as you contemplate your problem. You then make sure that the images or words you use to describe this felt sense are accurate.

Next you ask, "What is underneath or behind this?" And now you wait in silence for a physical sensation as a response. Opening your whole body and psyche so they can respond to your problem is your guide.

In the initiation of Chokmah, you enter into a state of Nirva Kalpa Samadhi, a sense of being united to everything that exists. Here too you wait in silence, listening, except you are not asking a question. You are listening for the right question to appear.

All the same, there are questions suitable for this kind of silence meditation: "What is missing from life? What is the highest purpose for my life? What events in the future must be prepared for now, if suffering is to be reduced on Earth? What part do I have to play in the unfolding of the world?"

We have touched on silence in other sephiroth. In the divine virtue in Malkuth, "In silence we shut down the world so it becomes still like a moment frozen in time. Though remaining completely detached, we look around in wonder."

In the magical virtue in Tiferet: "In stillness, things become calm, quiet, relaxed, and at peace. There is a sense that motion, movements in time, cease and then you perceive with great clarity."

And in the magical virtue of Binah we take "the void," a vast, empty state of mind, and meditate on it until it feels like home. Here in Chokmah, we are entering the silence of the Earth where we reach the highest state of receptivity, for the soul of the Earth feels one with all things.

As Franz Bardon has the student practice for each of his twenty-seven cosmic letters, you join yourself with Divine Providence in some aspect. And then, as you listen, it is your own voice that you hear speaking and pointing out where you should give your full attention. As in the quote, "Learn to listen so well that Divine Providence considers you part of itself."

If you should succeed in this initiation that involves listening, then, at least when you meditate, you will have the same awareness as Divine Providence. You will have the same purposes and you will plan the same actions. In which case, you have turned your soul into a pure, receptive, listening space, a magical silence, in which the voice of the divine world can be heard.

MYSTERY
Divine Missions

Franz Bardon refers to divine missions in a number of places in his writing. For example, in his book *The Practice of Magical Evocation*, Bardon describes Cigila, a spirit of the sign of Pisces in the Earthzone, in this way:

Since this head is a special initiator into, and a teacher of, magical kabbalistic mysticism, he can make the magician acquainted with secret methods which enable the latter to develop within himself in all three planes—the mental, the astral and the physical—the most perfect divine virtues by the help of magic and kabbalah.

Having developed within himself these virtues, the magician will then find it easy to acquire all those faculties which are connected to these virtues. The magician following these secret methods becomes more and more mature in fulfilling carefully certain tasks according to the will of Divine Providence.

However, Cigila only reveals these secret methods to the magician who has already reached a certain degree of maturity in magic and kabbalah during previous incarnations. A magician developed due to these methods in a god-like creature, a personified deity, equipped with all the virtues, powers and faculties, equal to Divine Providence.

If Cigila were incarnated, he would be the teacher I have always wanted to meet. He would be a student of the wisdom of all traditions. He would know more about the issues that concern our planet than any politician, scientist, ecologist, activist, or head of any intelligence service. And when he speaks, he would speak with the voice of the Earth about how you can use your life in the most beneficial and far-reaching way to assist mankind.

In other words, Cigila has a fabulous way of developing your spiritual identity. You perceive the world with great sensitivity and prophetic vision. The extent and strength of your perception are astonishing. Yet for Cigila, divine beings take responsibility for particular areas of life. Service keeps you grounded and practical. Without working on behalf of mankind, Cigila's transcendental powers could begin to dissolve an individual's ties to the world in which he has incarnated.

To meditate with Cigila is to perceive a thousand civilizations rise and fall before your eyes. And then the question is put to you, "What part will you play as you incarnate among these worlds? What divine gifts will you share and impart to others? What work will you accomplish as a token and symbol of the infinite light and love that shine within your soul?"

Another spirit says in regard to someone on a divine mission, "Most of all he will need to be able to relax and feel that he is at peace with the universe. When he meditates, he must be able to feel that every need and desire that he can feel, imagine, or dream is already satisfied."

In 1979, I placed an electromagnetic volt in a small horseshoe magnet following the instructions of Franz Bardon. This volt is a ball of electrical energy surrounded by a ball of magnetic energy. I used the vibration of Cigila in both the electric and magnetic fluids. I then placed within this energy medium a request for assistance.

I was after a sense of quality control. I was still at the beginning of my practice with Franz Bardon's Hermetics, and I wanted some sort of guidance and assurance that I would stay on track and follow through with the training. I sensed in advance that the stakes were high, and also the difficulties before me were immense.

Shortly thereafter, I had a waking dream in which I saw a conflict in the future between the United States and Russia that would lead to an all-out nuclear war. The dream in effect was saying, "OK. Here is a problem for the human race. Are you interested in helping solve it?"

This was a dream sent by Cigila. But he himself did not wish to oversee my work in this area. Instead at the time he referred me to two others spirits who specialized in resolving geopolitical conflicts.

Thus began forty-nine years of doing regular meditations on world leaders. This type of practice was within my capabilities. I already had a level of clairsentience that enabled me to read and study the aura of any human being or spirit. I had previous lifetimes where I engaged in the exact same activity. And I had the free time to do extensive research and training.

What I did not have was a manual on "How to Establish Peace Between Nations." If the U.N. Security Council did its job, then such magical activity would be totally unnecessary. Then my life could have taken a completely different course. But human beings are not enlightened when it comes to power. Power for nearly every politician is usually an uncontrollable obsession.

Work like this is rather consuming. It takes great effort to balance one's personal life with genuine magical training. It takes, as Bardon suggests, a near superhuman level of patience.

Ideally, then, to pursue a divine mission, you put yourself in a state of meditation in which you feel at peace with the universe—that a great peace, harmony, stillness, and wisdom govern the unfolding of all things. And from this state of mind, you consider what things you can do to reduce suffering on Earth and to assist mankind to attain maturity.

You need the inner peace because Uranian gifts are very stressful and cause a lot of tension. They do so because they are so new and unexpected, and they do not necessarily build on past traditions.

Without the inner peace and stillness, world teachers and revolutionaries have fanatical, rigid, and blind followers. These followers demand conformity. Others have to feel, think, and do as they do as they enforce narrow and rigid codes of morality and behavior. Without the inner connection to the divine, missions become crusades, acts of revenge, and power plays to take control and to dominate. These individuals are not on a divine mission. They are on an earthly conquest to enhance the interests of a specific group of people.

Pursuing a divine mission also places you in a crash course on resolving karmic issues. Some of these issues are personal. And yet when examined from the point of view of a divine quest, they take you down into the depths of the collective unconscious if you are to work through them.

On the one hand, you experience three or more lifetimes in one incarnation. On the other hand, the problems you confront are far beyond what other people have to address.

Put briefly, live a simple life free of conflict. Work hard. Demand assistance when you need it and you will be given it. But never relent or lose focus on your commitments.

You are journeying between worlds, casting aside what is no longer needed, and making friends of people and beings of which others have never dreamed. Then again, if you find this a natural calling, it is really just carrying on the same work you have pursued in other lifetimes. Now, however, in this age of the world there are so many more opportunities given to those who pursue ideals such as this.

Common Difficulties

The reason Cigila prefers individuals who have been magicians in previous lifetimes is because his level of power requires someone who has already worked through the basic issues of magic. The ability to shift in and out of a spiritual identity has already been established. The ability to take hold of karma and transform it through spiritual will—this too is a basic requirement. There is a need to look at your life situation from the point of view of your personality, and also from that of your spirit. This internal dialogue you have practiced many times before.

The personality says, "Here are my needs. I am not going to get very far without meeting them." And the spirit replies, "Since you have committed yourself to a higher purpose, here is what we can do with your situation. Your karma can be quickly resolved—hatred turned to love, obsession to wisdom, and fear to the power hidden within it."

There are other differences to consider. Individuals without a thorough training in magic from previous lives are involved in a discovery process. They ask themselves questions such as, "Is magic real?" "What should I believe in, and does my faith connect me to divinity?" "Am I pure enough to work with power without surrendering to selfish desires?" "Why don't other people recognize how important I am?"

Or, if they can prove to themselves that they are clairvoyant or telepathic, they ask, "What should I do with these abilities? Shall I use my supernatural gifts to make money or to get others to do what I want? Or shall I discover if there really is a spiritual world with beings of light and angelic nature hovering just out of sight?"

And they also sometimes say, "I shall be cautious with my powers. I do not want to know things that will make me different from others or that will disturb or threaten my identity." Individuals exploring magic for the first time have many issues to resolve.

Others who have been magicians before also may not be interested in working with divine missions. These are individuals whom Buddhists sometimes refer to as *arhats*. They have attained a degree of enlightenment through their own means. They are fiercely independent and cherish their autonomy. When they reincarnate, they automatically sense the power within themselves and desire to develop it further.

But the main theme governing their development is accomplishing things through their own efforts. They take pride in what they do, and they wish to be dependent on no one else. Such individuals may choose to become businessmen rather than magicians. This is because business celebrates and rewards in obvious ways those who are dynamic and powerful in accomplishing their aims.

A divine mission requires an individual to experience, to develop, and finally to identify with a transcendent awareness within himself. And it requires an individual to have a judicial temperament by being a person who can research and carefully weigh issues before making judgments. And these must be combined with an indestructible will and with compassion. Such an individual seizes opportunities as they arise and perseveres in his work over the course of a lifetime in order to make a better world.

RULE 1

KETHER/NEPTUNE

Crown, Oneness

Basic Quality	The higher self
Virtues, Vices, Negative	Higher conscience/Dreamy/Twisted
Challenge	A time to think, perceive, and act as a divine being
Magical Practice	Mindfulness—the great now
Common Virtue	The four aces of the tarot: the elements overflowing from within
Magical Virtue	Androgyny
Divine Virtue	Becoming a divine being
Dream	Imagine being whole and complete in every way
Initiation	Being your own guardian angel
Mystery	Multidimensional awareness

If you consider yourself a spiritual person, you are perhaps already in love with Kether. It feels like home. As one girl says, "I am already in heaven." To be aware of Kether is to feel heaven is close by and a part of you.

And yet, as some of the spirits of the sphere of Venus like to do, if you are passionate about another person and want to deepen your love, the spirit will advise you to work at what is weak in yourself.

If you want to become one with another, then become a person who is capable of such oneness. Strengthen your identity. Establish peace and contentment in yourself. And develop a clear and penetrating mind. Develop communication and problem-solving skills. Now you are able to deepen your connection to another so the relationship is stable and enduring.

Kether is like that. It insists you take a hard look at yourself. Do whatever you need to do to make up for the part of yourself that is still weak or undeveloped.

BASIC QUALITY
The Higher Self

The basic quality of Kether is the higher self. It is our inner source of inspiration. Put simply, developing an awareness of our higher self is learning to feel, think, and perceive as a divine being. There is transcendence—complete detachment. And yet there is total empathy—feeling one with everything within and around us.

VIRTUES, VICES, NEGATIVE

Virtues: Higher conscience, the wisdom and benevolence of a guardian angel, making things right. A still, quiet voice. A moral compass. Clear priorities.

Vices: Dreamy, otherworldly, ensnared in fantasies, not in your body, confusion over boundaries separating the inner and outer worlds, lack of respect for karmic limitations, lack of interest in mastering basic life skills, stuck—repeating experiences without learning. Loss of hope, inspiration, and a sense of who you are and who you are meant to be.

Negative: Twisted. Jaded. Possessed. Overshadowed by the will of others. You have destroyed your conscience. You are cast out, condemned, cursed. You feel that everything that makes life meaningful and worth living is taken from you.

CHALLENGE

In religious terms: "God is near. He is within each of us." Be still and sense this presence.

In terms of Kabbalah, you are a divine being. Put aside time to think, feel, perceive, and act as a divine being.

The challenge in Kether is to exercise oversight of all the previous sephiroth. You want to ensure that each gets the attention it needs to develop according to its own methods and purposes. Kether wants them equally developed and in harmony with each other.

We introduced the idea of magical equilibrium in Gevurah/Mars—we want to master all aspects of the self. Take weak traits and make them strong. Take passive traits and make them active. Take the negative and make it positive. What is involved here is giving your full attention to those things that are otherwise ignored.

There is one additional principle in Kether/Neptune—perfect all aspects of oneself. Take the human and what is of nature and transform it into divinity. Take an individual living within the limitations of an incarnation and turn him into a divine being.

In poetic format, when Jacob wrestles with an angel he is certainly engaged in the themes and purposes of Chokmah/Uranus—he is forming a partnership with a divine being in order to secure a blessing.

But more is implied. Jacob wishes to enter and participate in the divine workshop. He wishes to comingle with the divine and share in its creativity.

> *Grasping a better hold as he wrestled with the angel,*
> *Balanced, poised, muscles flexed, teeth clenched,*
> *Jacob spoke, his jaw next to the angel's ear:*
> *When you love,*
> *What is it like to love when your love*
> *Arises from a sea of infinite bliss*
> *So every abyss is filled*
> *And darkness*
> *Is forever banished from your vision?*
> *The Angel replies:*

When I meditate,
I become pure light.
And in this state of mind
I am united to all beings who love
Throughout the universe.
But know this:
I am but a small part
Of what you are destined to become.

MAGICAL PRACTICE
Mindfulness—The Great Now

The magician lives, if possible, exclusively in the present,
looking back only if the need arises.

FRANZ BARDON

Mindfulness is being aware of the internal and external experiences occurring in this moment. In focusing on these experiences, there are different things to consider. First, being mindful is a way of stepping back and looking at the context in which our thoughts, feelings, sensations, and actions occur. We can have strong emotions, but we are not those emotions. We can have strong sensations, but we are not those sensations. We can have compelling thoughts, but we are not those thoughts.

There is a distance between ourselves and what happens within and around us. Mindfulness is remaining aware of this open space of consciousness in which events occur. Second, humans have a subconscious. We have desires, motivations, and also inspirations and purposes that are hidden or barely perceptible to our conscious mind. Becoming aware of the subconscious is an ongoing process. The subconscious has its own language and its own ways of organizing experience. To be aware of this side of ourselves will require some detachment and an appreciation of the life unfolding within us.

Third, each of the five senses vibrates with pleasure, bliss, ecstasy, wonder, and rapture. To be mindful is to be in a constant attentiveness and exploration of the five sense perceptions.

Fourth, to quote Franz Bardon: "The faculty of concentration with respect to the elements depends on the magic equilibrium, and is the best standard to check which of the astral body's elements have yet to be brought under control. For example, if the Fire element can still get hold of the magician's astral faculties, he will not succeed very well in visualization exercises. In the case of the Air element, the acoustic exercises probably will become more difficult for him; as for the Water element, difficulties will arise from the concentration on the feeling; and in the case of the Earth element, the control of the consciousness will be impaired."

Mindfulness is being aware of the continuous revelations of Water's feeling, Fire's will, Air's clarity, and Earth's productivity, and how these interact in each moment. Awareness itself is shaped by the balance of the four elements within us. Our daily life is an ongoing study of how the different sides of ourselves interact.

Fifth, we do not live in a feudal society with extremely limited social mobility. Our democratic, postindustrial, pluralistic societies give us leisure time in which we are able to participate in many different endeavors and activities. And yet a modern society depends on its citizens to keep it running effectively. You do not want people checking out, living on the fringe, or off-the-grid. In a modern context, we need to sustain a sense of peace and also a willingness to participate. Being aware of the society in which we live is a part of being aware of ourselves.

Sixth, you will know when you meet someone who lives in the Akashic Now. He has an appreciation of how the unknown universe is continuously revealing itself as ever new in each moment. That is, wonder is always present.

He looks for harmony beneath every conflict; and he has a profound kindness, for he wishes to touch life with tenderness, realizing that the sacred is here and now and everywhere.

And this also—with such an individual, you will feel that no one has ever given you so much undivided attention. Truly, he looks at you with a sense of awe, respect, and appreciation, for he sees you as himself in another form.

Seventh, as the Heart Sutra asserts, "Form does not differ from emptiness, and emptiness does not differ from form. Perception, conception, volition, and consciousness are also like this." In each moment, we can sense Akasha, the fifth element. It is present as an awareness of being surrounded by a vast, empty space filled with infinite possibilities.

Eighth, each person will discover his or her own way of seeking to be fully aware in the present moment. Here are a few statements indicating a variety of responses:

> *My only wish is to be in the moment and to enjoy every second of it.*
>
> SUN TWIRL

> *There is no "I was" or "I will be." Only "I am."*
>
> MORAN

> *Heaven is not over yonder. I am already in heaven.*
>
> A MERMAID WOMAN

> *"Do any human beings ever realize life while they live it?—every, every minute?"*
> *The Stage Manager replies, "No. Saints and poets maybe . . . they do some."*
>
> OUR TOWN

> *A student asks his master, "What is Dzogchen?"*
> *The master replies, "Do you hear the sound of the dog barking?"*
> *"Yes," says the student.*
> *"Do you hear the sound of my voice?" asks the master.*
> *"Yes," says the student,*
> *"Do you see the stars in the sky?" asks the master.*
> *"Yes," says the student.*
> *"This is Dzogchen," says the master. "It is clarity of mind, spontaneity of response, and appropriate action in which separation, confusion, and conflict effortlessly dissolve into harmony."*
>
> FROM THE TIBETAN TRADITION OF VAJRAYANA

COMMON VIRTUE

The Four Aces of the Tarot:
The Elements Overflowing from Within

Thankfulness, gratitude, appreciation, and celebration of the four elements overflowing in one's soul.

Our breath joins us to the Air element and the atmosphere. Through the flow of Water and blood in us, we are joined to the Water element in the rivers, lakes, and seas.

Our physical body sustained by food and drink joins us to the physical world of nature. And our metabolism producing heat and energy joins us to Fire in nature and the radiance of the sun.

The physical elements also have their astral components. In Air are clarity of mind, a feeling of freedom, and harmony. In Water are innocence, love, and empathy. In Fire are vision, power, and will. And in Earth are stability and integration of consciousness and the ability to perform work in the world.

The elements of Earth, Water, Air, and Fire were introduced in Malkuth, Yesod, Hod, and Tiferet. In Gevurah, the elements were deepened, and the inner union with nature was presented as astral immortality. Here in Kether, where we meet divine creativity in its full measure, the four elements overflow from within us, enriching the world. There is no end to the giving.

MAGICAL VIRTUE

Androgyny

In Gevurah, masculine and feminine are approached in terms of self-mastery. If you are committed to something, you want to bring all of your resources to the task at hand. You want to use a will that expresses itself in dynamic action and resolve.

But you do not want to stop there. Certainly, you want to love what you are doing and use intuitive insight. Martial artists, in addition to their skills with weapons, are also known to have mastered internal silence, patience, and rugged endurance. Feeling is more important than thinking. In Gevurah, you master yourself in order to accomplish your mission.

In Kether, masculine and feminine are explored in their depths. The goal is a creativity that embraces all of life. This involves androgyny, an inner union of masculine and feminine. You unite these opposites in yourself so that life in every aspect is reflected in you.

And so immediately we are confronted by our culture. Once you give men a spear, a bow, a mallet, a knife, or a plow, the masculine in men becomes thirty, maybe a hundred times more powerful than the feminine in women. Giving women a dress to wear, a flower and hairbrush for her hair, laundry to wash, a kettle, a hearth, and fire to cook, perfume, lipstick, a lute to play, a dance, and a song to sing does not restore the balance.

For the last eight thousand years, we have been concentrating on developing the masculine with its emphasis on detachment, science, technology, control of natural resources, and, above all else, its will to power. The masculine has almost exclusively been focused on industry, productivity, and innovation.

To make matters worse, our entire civilization is fiery and electrical. We have individuals who act like incarnated Fire spirits. They reveal new applications of Fire to the world. For example, we have Edison, Tesla, Westinghouse, Nobel, Henry Ford, the Wright brothers, and Oppenheimer. We have the entire complex of computer and internet technology, mobility in transportation, and industrial powers that seize and transform nature.

This means the masculine (extroversion, external control of the environment, dynamic action, and applied force) is far more advanced in shaping human experience than is the feminine (intuitive perception, empathy, feeling, nurturing, inner soul-to-soul connection, and all-embracing love).

Lacking empathy, clairsentience, a direct connection to nature, and pure innocence, a man will tend to be narrow-minded because he clings to thoughts in order to think; he will be self-possessed because he has not learned to put his ego off to the side; he will be vain and selfish because he does not know how to give all of himself in every moment; and his will becomes twisted because he does not have a clue as how to join himself to the deepest purposes of life.

The Feminine

To review, feminine energy is cool, soothing, contracting, and attractive. It is nurturing and supportive. It contains within itself so as to shelter and protect. Instead of intense and explosive, it is rhythmic, receptive, and gentle.

In psychological terms, it is empathic, sensitive, and responsive. It draws together, bonds, joins, and unites. It accepts and affirms.

On the mental plane, the feminine presence calms the mind, exchanging the process of thinking for an expansion of sensory perception. It amplifies awareness so that Water becomes part of one's nervous system. You become aware of the subtle nuances of physical and emotional vibrations.

In spiritual terms, it reaches toward all-embracing, all-encompassing love. It presents us with astonishing states of awareness that transcend individual identity. Such states involve wonder, ecstasy, and beauty.

✴ Exercise: Feminine Energy in Nature

There are a great many ways that masculinity and femininity are brought into balance, harmonized, integrated, fused together, and united. I am emphasizing connecting to nature—seeing that human beings embody the energies of nature in a way that balances opposites in the individual and also furthers the evolution of the planet.

Imagine a still mountain lake behind the woman. It is early morning. There is a gentle breeze with mist dancing on the surface and rays of golden sunlight gliding down. The lake reflects the surrounding forest and mountains like a mirror. Look at the woman. The beauty of the universe is shining from her face.

And now visualize the sea behind the woman. Vast in expanse, it spreads out between continents. Ancient as the Earth, its shallows and depths have brought forth life, organic from inorganic being. The sea is also a magnetic field that supports and nurtures every dream.

Imagine this planetary magnetic field is within and around the woman. It is part of her, and she is in harmony with it. Sense what that would be like—there is no end to her attractive energies; the beauty of life is welling up inside of her; and she is one with anything she focuses on, bringing it to maturity and making it fully alive.

The Masculine

To review, the energy in men is hot, burning, expansive, dynamic, intense, powerful, and explosive in sensation. It has the capacity to produce great light. In psychological terms, it is commanding, full of faith and conviction. It reaches for sovereign power, seeking absolute control. It annihilates and destroys obstacles that stand in its way.

In more spiritual terms, it seeks to manifest its vision using all the previous qualities—with certainty, with dynamic will and expansive power, with implacable dedication and electrifying conviction.

Masculine energy can be very destructive as well. As such, its burning and consuming power acts to dominate the wills of others. It tortures and torments, hazes and subjugates. It absorbs others' wills into itself. It utilizes every means possible to corrupt, divide, undermine, and enslave others and society to its purposes.

For negative masculine energy, the light is there but it lacks purity and clarity—the vision is distorted and twisted. The faith and conviction are there but are often expressed in a degraded form, such as through arrogance and self-righteousness.

✭ Exercise: Energy of Water Flowing to the Masculine

As a woman, visualize a man in front of you. Get a sense of that rough magma of the outer core of the Earth, that burning, raging fiery energy that makes a man a man.

As you visualize a man in front of you, imagine that you are extending to him the energy of a bubbly, effervescent mountain pool and falls. Instead of identifying with your social identity, you are identifying with the energy of nature and flowing this toward the man. There is now a current of watery, renewing, life-giving energy circulating between the two of you.

In psychological terms, this is being vivacious, receptive, responsive, empathic, and 100 percent focused in a sensual way on the man. This meditation is not a concept. It is not even a set of images. It is an actual watery energy you can feel flowing in and through each other.

Now imagine you are extending to the man the feeling and vibration of a quiet lake. The water is still and the feelings calm, relaxing, soothing, and peaceful. That cool, soothing, and calming energy encircles the man, embracing him from all sides.

I looked at a picture of a man and woman together. And I said to the woman, "To keep this relationship in balance, whenever he thinks about you, he needs to feel peaceful, calm, and safe. This is easily within your ability to accomplish." It is the nature of the feminine to be able to take any man and hold all that he is within your heart.

And finally, extend to the man the vastness and magnetism of the seas that encompass the Earth. The open ocean is pretty much the same for the last billion years. Take a moment and imagine you are the one sea of the Earth. Extend that watery, cool, blue-green energy around the man.

Going on. While surrounding the man with the watery feeling of the sea, extend through him the magnetism of the oceans of the Earth. The magnetism flows through and unites with him. Without dampening or freezing his masculinity, you become 100 percent one with all that he is. You are focusing the entire magnetic field of the planet Earth on the individual man in front of you, uniting him with it from within.

When you get this right, that hot, raw, burning, and explosive energy of the male transforms into light; that is, it becomes intuitive and aware rather than aggressive and controlling. This is one aspect of androgyny in which the masculine and feminine energies unite.

The outer core of the Earth, around five thousand to ten thousand degrees, is the same temperature as the surface of the sun. The planet itself is conflicted from within. The elements in nature—Earth, Air, Fire, and Water—are profoundly rich and contribute to the biosphere. Yet they are not in harmony, just as will, intellect, feeling, and conscious endeavor are not in harmony in society or in individuals.

In esoteric lore, the microcosm reflects the macrocosm. Men and women are a reflection of the energies of the greater universe, and specifically the planet Earth. For example, a ring of fire of volcanoes encircles the Pacific Ocean. In a similar way in society, women are surrounded by masculine technology and institutions. To attain harmony, we need to accomplish the opposite: in magical androgyny, the feminine encircles and encloses the masculine within itself. The mystery, then, is the magical ability of the feminine spirit to contain within itself the soul of any man on Earth, purifying, renewing, uniting, and transforming him into the person he is meant to be. This embracing love is in the ocean and in the magnetosphere. As a woman, this love is imprinted on your soul and woven into your DNA. There is a direct connection between your body and nature. Find it and activate it and the human race will enter a new age of beauty and wonder where love is triumphant and justice fills the Earth.

DIVINE VIRTUE
Becoming a Divine Being

The divine virtue of Kether is operating as a divine being. Here are a few reference points that suggest how to do this.

In 1976, I spent a half hour each day for six months imagining I was each of three tarot cards—Isis, The Magician, and The Fool. In some tarot traditions, the major arcana tarot cards represent paths between the different sephiroth.

Shortly after this practice, I dreamed of finding four magical books—three of which were Isis, The Magician, and The Fool. Soon a friend gave me my first Franz Bardon book, *Initiation into Hermetics*. Each of Bardon's three books is based on a different tarot card.

The Magician

The Magician is the path between Binah and Kether. Isis is the path between Tiferet and Kether. And The Fool is the path between Chokmah and Kether. Here are brief descriptions.

The Magician controls the four elements and works with Akasha. He is at the beginning originating, and he is at the end having already entered the future and experienced his vision becoming reality.

If I imagine I am The Magician, I stand in front of a table with symbols of the four elements on it—a wand, a chalice, a sword, and a pentacle. As I move my hand over each of the symbols, the kings and queens of the four elements briefly appear and disappear before me.

The harmony of the magical equilibrium established in Gevurah is present. And from Binah, the magician identifies with the fifth element, the void, nothingness, and Akasha. The magician is able to create each element out of nothing through a massive amount of experience, and through force of spiritual will. He stands at the center of a magic circle joined to divinity.

You do not go around wearing your magician robes every day. But from time to time, you turn to the fifth element of Akasha to further your plans. The question for the magician is, "What wonders will you create from out of nothing through your mastery of the five elements?"

Isis

Isis is the path between Tiferet and Kether. Isis has a stillness that is at the center of the unfolding of history and the universe. In a state of timelessness, she experiences completion.

If I imagine I am Isis, there are two themes that stand out. The mermaid queen Isaphil says, "It does not matter in what realm you dwell, as long as in your soul you feel free." For Isis, there is a joining of opposites: time and timelessness, physical reality and divine being, historical experience and a spiritual dream.

And there is a second emphasis. It is the prime directive for all souls that incarnate on Earth no matter what their origins. In my story "The Prime Directive" from *Stories of Magic and Enchantment,* an angel is directed to incarnate on Earth as a human being. The angel asks the Creator, "Why then have you set before me a quest that will take me into the depths of darkest matter? What more can I be than what I already am?"

And the Creator replies, "What I am asking you to do is quite simple. Put aside your light, your wisdom that shines so bright, your bliss and boundless happiness, your ecstasy of oneness with so many others— put it all off to the side for a little while. In this way, you will be able to be born as a human being in a realm of linear time where consciousness is shaped by weight, density, and form. You will then attain self-awareness under situations and circumstances you do not control. And you will grow through your interactions with others who will be quite different from you.

"Slowly over many lifetimes you will increase in experience until one day you shall finally ascend and stand right here before me again.

This is the only way that the glory and beauty of the universe can be put on display."

And the angelic being says, "I get it—I am to become my own creation."

And the Creator replies, "Ah. There. What you have just said cannot be stated more clearly. Now then be off and the best of luck to you."

The prime directive is to decide what you wish to become and then take the time and make the effort to become it. In Tiferet there is an exercise for putting together your own source of inspiration that will enable you to become transformed into the person you wish to be. Here in Kether, this exercise is perfected. And so we have the question Isis asks, "What divine dreams will you bring into being by embodying them in yourself?"

The Fool

The Fool oversees all ten sephiroth, the entire deck of the tarot, both major and minor arcana. In doing so, he surveys the entire spectrum of life—all dreams, all desires, all ideals, and all that men pursue through work. Wherever is the weakest link, or most neglected thing in the entire Tree of Life, he is there filling in, offering what is needed so that everything else can continue uninterrupted. The Fool is the path between Chokmah and Kether.

In Binah, the challenge is to discover what your deepest lessons are in life, and now take the time and energy to learn them. The Fool card is more encompassing. The question is, "What is missing from life? Now take the time and make the effort to find and share it with others."

To do this, The Fool is master of the beginner's mind. He is always learning and starting something new. How do you tell who the master is among any group of people? You carefully observe who is learning the most. That individual is the master.

If I imagine I am The Fool card, I see myself floating in the sky far above the planet Earth. And then I ask, "What is missing from life?" For me, the answer is justice. There is no religion or wisdom tradition that is committed to establishing justice between nations and eliminating corruption in governments.

The United Nations Security Council could go a long way toward accomplishing this. After all, the World Health Organization through a global effort eradicated smallpox, one of the deadliest diseases facing mankind, from the Earth in 1977. But the members of the Security Council are committed only to furthering the interests of their own nations.

Israel had prophets for a thousand years. Among other things, the prophets anointed and advised kings. In Deuteronomy, a command is given that includes the kings of Israel: "Justice and only justice shall you pursue."

But historical Israel was often under attack from foreign powers, sometimes successfully defending itself through amazing victories, and other times suffering defeat and exile. As with Isaiah's prophecy—war shall be no more—we have yet to witness these commands and prophecies coming into being.

From *Stories of Magic and Enchantment,* God turns to the archangel Michael and says, "As once before with Neanderthal, now is a time of reckoning. Go forth and see what part *Homo sapiens* has chosen to play in the unfolding of the universe. Discover if they are like Neanderthal—having attained their dreams, survival is no longer a priority."

Michael searches through all minds that exist upon the Earth and finds one individual that can speak on behalf of the human race. And appearing before him, the angel says, "I am the archangel Michael commissioned by the Creator to determine the fate and destiny of your race. Therefore, answer my question, 'What part has *Homo sapiens* chosen to play in the unfolding of the universe?'"

After giving his answer, Michael questions him further, "You appear to be constructing a new purpose for the human race. And so I am required to ask you, By what authority do you intervene to create peace where there is war, justice where there is injustice, and to eliminate from governments those who abuse their powers? You intend to set an example down through the ages to other races in this galaxy about how to mediate every conflict and resolve every dispute.

"You are unleashing a love on Earth that annihilates every obstacle and barrier that separate one person from another. From where does your inspiration arise?"

The man replies, "When I listen, I can hear the song of every star in this galaxy. And further, beyond this wondrous, whirling, living being that is our galaxy, I can hear the song of every galaxy in the universe. The beauty is incomprehensible. By comparison, my contribution to the human race is next to nothing. It is the least I can do."

For me, the first test of a genuine cosmic religion, one in harmony with the greater universe, is that it eliminates all wars on Earth forever. Such a religion does not yet exist on Earth. For me, that is what is missing from life. It is a dynamic spirituality in which love, wisdom, power, and justice are equally honored and pursued.

In summary, as we review the three tarot cards, completion, satisfaction, closure, and fulfillment are embodied in the divine virtue of Kether.

DREAM

The dream of Kether is in any moment being able to imagine, with ease, that your every need is met, your every desire satisfied, your every purpose fulfilled, your every mission accomplished, and your every ideal made real. In other words, any weakness or obstruction you feel in yourself vanishes. This takes the tension out of living in circumstances and conditions that are, in fact, quite challenging.

INITIATION

The initiation in Kether is to become your own guardian angel. In Tiferet, we can talk about conscience and listening to the still, quiet voice within us. If you listen well, your conscience will direct you to discern good from evil and do the best things instead of something less.

In Kether, we identify with the divine within ourselves and so are more active. In the Kether initiation, we enter the consciousness of our guardian angel. What does a guardian angel do? It is watchful and vigilant. It guards and protects.

Without interfering with the freedom of choice belonging to the incarnated individual, from time to time it sends promptings, visions, and dreams. It says, "You have to deal with necessities of life. You are a member of society and so have social obligations to fulfill. You have personal needs to meet and desires to satisfy. But you are also part of something far greater."

In the initiation of Kether, you are aggressive in meeting your social needs, and you are equally aggressive in meeting your spiritual needs. The human personality can say to itself, "Ah. This is something I have been looking for."

And the guardian angel part of oneself can also say in the same moment, "This situation is not right. It is too risky. It has no deeper, underlying purpose, and it contributes nothing in becoming the person you are meant to be. Let's find something better."

In this case, the conscious self and the divine self are working together as equal partners in achieving their ends.

MYSTERY
Multidimensional Awareness

The magician calls many realms his home and many races of beings consider him one of their own.

The mystery in Kether is straightforward. In our modern society, the freedom to choose different courses of action are vastly increased. You can belong to a church, a political organization, an investment club, a dance group, an alumni association, and any number of other groups. A firefighter can be training for the Olympics. An accountant can be a colonel in the Army Reserves, and teach basketball in a youth group. One moment you can be day trading stocks, and the next moment you can be leading an online yoga class.

We are also surrounded by many different worlds and realities. We can be active in this physical world we share in common with others, and we can also be active in worlds that are invisible to other people. As we extend our spiritual perception, we naturally begin to explore other frontiers.

My awareness of other worlds comes from studying the Franz Bardon Hermetic training system. The procedure in Franz Bardon's system is for the student to first work extensively on training his body, soul, and mind through intense concentration and a variety of related practices. The goal is to bring the individual in harmony with the greater universe.

At this point, Bardon introduces the student to the four elemental realms underlying the elements of Earth, Water, Air, and Fire in nature. These are the realms of gnomes, mermaids, sylphs, and salamanders. You explore their realms one after the other. You learn to perceive, feel, think, and act as they do. You are then instructed to learn all you can about these realms and in effect make them like a second home.

Salamander Realm

I am fortunate to know a girl who is an incarnated Fire spirit. She grew up in a human body in a human family and did normal things like attending school. But she thinks of Fire as being healing, as loving, and as wise. She is energized and inspired by Fire.

For her, Fire is home. I can feel what she feels and look at the world through her eyes. Her view that Fire is friendly and is a source of soul illumination is outside of normal perception.

We do, of course, have individuals who have played major roles in unfolding the technology of Fire. These men act exactly like a Fire spirit would act if it had incarnated. They reveal to the world new applications of Fire—Nobel, Westinghouse, Tesla, Edison, Oppenheimer, Niels Bohr, and others give us explosives, electricity, nuclear power, lasers, and solar energy.

These individuals are not very concerned about ethics and preserving life on Earth. Like salamanders, their interest is in vastly increasing our power, mobility, and overcoming our boundaries. They take iron and with a blast furnace make steel. They take electricity and gasoline and make an engine to propel boats, cars, and airplanes. They take oxygen and hydrogen or various propellants to fuel rockets. Like it or not, the realm of Fire spirits has already made itself a part of our world.

Mermaid Realm

I have also entered the realm of the mermaids. Bardon describes eight different mermaid queens and mermen. I have written about all eight of these beings through my encounters with them. Using the genre of fairy tales, I have a collection of stories about incarnated mermaids in my book *Mermaid Tales*. I describe my interactions with various mermaids in *Undines: Lessons from the Realm of the Water Spirits* and also in *Mermaids, Sylphs, Gnomes, and Salamanders*.

Only in the last few years have incarnated mermaids begun sharing themselves with the world. Previously, due to their powers of attraction and unfamiliar watery mode of love, they have been either stalked or killed. So they have had to keep their existence secret or else go to great lengths to pretend they are human.

Lately, the idea of being a mermaid has become popular with some people. The imagery of a mermaid does carry with it a feeling of relating more deeply to nature and of gaining a natural sense of feminine sensuality. Mermaids themselves, however, have no egos, are not jealous, love everyone equally, and never lose their sense of innocence.

In their own realm, they have no group identity or affiliations. They do not compete with each other to win prizes. They need no social support to affirm their identities. When they relax, they spontaneously take on the vibration of some aspect of Water in nature.

To protect the mermaid realm from human beings, it appears that certain safeguards have been put in place. For example, an individual, like a mermaid herself, has to set aside his ego, change his brain waves so they reflect the vibration of Water, and also seek to love as mermaids love in order to feel comfortable in their realm. Nonetheless, without joining the mermaid realm to human history, human beings are in great danger of producing megadisasters that threaten their own survival.

Sylph Realm

The planet Earth also has a fantastic atmosphere within which is the realm of sylphs—the Air spirits. These beings celebrate their freedom and independence. They love finding harmony amid discord and providing balance between opposites—hot and cold, moist and dry, high and low pressure, calm and turbulent, electric and magnetic, evaporation and condensation, and so on.

We encounter the acute sensitivity of the airy temperament in artists such as Beethoven and Shakespeare. For such artists, the nuances of perception in each moment reveal the newness of life and experience.

Whether in human form or in their own realm, sylphs have a telepathic awareness of how others' minds operate. All the same, their hypersensitivity usually causes them to stand back and so, like the mermaids, though they make great lovers, they usually refrain from bonding in a normal human sense of "I need you and you need me."

Though Franz Bardon says it is quite difficult to interact with sylphs in nature, I find the sylph realm to be quite enchanting. It feels like home when I reflect the sky in my mind.

Gnome Realm

Gnomes live in the earth. They like to study and work with minerals, gems, trees, plants, flowers, organic processes, and the feng shui of the land. They feel very down-to-earth and grounded, solid, and persevering. They involve themselves in whatever they work on as if time does not matter, only their desire to finish what they have begun. Gnome-type individuals are like scientists who discover the double helix in DNA or make a new kind of ceramic, or they contribute to society like the U.N. project that eliminated smallpox from the Earth.

Through science, we are gradually extending our life spans. In the next century, we will no doubt make amazing discoveries in the area of medicine. But if the king of gnomes—named Mentifil—was incarnated, one of the first things he would do would be to teach human beings to become immortal simply through meditation. We have a lot to learn from these beings.

I only know four incarnated gnomes. Of the elemental beings, gnomes feel most at home being here in a physical body. All the same, they can be quite reclusive. How do you explain to human beings that flowers blossom as you walk by or that plants move when you place your hands near to them?

Fairy Realms

Unlike elemental beings, fairies have a history and a social identity. They go on quests and, like human beings, they make choices that define who they are and what they wish to become. They belong to groups and have traditions.

And they have close associations through historical ties with human beings. There are Celtic fairies and even book fairies. There are flower fairies and fairies that live in trees and streams. There are serious fairies who are passionate about healing plants and fairies that embody laughter, play, song, and dance.

For those who see fairies, they are everywhere. A patch of grass—there is probably a fairy there. Fairies fly through a room as a ball of energy, and oftentimes it seems fairies are more inclined to adopt a human form when they are near the aura of someone who can sense them.

Fairies are beautiful, innocent, and creative. There are perhaps thousands of different kinds. David Bowie has that feel of a fairy, and an Irish band with pipes, drums, and violins jamming has the Celtic fairy vibration.

How to regain the innocence of mermaids who give all of themselves in every moment without hesitation or limitation? How to be as innocent and playful as fairies who embody laughter, joy, and the enchantment of a moonbeam or a ray of sunlight at dawn? Become as innocent as a child, become love that knows no fear, trust that is free of vulnerability, and assume an identity that is forever pure.

Where to go from here? What of dragons and unicorns? I have met those who carry those soul vibrations. What of wood elves and all manner of sprites, nymphs, and jinn? The astral plane, like the master said, is a house with many mansions. Humans are attuned to only a few.

As we ascend into the realms of light, the Earth, the moon, and each planet also have a vast array of beings. If you want to read about some of these, try Franz Bardon's second book, *The Practice of Magical Evocation*. He mentions over five hundred different spirits and offers brief descriptions of four hundred.

Bardon's idea, again, is that you make friends with a few of the higher intelligences in each of these spiritual domains. They offer assistance and you can learn from them until you are able to do what they do—oversee, guide, and inspire all aspects of evolution.

Of course, you can meet human gurus who are conscious of other realms. The lineage masters of a tradition from centuries before still appear to and guide those who are in incarnation. During rituals and ceremonies, some human gurus will channel these masters who still speak with insight and authority. You could say that a strong spiritual lineage has created its own kingdom or realm on the astral plane.

When you have a spirit guide, those guides in effect are from another realm or part of the astral plane. You are joining two worlds when you interact with them.

◆

One day a girl said to her mother, "I am not like other people. Is there something you are not telling me?" Her mother replied, "You are of Water. You are a mermaid."

When she searched on Google under "mermaid woman," she found my essay, *Traits of Mermaid Women*. She then emailed me and I confirmed that she had the Water in her aura typical of mermaids.

But she also belongs to other realms as well. She is the incarnation of a fairy queen who has her own kingdom on the astral plane. The fairy queen part of herself that remains on the astral plane argues with the part of herself that is in a human body about who she is to marry and whether or not she will have a child. When you are in a human body, you get to make your own choices about what you wish to do with yourself. This rule is like a prime directive governing all those who incarnate on Earth.

Not all incarnated mermaids are stone broke. This one is extremely successful in her profession and very handsome billionaires ask her out on dates.

A different woman can speak to departed souls as easily as she does to human beings who are alive. They appear to her just as clearly as regular folks. In fact, she is so familiar with the astral realm of departed human souls that she acts in an official capacity as a "greeter." She welcomes newly departed human beings and helps them adjust to the afterlife on the astral plane.

In addition to this, nearly every night when she sleeps, she sits as a member of a group of twelve who review individuals' lives when they are ready to look back on the life they left behind after they have died.

Once dead, there comes a point where you reexperience every moment of being alive, except now you also feel what others felt when you were with them. She says these roles she plays on the astral plane during lucid dreams are more real to her than the life she lives in the outer world.

And yet this woman is also a mermaid. With ease she enters the mermaid realm and wears the form of a mermaid when she is there. Like many incarnated mermaids, she likes to spend time in the water every day. In her case, she will spend hours meditating in the bathtub with only her mouth and nose above the surface of the water.

In addition to interacting with departed souls, there are a vast range of beings who appear to her in her house whether she is asleep or awake. She loves all of them and they discuss with her the purposes they pursue, which are quite different from those of humans.

Unlike the movie *Ondine,* some of the incarnated mermaids do not need to call fish with a song. If they step into a lake, hundreds of fish swim up to them. But they would never use their power to harvest fish. It appears that when fish are around them, the fish begin to act like human beings expressing concern, feelings, and insight into human activities.

Imagine that you have memories of another lifetime on Earth that seem more real to you than the life you are now living. And this is a different woman who feels each moment is equally real whether it is the present or the past.

Another woman interacts with the souls of dead people. They are just as real to her as living people. Even though she has a wonderful husband, she also considers herself married to one of these departed souls.

And there is a man who is a successful businessman and who has a lovely wife. But he is also married to a fairy queen. This fairy queen appeared in a novel written a hundred years previously. Add to this that he belongs to a group of six other men each of whom is married to a fairy.

Starseeds

Some of the individuals have auras that do not belong to any of the planets in our solar system. These individuals are called *starseeds* since their souls are from another star system, even though they are now incarnated in a human body. Some of these individuals have no idea about their origins. And others, if you ask them, will tell you straight out, "Yes. I am from a planet that circles a different star."

Some have a stream of energy flowing through their auras that continues to connect them to their home world. In most cases of starseeds, however, life on Earth makes no sense. The planet Earth appears to be quite unusual for the speed with which we are evolving in technology while at the same time remaining quite violent and emotionally unstable.

Life on Earth is governed by scarcity, survival, and competition. Even love is viewed in a competitive context. You have to "court" someone to "win" that person as a marriage partner. Love is so rare on Earth that some will die without ever tasting its bliss. And then too the nature of government is constantly changing as reformers and revolutionaries rewrite the rules of society as they pursue their social and political experiments.

Some starseeds are like normal people. There is that enthusiasm and positive outlook of a high school cheerleader. There is that attractive aura of a prom queen. There is that desire for harmony in relationships like a female with a Libra sun sign.

But then you ask questions, and you discover they feel they are a part of multiple dimensions and alternate realities. One woman has always seen fairies. They guide her whenever someone or something needs help when she enters a forest. And she has a spirit guide that worked with humans during Atlantis.

But when she falls asleep at night, she enters a lucid dream in which she lives moment by moment in a parallel incarnation on another planet as a member of the race of Pleiadians. And among the Pleiadians she is a first contact specialist. Over the span of her incarnations, she has contacted thousands of races throughout the galaxy who are ready to join the galactic community.

Her intuition is such that she can read the archetypes of a planet to find the best way to present herself to whichever race of beings she is contacting. Some of these galactic races are similar in form to human beings. Some are reptilian or mantis in shape. Some are silicon- or sulfur-based life forms. Some have evolved from crystals or minerals and have little if anything in common with life as we know it.

She says that some races in the galaxy, like the Yahyel, do not exist within linear time. Like the Pleiadians, they have to make their vibration denser so their spaceships can be seen by humans. For this woman, past lives and future lifetimes are equally real. They are all occurring now.

One thing that can be observed about her is her connection to wild animals. Whenever she meets bull sharks, mountain lions, wolves, or wild horses, the animals treat her as if she is the alpha. Or probably more accurately, they see her as a goddess.

To summarize, in ethnography, the researcher immerses himself in the world of the individual he is interviewing. He listens to how the individual describes his own experience. If you listen carefully as someone speaks about his life, you will meet individuals who participate in multiple worlds. Sometimes their otherworldly experiences add to and enrich their life in this world.

At other times, participating in more than one reality is exhausting, time-consuming, and bewildering. The individual may not have an effective paradigm or interpretative framework to understand his experiences. For some individuals, such experiences are kept private. Others are willing to talk and some write books about what they have learned from participating in other worlds.

And yet, all worlds, all realms, and all lifetimes are arrayed around us. Whatever race of beings we are, we evolve by expanding our awareness to include and then move beyond the boundaries and limitations that define our lives. In the end, to know ourselves is to become one with everything.

Common Difficulties

Sometimes the nervous system relating to Kether can be overstimulated. This may result in the individual being dreamy, otherworldly, and detached from his body. He may be confused over the differences between the inner and outer worlds, lack respect for karmic limitations or the value of physical existence, and he may lack an interest in mastering basic life skills. The individual also becomes stuck—repeating experiences without learning.

To stop an individual's spiritual growth, all you need to do is control one of three things: an individual's physical actions, his feelings, or his thoughts and/beliefs. For example, if you are bogged down or oppressed in the physical world, you do not have time or the energy for spiritual pursuits. Conscience then seems like a luxury. You need to survive. What else matters?

Or if your emotions are conflicted or confused, spiritual intuition shuts down. A turbulent emotional life interferes with the ability to receive more subtle intuitions. And if an individual's thoughts are rigid or his beliefs are narrow-minded or forced upon him, he is too insecure to pursue the truth.

Unable to think symbolically, use his intuition, or reflect accurately on his life, he tends to be materialistic, selfish, trapped in his ego, insipid, and without empathy. Whether a rebel, reformer, or even an idealist, he cannot think beyond the conventional views of his world.

On the other hand, in the case where Kether's development is stronger than the other sephiroth, the individual's conscience may be overdeveloped. In this case, it is easy for him to feel guilty, or he feels an urgent need to accomplish certain missions while lacking the preparation necessary to do so. Or he knows the right course of action but he lacks the will or emotional strength to follow through.

One result is that a person is then oversensitive, self-sacrificing, sometimes a fanatical idealist, or overwhelmed by depths of feeling that have nothing to do with his daily life. The individual's inner world operates without any points of contact with his personal life.

Or, with an overexposure to Kether, an individual can end up attaching his personal ego to some deity. And then all the prepackaged doctrines and moralities of a religion substitute for the individual's inner voice of conscience. And again, out of touch with the real world, he may begin to think of himself as some great being with powers far beyond those he actually possesses.

How do you get back to Earth? Get a job. Make money. Run a company. Be productive. Participate in society and do something that benefits others. These are the actions of Malkuth where the basic quality is focusing 100 percent of your attention on the physical world.

There are other ways Kether and conscience close down. For example, attachment of a psychic entity to an individual's aura tends to dampen or shut down his conscience. And this can be a matter of degree or total. In other words, the individual ends up thinking the thoughts and taking the point of view of the being or thoughtform that has attached itself to him.

Or, as is more easily observed, someone falls deeply or passionately in love. This may be a complete disaster. If through fear or love someone creates a captivating dream for you, then your own conscience may cease to function.

Obviously, sometimes an entire nation or set of nations are charmed and obsessed with some idea, ideology, or political leader. And then vast numbers of people are unable to hear the voice of their conscience. The "superego" takes over—the politically correct doctrines of what is right and wrong—and only later, after the government falls, are individuals left wondering how they could have been so cruel, callous, or stupid.

Another problem is when kundalini, a primal energy "sleeping" at the base of the spine, awakens. This primal energy, when activated in the lower chakras, can also destroy conscience as obsession overrides common sense and pushes aside the values an individual otherwise lives by.

An overwhelmingly blind and impersonal power, kundalini seeks only one thing—to move upward and unite with its consort in the crown chakra. But if it is directed away from this objective, she becomes extremely hostile. She seizes whatever life experience is available— sensations of pleasure, control of others, or possession of physical resources—in an act of desperate craving, like a drowning man clinging to the one who would rescue him.

Your spirit guide or spiritual therapist could restore the individual's own feelings through empathy. And with great detachment and clarity, he can remind the individual about his goals and values.

Some of that clarity and empathy—the sense of being fully alive— can be transferred to the other person so he becomes free of his obsession. The overstimulated kundalini returns to a sleeping state where it no longer torments the individual. Or it remains active but now cooperates in fulfilling the individual's purposes.

And then there are individuals who enter life without a functioning conscience. Ask him, What is in your heart? He may have a negative response based on revenge, hatred, fear, lust, or greed. Kind of like,

"I want to destroy something—that is what is in my heart." And this tendency toward destruction or domination can operate outside of the individual's awareness. It is covered over with rationalizations, as in "When I did that it was not me." They deny that the malice or aggression was their own.

In such cases, these individuals may join themselves to a group—a church, an organization, a team, the military, and so on. In accepting and submitting themselves to the external values and goals of the group, they acquire a functioning conscience in a surrogate manner. After enough time, they may internalize the values of the group and slowly begin to sense for themselves the difference between right and wrong.

Saturn too has its own operating manual when it comes to conscience. Some individuals can sense the difference between right and wrong, but they choose to ignore their inner voice, turning it off until it is no longer heard. We see this often with individuals who abuse their power. Power becomes an addiction, in which case acquiring more power is the sole objective.

This can sometimes result in a neurological dysfunction, a form of self-induced frontotemporal dementia. The individual speaks with clarity and sets forth persuasive reasons that defend his actions. But, in fact, this individual can no longer think about consequences. He is blind to what is obvious—if you do such and such, then this is what will follow. He can no longer evaluate the probability of future events.

For example, Alan Greenspan, chairman of the Federal Reserve, testified that the crisis in subprime mortgages would not spread to the rest of the market. Look inside Alan's mind—he believes and perceives that the great financial institutions like Leman Brothers and Bear Sterns, like Merrill Lynch and insurance companies like AIG, are too big to fail.

Pull Alan Greenspan aside and ask him at that time, "What are the conditions under which they could fail?" Greenspan would most likely reply, "You are asking a hypothetical question that is outside of reality." Greenspan's brain is locked into a set of interconnected ideas that interfere with normal brain functions, like being able to imagine different outcomes.

This happened to Saddam Hussein, who did not believe the United

States would invade Iraq. It happened to the news media in covering the 2016 presidential election. It happens to large organizations and it happens to individuals.

We can call this frontotemporal dementia effect the affliction of Saturn. Saturn takes away until the individual chooses on his own to develop a conscience. As mentioned previously, the Saturn return (roughly every thirty years) is a chance to consider whether the choices you are making are in accord with your deepest values; if they are not, then what you depend on will fail.

Conscience requires a balance between all five elements—Earth (productive actions in the physical world), Water (feeling and empathy), Air (clarity of mind and intellect), Fire (willpower), and Akasha (the deeper purposes of life).

Yet with human beings, all five elements are only partially operational. In general, however, human beings lack the presence of Water (feeling and empathy). The Water element, among other things, gives an individual a graphic imagination—if you think about something, you are there with it right now. If you think about the future, you are in the future where you are able to examine the results of current decisions.

This is what Greenspan and Saddam Hussein and the news anchors failed to do. They could not imagine something happening that is outside of their comfort zone or in contradiction to the thoughts and beliefs they hold dear. At the least, Kether offers a degree of transcendence in which the individual is able to step back, view life with some degree of clarity, and decide to pursue the best outcomes.

AFTERWORD

In this book, I explore some of the possibilities we have for personal and spiritual development. Consider Hod/Mercury. I started with the familiar. For example, active listening is a skill readily available to anyone. As you listen to someone talk, you assume a stance that allows you to reflect back to the person his own thoughts and feelings.

Developing a judicial temperament is slightly more difficult, but still within nearly everyone's reach. With it, we strive to understand—in a fair and balanced way—the feelings and thoughts of those on both sides of a conflict.

Using visualization to imagine the future is also accessible to nearly everyone. There are lots of seminars on how to master this skill. Learning to perceive without thoughts arising in our minds is definitely more challenging, but it is worth the effort. The experience of the enlightened mind is certainly a supreme accomplishment. But it is important to realize that the enlightened mind is always with us and that it supports all thought processes.

Reviewing the sephiroth, there is a movement from familiar to unfamiliar.

In Malkuth/Earth, we can review our daily routines. We can also find nature inside of ourselves and make a study of silence.

In Yesod/the Moon, we can practice directly interacting with our subconscious. And we can learn to change negative emotions into positive emotions.

In Hod/Mercury, we learn to communicate in a clear and concise manner. But to make our best choices and better solve problems, we develop a heightened mental clarity and a powerful conviction.

In Netzach/Venus, we consider focusing on life goals that supercharge our motivation and help integrate our personalities. At the same time, Venus is about personal love. Why not study the art of empathy if we seek oneness with another?

In Tiferet/Sun, the opening exercise is straightforward and simple. Make your own book of inspirational experiences. Collect in one place your favorite writings as well as describe moments in your life when you have been touched by beauty, wonder, and the sacred. Later on in Tiferet, we encounter the dream of uniting with the source from which all inspiration arises.

Gevurah/Mars likes to point out that the energy someone puts into whining, complaining, and blaming others can be redirected so that it is used to strengthens one's will. In fact, if you want to work on mastering yourself, balancing the four elements in your personality is a fabulous beginning as well as a lifelong practice.

In Chesed/Jupiter, the question is, what can we do with our lives that will enrich the world? To get the most out of life, to make the best choices, we might consider practicing some sort of advanced magical or spiritual training system.

In Binah/Saturn, right from the beginning we take on the idea of learning our deepest lessons in life. Here there is a feeling close to us but easy to ignore—the realization of how fragile and precious life is. And here is one of life's greatest mysteries—to create love where love does not exist.

In Chokmah/Uranus, we take the idea of visualization to a professional level through role-playing the future. And then there is another supreme accomplishment open to us—learning to listen, not just to silence, but with such depth and freedom from ego that we can hear the divine speak to us.

In Kether/Neptune, I present the familiar practice called mindfulness with a few uncommon additions. But Kether oversees all the
sephiroth. And so this is a place where we exercise our oversight
in its full measure by considering how to act, feel, and perceive as
a divine being. Pull out all the stops. Become your own guardian
angel.

And so, on our journey—for all the horror and suffering we encounter
in life—wonder, beauty, and awe are always by our side. And, in spite of
all the complexities and difficulties we face, there remains a final attainment, to become our own creation.

And how shall we measure this attainment? Not just our own, but
other's lives are enriched and dreams fulfilled.

APPENDIX

GUIDE TO THE SEPHIROTH

Rule 10. Malkuth/Earth: Kingdom, Physical World
Basic Quality: Focus on physical reality
Virtues, Vices, Negative: Solid/Rigid/Oppression
Challenge: Pursue something of value that you are passionate about
Magical Practice: Observe your routines
Common Virtue: Well-being
Magical Virtue: A quiet ecstasy
Divine Virtue: Silence
Dream: Mastery and love
Initiation: Bringing nature into one's role in society
Mystery: The five elements in the personality, society, and the
biosphere

Rule 9. Yesod/the Moon: Foundation, Soul, Astral Plane
Basic Quality: Entering dream states at will
Virtues, Vices, Negative: Strength/Idleness/Narcissism
Challenge: Discover what makes you happy, fully alive, and at peace
Magical Practice: The five senses
Common Virtue: Self-acceptance as a gate to the inner self
Magical Virtue: The element of Water
Divine Virtue: Creating peace, happiness, contentment; compre-
hending opposites
Dream: Physical bliss

Initiation: Self-renewal

Mystery: The astral plane, spiritual anthropology, global dreamtime

Rule 8. Hod/Mercury: Glory, Splendor, Quest for Truth

Basic Quality: Clear and concise speech

Virtues, Vices, Negative: Alert/Dull/Criminal

Challenge: Develop clarity of mind

Magical Practice: Observing without thinking; understanding all
sides, contemplation

Common Virtue: Vivaciousness

Magical Virtue: The element of Air

Divine Virtue: Faith and conviction

Dream: Making others more alive and words that transform the
world

Initiation: A clear mind amid confusion

Mystery: The enlightened mind

Rule 7. Netzach/Venus: Victory, Poise, Charm, Charisma, Personal Love

Basic Quality: Relating to others

Virtues, Vices, Negative: Unselfish/Lustful/Treachery

Challenge: Find someone or something you love completely

Magical Practice: Two examples of pursuing life goals

Common Virtue: Empathy

Magical Virtue: Magnetic love

Divine Virtue: Purity of motives

Dream: Oneness

Initiation: Personality integration

Mystery: Zen of love

Rule 6. Tiferet/Sun: Beauty, Harmony, Uniting Opposites

Basic Quality: Inspiration

Virtues, Vices, and Negative: Humility/Pride/Domination

Challenge: Find the inspiration that guides you through life

Magical Practice: Make a book of inspirational sayings;
reinforce your inspirations

Common Virtue: The better self

Magical Virtue: Stillness

Divine Virtue: The ability to heal others

Dream: Equanimity

Initiation: Make the divine world a part of yourself

Mystery: The relation of the personality and the Higher Self

Rule 5. Gevurah/Mars: Self-Mastery

Basic Quality: Daily practice in arts of self-mastery

Virtues, Vices, Negative: Strength/Fear/Terror

Challenge: Find an ideal or purpose that inspires you to master yourself

Magical Practice: Develop balance between your personality traits

Common Virtue: A quiet exuberance

Magical Virtue: Astral Immortality

Divine Virtue: Embodying the energies of nature

Dream: Having the power you need to accomplish your purposes

Initiation: The process of acquiring power

Mystery: The four elements unite to become one energy field comprising two opposites of masculine and feminine

Rule 4. Chesed/Jupiter: Wealth in All Aspects

Basic Quality: Participation in groups

Virtue, Vice, Negative: Leadership/Hypocrisy/Dystopia

Challenge: Imagine you possess the material and spiritual wealth that enables you to enrich others' lives

Magical Practice: Consider practicing a high-level spiritual or magical training system to get the most out of life

Common Virtue: Universal love

Magical Virtue: Transformation

Divine Virtue: Magical Blessing

Dream: Imagine belonging to an ideal community committed to assisting mankind

Initiation: Work at making the world a better place

Mystery: Spiritual community/A genuine cosmic religion

Rule 3. Binah/Saturn: Limitation and Enlightenment

Basic Quality: Appreciation

Virtues, Vices, Negative: Judicial temperament/Negligence/Treachery

Challenge: Overcome your limitations

Magical Practice: Master your deepest lessons in life

Common Virtue: Appreciation of the gifts of the past

Magical Virtue: Identifying with the void

Divine Virtue: Dissolving negativity, malice

Dream: Placing causes in Akasha

Initiation: The feeling of how precious life is

Mystery: The final test of enlightenment: creating love where love does not exist

Rule 2. Chokmah/Uranus: Wisdom, Destiny

Basic Quality: Revealing new things

Virtues, Vices, Negative: Creativity/Failure to prepare/False prophets

Challenge: Work with the divine world in fulfilling a task

Magical Practice: Dialoguing

Common Virtue: Appreciation for the gifts of the future

Magical Virtue: Role-playing the future

Divine Virtue: Revealing new magic to the world

Dream: The dream of magic

Initiation: Listening

Mystery: Divine missions

Rule 1. Kether/Neptune: Crown, Oneness

Basic Quality: The higher self

Virtues, Vices, Negative: Higher conscience/Dreamy/Twisted

Challenge: A time to think, perceive, and act as a divine being

Magical Practice: Mindfulness—the great now

Common Virtue: The four aces of the tarot: the elements overflowing from within

Magical Virtue: Androgyny

Divine Virtue: Becoming a divine being

Dream: Imagine being whole and complete in every way

Initiation: Being your own guardian angel

Mystery: Multidimensional awareness

INDEX

About the Author

 After graduating from Wheaton College in Illinois in 1969 with a bachelor's degree in philosophy and economics, William R. Mistele began studying esoteric oral traditions, seeking the oldest, intact lineages from around the world. For his field research, he lived in a Tibetan Buddhist monastery in Berkeley, California, and he later studied Hopi culture and language at the University of Arizona, where he received a master's degree in linguistics. At that time, he became the only student accepted by a Hopi shaman.

While living in Tucson, Arizona, Mistele began studying the Western Hermetic traditions and nature religions of Wiccans and Druids. He also worked with a number of gifted psychics and parapsychologists and practiced evocation with a Sufi master. Mistele moved to Hawaii in 1982 to study with a Chinese Taoist master, a Vietnamese Zen master, and one of the foremost Tai Chi Chuan masters of China. Since 1975 he has been a student of Franz Bardon's teachings on Hermetic magic, a system of training that includes the evocation of and communication with nature spirits.

William Mistele calls himself a spiritual anthropologist and a bardic magician. As a spiritual anthropologist, his interest is in extracting and integrating the universal contributions from all spiritual and wisdom traditions. Spiritual anthropology asks these age-old questions: What is it to be a human being? What is human nature? What are we capable of becoming? And what is it to be and to feel fully alive?

As a bardic magician, he uses the medium of poetry, short stories, novels, and screenplays to present modern fairy tales and mythology. This genre asks questions like, How do we discover the divinity within ourselves? And how do we apply our divine powers so they are effective in transforming the world in which we live?

For Mistele, magic is a study of how to make the best choices in life. For those who are up for it, a study of magic accelerates your learning process and grants you greater depth and variety of life experiences. After forty-five years of studying Bardon's system, Mistele has gone on to apply his magical skills to establishing justice between nations.

See also his videos at youtube.com/emedetz in which he, Avaah Blackwell, and Aaron interview a number of mermaids and mermen described in Franz Bardon's book, *Practice of Magical Evocation*. He also has a large number of videos on facebook.com/williamrmistele.

His published books are *Undines: Lessons from the Realm of the Water Spirits; The Four Elements; Mermaids, Sylphs, Gnomes, and Salamanders; Stories of Magic and Enchantment; Mermaid Tales;* and his upcoming series of novels, beginning with *The Admiral's Mermaid.*

A new edition of *Undines* will be published under the title *Encounters with Mermaids* by Destiny Books, as part of its Sacred Planet Books collection, in the spring of 2024.

BOOKS OF RELATED INTEREST

The Kabbalah of Light
Ancient Practices to Ignite the Imagination and Illuminate the Soul
by Catherine Shainberg

The Hermetic Marriage of Art and Alchemy
Imagination, Creativity, and the Great Work
by Marlene Seven Bremner

The Path of the Warrior-Mystic
Being a Man in an Age of Chaos
by Angel Millar

The Alchemical Search for the Unified Field
Pythagorean, Hermetic, and Shamanic Journeys into
Invisible and Ethereal Realms
by R. E. Kretz

Alphabets and the Mystery Traditions
The Origins of Letters in the Earth, the Underworld, and the Heavens
by Judith Dillon

Theurgy: Theory and Practice
The Mysteries of the Ascent to the Divine
by P. D. Newman

Gnostic Philosophy
From Ancient Persia to Modern Times
by Tobias Churton

Elemental Magic
Traditional Practices for Working with the Energies of the Natural World
by Nigel Pennick

INNER TRADITIONS • BEAR & COMPANY
P.O. Box 388
Rochester, VT 05767
1-800-246-8648
www.InnerTraditions.com
Or contact your local bookseller